THE COSTS OF INEQUALITY IN LATIN AMERICA

Lessons and Warnings for the Rest of the World

Diego Sánchez-Ancochea

W0006659

I.B.TAURIS
LONDON • NEW YORK • OXFORD • NEW DELHI • SYDNEY

I.B. TAURIS
Bloomsbury Publishing Plc
50 Bedford Square, London, WC1B 3DP, UK
1385 Broadway, New York, NY 10018, USA

BLOOMSBURY, I.B. TAURIS and the I.B. Tauris logo are trademarks of
Bloomsbury Publishing Plc

First published in Great Britain 2021

Cover design by www.paulsmithdesign.com
Cover images: [left] Brazil © Patrick Altmann/Getty Images;
[right] Mexico © grandriver/iStock.

A catalogue record for this book is available from the British Library.

A catalog record for this book is available from the Library of Congress.

ISBN: HB: 978-1-8386-0624-4
       PB: 978-1-8386-0623-7
       ePDF: 978-1-8386-0626-8
       eBook: 978-1-8386-0625-1

Typeset by RefineCatch Limited, Bungay, Suffolk
Printed and bound in Great Britain

To find out more about our authors and books visit www.bloomsbury.com
and sign up for our newsletters.

CONTENTS

ACKNOWLEDGMENTS

At the time of writing the final pages of this book, the world is in the midst of an unexpected health and economic catastrophe created by the outbreak of the COVID-19 pandemic. In recent months, many of us have been in a lockdown that has saved millions of lives while also creating significant economic collateral damage. When this book is finally out, most people will still be focused on the implications of the pandemic for their lives, their countries, and the whole world. There is a risk that we stop paying attention to problems like inequality that just months earlier were at the heart of the public agenda.

This reaction would be understandable but mistaken. In fact, the pandemic is likely to exacerbate the concentration of income and power, further threatening our democracies and challenging our economic model. It is thus even more important than ever to consider the costs of income inequality and debate the ways to overcome it. To do so, the historical experience of Latin America—a continent with more than 600 million people and four times the size of the European Union—will be particularly relevant.

Given the growing challenge that inequality poses, academics must make an effort to go beyond university walls and participate in public debates. This book is my first attempt to do so. I could not have done it without my wife Rosa's unremitting backing. She encouraged me to write a book for a general audience, supported my sabbatical plans enthusiastically, and patiently listened to my worries and concerns.

Three friends supported this project from beginning to end. Jill Hedges was instrumental in the initial phases. She liked my original idea, put me in touch with her publisher, and commented on early drafts—making sure that I did not make glaring mistakes in my discussion of Perón! Salvador Martí i Puig read the full manuscript, making thorough suggestions and providing additional readings. Thanks to him (and to Ben Phillips) I ended up writing Chapter 6 on Latin America's positive lessons. I hope we can together write our planned sequel to this book in Spanish. Juliana Martínez Franzoni has been my coauthor and close friend for many years. Much of what I have written here, particularly about social policy, results from hours of hard work and fun conversations with her.

Others read either the full draft or at least some chapters. I thank my aunt Margarita Sánchez Castilla and my sister Milagros Sánchez

Ancochea as well as Ludovic Arnaud, Ana de Vicente Lancho, Mateo García Cabello, Ben Phillips, and Pablo Sánchez-Blanco for their constructive comments and appreciation of the project. Geoff Goodwin deserves a special mention: during the editing phase, he commented on several chapters at lightning speed.

I wrote the book while spending a sabbatical year at the Kellogg Institute for International Studies. It is hard to imagine a more welcoming place: everything there is organized to make the life of its fellows easy and productive. I thank all its staff, particularly its director Paolo Carrozza, its managing director Sharon Schierling, and its fantastic assistant director Denise Wright for all their support. Being at the Kellogg also gave me the opportunity to share time with a unique group of visiting fellows. With two of them (Ben Phillips and Vicky Paniagua) and with Ray Offenheiser I co-organized a conference on inequality and democracy that helped develop some of my thinking for the book.

At Notre Dame, I also had the opportunity to present the book's argument at the Higgins Labor Program lunch seminar series. I am thankful to its director, Daniel Graff, for the opportunity and for great conversations on inequality, labor rights, and social justice over lunch and dinner. I was also invited to discuss parts of the book in the International Seminar "Culture and the SDG" at the Universidad Tecnológica de Bolívar in Cartagena, the Labour Party constituency of Banbury and Bicester, the MA in Development Strategies and Technologies in Madrid, Mount Holoyke College in the United States, and the universities of Chile and Helsinki. I am very grateful to participants in all these events for their comments and to the following friends and colleagues for their invitation: José Miguel Ahumada, José Antonio Alonso and Iliana Olivié, Tania Jiménez and Lizzette Robleto, Jussi Pakkasvirta, and Eva Paus—always a great source of ideas and inspiration. Agenda Pública also provided a unique opportunity to publish some of my ideas on inequality, democracy, and Latin America, and I thank Marc López for it.

I could not have written this book without the sabbatical leave given by the University of Oxford. Over more than a decade, the Latin American Centre and the Oxford Department of International Development (ODID) have been great homes, full of interesting, committed, and supportive colleagues. Much of what I know about inequality comes from discussions with them. In the last few months I have had the pleasure to head the ODID; I appreciate its staff's patience in the run-up to the book's submission. Outside Oxford, I have benefited from endless support over many years from Maxine Molyneux and Ken Shadlen.

Joanna Godfrey from I.B. Tauris/Bloomsbury encouraged the idea from the very beginning. I am thankful to her and to Olivia Dellow for their support in every step of the process. Two anonymous referees also provided useful comments. I also thank Robert Davies for his great copy-editing job.

My interest in inequality and development comes from my parents Diego and Milagros. They made sure that my sister Milagros, my brother Ramón, and I understood how much the world has to change and that we embraced the need to contribute to a more just world. This is a great opportunity to acknowledge the support the four of them have always given me.

My wife Rosa and my daughters Silvia and Maya have shown great patience while I was writing this book. They always make life interesting. Rosa is one of the most creative, supportive, and brave people I know. Her commitment to fighting all kinds of inequality is inspiring. Silvia is one of the most thoughtful and critical teenagers I have ever met (of course I am biased!) and Maya is daily fun. I dedicate the book to the three of them.

Chapter 1

INTRODUCTION: LESSONS FROM THE LAND OF INEQUALITY

Occupy Wall Street, anti-austerity protests in Spain and Greece, the electoral successes of Trump, Salvini, Erdogan, and Brexit, the 2008 financial crisis, the casualization of work... We thought that the first two decades of the twenty-first century had been turbulent and then the COVID-19 outbreak made things even more complicated. The world seems to be in a continuous state of shock, with millions of people struggling.

Although poverty has been reduced in many countries and the world is wealthier than ever, a growing number of people are discontented. They see the rich becoming richer and worry about their own stagnant living standards. Many believe their children will fare worse than them, suspect that the economy is rigged, and doubt that politicians will do much to change things. The pandemic may have diverted our attention in the short run, but it is likely to make things worse, creating even larger income gaps.

The growing instability in the face of inequality is unsurprising for those of us who study Latin America. We know well the catastrophic consequences of the concentration of income and opportunities in a few hands. In Latin America—one of the most unequal regions in the world—inequality has historically contributed to many social ills, from low economic growth to weak democratic institutions and high levels of violence. Populism, financial crises, bad jobs, social polarization: Latin America has struggled with all these problems for more than a century.

This is why I decided to write this book. Little by little I have come to realize that much of the world—from the US all the way to India—looks more and more like the region I study and love. "As some western economies have become more Latin American in their distribution of incomes, their politics have also become more Latin American," the *Financial Times* commentator Martin Wolf wrote recently.[1] If you want to understand why our economies are failing to sustain growth and create good jobs for all, why our politics is increasingly broken, and why social trust is at risk, you would do well to learn more about Latin America's struggles.

Recent events in the continent have only increased the relevance of this book. Social protests in Chile and Colombia, indigenous revolts in Ecuador, and political tensions in Bolivia have shown once again how difficult it is to sustain democratic institutions and economic development in highly unequal environments. These cases also point to a growing risk across the world: the consolidation of vicious circles that become increasingly hard to break. As the wealthy become more powerful, they exert more control on the political system, people become more dissatisfied, and economic and social instability intensifies, resulting in an even worse distribution of income.

This book thus uses the Latin American experience to show the economic and political costs of inequality. We will see how large income gaps between rich and poor can hamper economic growth and contributed to a lack of good jobs. Across Latin America, the wealthy have faced limited incentives to invest in new sectors—they make healthy profits anyway—and have been unwilling to pay enough taxes to fund public social spending. Inequality has been one of the drivers of weak institutions and the emergence of anti-system politics. The poor and the middle class—losers of what they consider a rigged system— have tended to distrust traditional political parties. Often in Latin America's history they have gravitated toward leaders who promised rapid gains based on easy solutions. Inequality has also had serious social costs, from high levels of violence to urban segregation, ethnic discrimination, and lack of social trust.

The book will also help you understand how vicious circles contribute to the perpetuation of income polarization. It is not only that inequality has shaped political and economic institutions in Latin America; these institutions have in turn contributed to more inequality. For example, labor market duality (with large differences between good and bad jobs) has led to growing income gaps between workers. Politics and economics have also reinforced each other: inequality has contributed to the election of leaders who, in their search for easy solutions, have ended up triggering economic crises and ultimately favoring the wealthy.

Although the book primarily constitutes a warning, it also provides ideas on how to change path. Drawing from the Latin American experience as well as broader policy debates, I emphasize the link between ideas, policies, and politics. As you will see, I do not propose radically new solutions, because we already know much of what needs to be done to create a more equitable future. We need to strengthen social movements and make them more politically influential; we must consider distributional implications when making any policy proposal; we should renew our belief in the power of democratic institutions and also reject dominant individualistic ideals. Let's only hope that the way we react to the COVID-19 pandemic and its aftermath reinforces these messages.

I hope that readers attracted to Latin America find this account of the region's long struggles with inequality insightful. More broadly, the book should be of interest to anyone concerned with the high costs of inequality today and in the future. As we will see in the next chapters, Latin America's history provides a painful reminder of the dangers of income concentration and the urgent need to reduce it. While focusing on income, the book will consider at times its connections to inequalities in gender, race, and ethnicity.

The following pages show how much inequality has increased in developed countries in recent years and why we should be worried about it.[2] The chapter also explains why Latin America is *the* region to study if we want to understand the long-term costs of a bad distribution of income. It also describes the main tools used in this book—case studies—and why they constitute an important (if at times undervalued) approach to making sense of the world. In the concluding pages, I describe the argument of the book and reflect on some potential ways to tackle the inequality plague we are witnessing.

Inequality is Growing in Developed Countries. . . and it is Even Higher in Latin America

Here (on Nantucket in Massachusetts) "you don't feel bad because you want a nice bottle of wine. If you order a $300 bottle in a restaurant, the guy at the next table is ordering a $400 bottle" explained Michael Kittredge, an entrepreneur then worth half a billion US dollars, to a *New York Times* journalist in the mid-2000s.[3] Kittredge was part of the small elite of American CEOs, hedge fund managers, and entrepreneurs who most benefited from changes in US policy since the early 1980s.

In the last decade, the power and influence of this economic elite has become even more evident in politics and the media. In 2013 President Obama warned Americans that "the combined trends of increased inequality and decreasing mobility pose a fundamental threat to . . . our way of life," decreasing the trust in institutions, reducing opportunities for personal growth, and weakening democracy.[4]

The data on the growing concentration of income in a few hands—made popular by Thomas Piketty's bestseller *Capital in the 21st Century* (2013)—is staggering. Figure 1.1 compares the share of the total income generated in each economy of the wealthiest 1 percent in 1980 and 2015. In the US, the share of pre-tax income in the hands of the top 1 percent almost doubled between the early 1980s and the present, going from 11 percent to 20 percent. Between 2000 and 2007 this group received 65 percent of all economic growth generated in the country![5] In social democratic Sweden, the share of the top 1 percent more than doubled during the same period—from 4 to 9 percent. The US and Sweden were not exceptions: in fact, in the last 25 years, the income share of the wealthy has increased in every developed country in the graph. Things are likely to worsen as a result of the COVID-19 pandemic, as many workers lose their jobs and struggle for new opportunities, while the wealthy rapidly recuperate from the crisis.

Wealth inequality—i.e. the gap in the amount of assets such as stocks and houses owned by different groups—is even higher. Today the top 1 percent controls around 40 percent of US net wealth, compared to 25 percent in the late 1980s.[6] In the more egalitarian Norway, the share of wealth controlled by the top 1 percent has grown by seven percentage points, from 16 to around 23 percent. The rich compete with each other

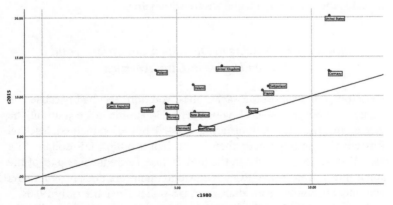

Figure 1.1 Income share of top 1 percent in some wealthy countries, c.1980 and c.2015. Source: Author's own, based on data from the World Income Inequality Database.

for the best paintings, yachts, and palaces in the French Riviera. In 2010 many people were scandalized when an Andy Warhol self-portrait sold for $32.6m—more than twice the expected $15m.[7] Nevertheless, just three years later, another Warhol reached the astonishing price of $105m.[8]

The bestselling book *The Spirit Level* (2011) demonstrates how this high inequality contributes to many social ills, including mental illness, drug abuse, homicides, and lower life expectancy.[9] It also has negative implications for politics. The "winner-takes-all" economy in which a few company managers, financial investors, and successful professionals receive huge rewards has also contributed to a "winner-takes-all" politics. This is a term coined by political scientists Jacob Hacker and Paul Pierson to describe the outsized influence that the wealthy exert in policy decisions in the US. Rich individuals and large firms have used campaign contributions, media influence, and lobbying to push for pro-rich measures in areas such as taxes, social program reform, and financial (de)regulation.[10] In Europe, lobbying is more constrained, but the economic elite (and right-wing parties) have still found alternative ways to promote a regressive agenda.[11]

None of this is surprising for Latin American experts. For a century—if not more—wealthy Latin Americans have controlled a larger share of income than anywhere else in the world. The region's staggering inequality can be illustrated through the Palma ratio, based on the work of the Chilean economist Gabriel Palma. In several studies published in the last few years, he compares the income of the richest 10 percent with that of the poorest 40 percent across the world. In many developed countries, this ratio hovers around 1:1; that is, both groups receive a similar income share. The situation in Latin America is quite different. The average Palma ratio in the region is 2.75:1—the income share of the top 10 percent of the population is almost three times higher than that of the bottom 40 percent. The economic power of the wealthy is particularly high in Colombia and Brazil—despite improvement in the latter under the Partido dos Trabalhadores (Workers' Party, PT) during the 2000s.

What's more, these numbers underestimate the actual level of inequality because they are calculated using household surveys—questionnaires about income and expenditure distributed regularly to a small sample of households. This kind of survey does not measure the income of the rich particularly well: in every society, there are just a few wealthy individuals who often refuse to answer income questions and when they do, they are not always truthful.

As we just saw for the case of developed countries, tax-based data on top incomes provides a more accurate perspective on the growing

Table 1.1 Income share of the top 1 percent in some Latin American countries, 1997–2014

	Argentina	Brazil	Chile	Colombia	Mexico	Uruguay
1997	12%			21%		
2000	14%			17%	27%	
2003	17%			20%		
2004	17%			18%	25%	
2005			22–32%	19%		
2006		23%	21–31%	20%	27%	
2007		24%	21–31%	21%		
2008		26%	24–36%	20%	27%	
2009		25%	22–33%	20%		14%
2010		25%	20–30%	20%	26%	14%
2011		27%	20–30%			14%
2012		26%	20–30%		27%	
2013						
2014					30%	

Source: Author's own, based on data from several studies.

concentration of income. Unfortunately, the same kind of data is only available for a handful of Latin American countries. The results from these studies are astonishing. As reflected in Table 1.1, the top 1 percent control 30 percent of total income in Chile and Mexico and around a quarter in Brazil. While Argentina and Uruguay perform comparatively better, the income share of the wealthy there is still high by global standards.

Behind these numbers lie disparities that are evident in all sorts of ways. Think, for example, about São Paulo, where millions of workers struggle daily with notoriously bad traffic—a two-hour commute is common—while 500 helicopters, more than in any other city in the world, fly the wealthy from one business meeting to another at lightning speed.[12] In Mexico, the wealth of Carlos Slim, owner of the mobile company América Móvil and investor in well-known international firms like the *New York Times*, is equivalent to 5 percent of the whole country and could fund its education budget four times over.

Exploring Inequality Through Case Studies

In the era of big data and powerful computers, quantitative methods have become the dominant approach to analyzing social problems.

Studies that explore correlations between numbers are supposed to be objective, because they use data collected through independent surveys; reliable, because they can be replicated; and generalizable, because they incorporate information from many different countries and/or periods. Using other sources and methodologies to study issues like inequality is almost unimaginable for many mainstream academics and policymakers.

Despite their popularity, studies of this kind are not without problems. Many use data uncritically, failing to fully understand its sources and acknowledge its limitations. Data mining is not uncommon: some researchers search for the relations they can find in their data without reflecting on their meaning or linking them to specific theories. Even more problematic is the emphasis of most researchers on simplicity: they systematically ignore the complexity of human life, struggle to uncover causal relations, and disregard the complex links between economic, political, and social processes.

Case studies constitute a powerful alternative and can solve many of these problems. They are in-depth explorations of countries, regions, or cities, and of other social processes such as revolutions, democratic transitions, and development "miracles." Case study research relies on multiple sources, including books, official memos, interviews, newspaper articles, and documents from archives, as well as statistics. Researchers triangulate all this data, comparing and contrasting different sources in order to make causal claims about the world. They may explore how wealthy individuals influence politicians, how the poor fight for social rights, or how political and economic inequalities interact in specific countries and/or periods of time.

There are all kinds of case studies—some are comparative while others rely on a single unit; some aim to propose new theories while others focus on testing old ones—and many ways to implement them. Discussing all possible alternatives would require a totally different book. What is most relevant for us is that all case studies provide a unique opportunity to explain complex relations between income distribution, democracy, and development, drawing on a range of examples and experiences.

This book considers the case of Latin America to explore the consequences of inequality. To justify why this selection makes sense, it is useful to consider two questions. Can we really talk about "Latin America" as a single unit? Can we draw lessons from the Latin American experience?

There is no doubt that Latin American countries are different in size (Brazil is 400 times bigger than El Salvador), population (Brazil and

Mexico together have more people than all the other countries combined), income (Chile's gross domestic product per capita is closer to Spain's than to Bolivia's), and racial composition. Yet all of them share enough similarities to be grouped together. All Latin American countries have a similar history: they became colonies of Spain and Portugal during the sixteenth century, gained independence during the nineteenth century, and then had to deal with similar obstacles to building effective institutions. The state is weaker than in developed countries: corruption is an endemic problem, changes in rules and regulations are common, and policies are often inconsistent. They have always had to deal with influential external actors, including the US, and struggled with external dependence. Latin American countries also share some cultural traits, including a common language (with the exception of Brazil ... but Portuguese and Spanish are similar), and many social similarities. They are some of the most urbanized countries in the developing world, and most have large non-white minorities.

Particularly important for this book—and relevant to answering our second question—is the fact that all Latin American countries suffer from a highly unequal distribution of income. Of course, inequality is not exclusive to them; countries at different levels of development (from the US to China and India) have witnessed large gaps between the rich and poor at different points in their history. What makes the region unique is the persistence of high inequality over long periods of time. Although academics conduct heated debates over whether this problem began in colonial times or during the late nineteenth century, there is little doubt that inequality has been high for decades.

But can we use the example of Latin America to draw lessons for other countries and regions? Many readers will be skeptical and believe that the Latin American experience can teach little to countries like the US, the UK, or India. You may wonder how anyone can compare a poor region specialized in mining and oil with wealthy countries that have diversified economies and strong institutions. Many will believe that stable countries with durable political parties and consolidated democracies cannot learn anything from extreme cases.

Paradoxically, most people do not have the same queries when the experience of developed countries is used to draw lessons. Studies about how Sweden created its welfare state, why the US has repeatedly succeeded in introducing technological innovations, or what led South Korea, Taiwan, and Singapore to transform their economies so successfully often conclude with policy lessons for other parts of the world. In fact, our understanding of economic development still relies heavily on our interpretation of the historical experience of wealthy countries—despite obvious cultural, historical, and institutional differences.

If developing countries can learn from developed ones, we should also be able to draw lessons in the opposite direction. Latin America's experience can be particularly relevant. Its countries are older and richer than many others in the developing world, and benefit from longer democratic traditions and better institutions. Three of them (Chile, Colombia, and Mexico) have even become members of the Organisation for Economic Co-operation and Development (OECD), the "rich country club." Additionally, Latin American societies have historically been characterized by the kind of ethnic diversity and economic duality that is now becoming the norm in many other parts of the world.

The Book's Arguments: The Economic, Political, and Social Costs of Inequality

"Although the region has achieved significant success in reducing extreme poverty in the last decade, it still shows high levels of income and wealth inequality, which have been an obstacle to sustainable economic growth and social inclusion." Thus proclaimed the heads of the Economic Commission for Latin America and the Caribbean (ECLAC), Alicia Bárcena, and Oxfam International, Winnie Byanyima, in 2016.[13] Years earlier, in an influential regional report the World Bank warned that economic and political inequality have limited economic development.[14]

Following these statements from leading international institutions, this book will show how more than a century of inequality in Latin America has contributed to poor economic performance, weak political institutions, and social problems. In turn, low growth, exclusionary politics, and violence and social mistrust have reinforced the concentration of income, generating vicious circles.

Several mechanisms explain these pernicious relations. First, and starting from the economy, a small elite, which has always controlled a large share of land and financial resources, has faced limited incentives to increase productivity and invest in more advanced economic sectors. To be sure, the business elite has diversified into new activities at different times, but they have generally been low risk, not particularly sophisticated, and/or dependent on the government. This is still evident, for example, when considering the list of the ten wealthiest Latin Americans, a group made up of nine men and one woman coming from just four countries (Brazil, Chile, Colombia, and Mexico). Their revenue comes from highly regulated telecommunication services (Carlos Slim), finance (Jorge Paulo Lemann, Joseph Saphra, Luis Carlos Sarmiento Angulo), food and drinks processing (Marcel Herrmann Telles, Iris Fontbona, Carlos Alberto Sicupira), and mining (Iris Fontbona, Germán Larrea Mota Velasco, Alberto Baillères González).[15] Why would they move into new, high-tech sectors when they can secure huge returns in low-risk activities?

Lack of systematic innovation has gone hand in hand with insufficient investment in education. Together, both processes have contributed to a relatively low number of well-paying jobs. In fact, the kind of labor market polarization evident in many wealthy countries today has been a feature of Latin America for quite some time. During much of the twentieth century, economic activity concentrated on large plantations, mining, and some manufacturing production—activities that created limited formal employment. Most workers had bad jobs that paid little and did not provide access to social benefits. The process of market liberalization promoted by orthodox economists in the 1980s and 1990s did not change this negative relationship between inequality and the economy: a small number of well-connected men (unfortunately they are still mostly men) benefited from the privatization of public companies, while few domestic firms were able to successfully compete internationally. As a result, informality—that is, poorly paid jobs with no social benefits attached—remained high across the continent from Mexico to Paraguay.

Second, the lack of economic dynamism has much to do with the control of policymaking by the wealthy—politics and economics can seldom be separated. The top 1 percent successfully pressured for low taxes: most Latin American states collect less than they should, given their level of development.[16] Personal income taxes are particularly low: in 2015 they accounted for less than 10 percent of total tax revenues compared to almost 25 percent in OECD countries.[17] At the same time, most Latin American countries have failed to spend enough on basic public healthcare and education. Until very recently, support for universities and sophisticated hospitals for the rich was high, while spending in primary education and rural health clinics was insufficient. Adopting effective macroeconomic policies and avoiding financial crises has also been harder due to inequality.

Third, given these exclusionary policies and lack of economic dynamism, it is not surprising that citizens have repeatedly supported populist responses. Leaders like Juan Domingo Perón in Argentina in the 1940s and 1950s or Hugo Chávez in Venezuela more recently promised to provide good jobs and adequate social benefits to the poor and the urban middle classes. Unfortunately, their governments often ended up implementing unsustainable economic policies, while proving unable or unwilling to systematically confront the power of the wealthy—a lesson voters in developed countries would do well to remember.

Inequality has affected politics negatively in Latin America in many other ways. It has contributed to polarization and reduced the space for political compromise. The elite has never shown a willingness to strengthen state capacity or promote effective anti-corruption measures, while social movements have seldom been powerful enough to advance reform agendas. Brazil's instability in recent years constitutes a great example of the negative links between weak institutions, corruption, and inequality-induced political conflict. Under presidents Lula and Rousseff, the government implemented redistributive policies that favored the poor, yet failed to promote transparency and reduce corruption. Conservative forces—which have always protected the rich in Brazil—took advantage of this failure to reverse most progressive policies, halting the reduction of inequality.

Fourth, inequality has also been linked to various social problems from violence to social mistrust. Latin America is not only the most violent region in the world but also one where people have little trust in each other—problems that are at least partly caused by large income gaps. High income inequality is also linked with disparities in many other dimensions, including gender and ethnicity. Inequality has also contributed to urban segregation and to ethnic and racial discrimination. In turn, these social problems have hampered the growth of coalitions between the poor and the middle class, which are required to implement more redistributive public policies.

In sum, Latin America's experience shows the negative impact of income gaps on the economy (by leading to underinvestment, particularly in dynamic sectors and human capital, and to periodic economic crises), on politics (by contributing to weak democracies and promoting personalistic politics), and on the social fabric (by contributing to violence, social mistrust, and lack of cohesion). The region's history also demonstrates the high probability that inequality persists over time, further reducing the chances to create dynamic and integrated societies.

What makes the Latin American discussion particularly relevant today is that similar problems are increasingly evident in many other countries. Inequality, labor market dualism, financial crises, and political instability are growing everywhere. Wealthy countries like the US look more and more like Latin America and—if they do not reverse direction—could suffer many of the same negative interactions over the long run. Unfortunately, avoiding the costs of inequality will become harder and harder: Latin America shows that reversing the income gap is difficult precisely because of negative political and economic feedbacks.

Our discussion in this book may also be relevant for large emerging economies such as China and India. In recent years, both Asian giants have grown rapidly while experiencing a growing concentration of income at the top. As a result, they are witnessing the type of elite-driven politics and institutional weakening that was evident in Latin America for more than a century. If their economies were to slow down—as a result, for example, of the COVID-19 pandemic—the negative impacts of income inequality could become more evident and feed into social discontent. In other parts of the developing world, inequality is already a growing source of economic and political tensions as well.

How Do We Move from Here? Some Latin American Lessons

This book constitutes a warning: it draws on Latin America's experience to highlight the political and economic costs of inequality. Vicious cycles of high inequality, economic underperformance, and anti-system politics can easily become a norm more than an exception and will be hard to reverse. If we do not act now, things could easily go from bad to worse in the twenty-first century.

Yet Latin America's history also offers positive lessons. The region has become a hotbed of progressive ideas that provide unique perspectives on inequality and exclusion. Appalled by their everyday experience, economists, sociologists, theologians, and educators have elaborated original theories and pushed for ambitious policy and political reforms. Some of the most creative and active social movements in the world can be found in Latin America. From the *Movimiento dos Trabalhadores Rurais Sem Terra* (the Rural Landless Movement, MST) in Brazil to the *cocalero* movement and its political party, the *Movimiento al Socialismo* (Movement toward Socialism, MAS) in Bolivia, activists in Latin America have successfully pushed for more rights. Although they have not been able to reduce inequality as much as they would have liked, these movements can teach much to activists in other parts of the world. Their experience demonstrates, for example, the importance of pressure from below on unresponsive states; the need to link local and national struggles; the usefulness of connecting concrete needs with broader development agendas; and the relevance of building cross-class coalitions. Latin American movements have also been extremely successful at combining traditional mobilization techniques with the use of social media.

Latin America's recent trajectory also offers some room for optimism: inequality can be reduced even in this period of (neoliberal) globalization and in difficult institutional environments. Between 2003 and 2013, most Latin American countries improved their distribution of income, precisely at a time when income gaps were increasing in the rest of the world. Some of the drivers of this recent improvement are not particularly relevant for wealthy economies but may be important for developing countries. In some Latin American countries, the poor became the subject of social rights for the first time in history, contributing to a rapid increase in their income. The power of electoral competition to promote some level of inclusion is a second useful lesson.

Other lessons are relevant for developed and developing countries alike. The policy effort that some governments undertook to unify the social benefits that different people receive is particularly interesting. In Uruguay, for example, the healthcare system was revamped so that everyone—both those contributing to social insurance funds and those who were part of the public system—could receive the same basket of benefits.[18] The arrival of a left-wing government with a historical commitment to equity and close links to social movements was—at least in part—behind this reform. Uruguay also implemented a new National System of Care, which simultaneously supported the elderly in need and pre-school children.[19]

In Brazil, a drive to formalize many unskilled jobs together with steady rises in the minimum wage contributed to a rapid improvement in income distribution. Between 2002 and 2008, the share of formal workers increased by six percentage points. Economic growth was partly behind this positive trend, but progressive policies (including the simplification of taxes for small firms and the expansion of labor inspections) were also important. Efforts to increase formalization went hand in hand with a rapid expansion of the real minimum wage, which went from R$263 in 2000 to R$465 in 2009.[20] Brazil's experience thus questions the much-repeated argument that minimum wages have a negative impact on job creation.[21]

The 2000s in Latin America thus demonstrate that, even in weak institutional environments, public policy matters in the fight against inequality. There are also more policy options than usually recognized. Of course, I should not exaggerate Latin America's recent success. Inequality remains high across the region and its reduction has been moderate. Moreover, recent improvements may not be sustained: now that the Latin American economies are growing less, the reduction of the income gap has slowed down.

Countries in both Latin America and other parts of the world need to move urgently to promote equity. The book concludes with an exploration of policy options and political requirements to make that happen. The fight against inequality will demand concerted efforts in many areas from wealth taxes to financial regulation and from stronger democracies to more ambitious social policies. At a deeper level, it requires a reframing of what a good society is, moving away from our current focus on individualism and meritocracy and embracing solidarity and community across the world. Will the COVID-19 pandemic make this reframing more likely, or create even more obstacles for it?

The Rest of the Book

The rest of the book illustrates the negative relation between inequality, economic development, and political institutions in Latin America. I show how income gaps are related to negative political economy outcomes—and how those outcomes often feed back into an even worse distribution of income. Each chapter relates the Latin American experience to the current situation in OECD countries. For example, I show how economic problems such as labor market dualism and financial crises are increasingly evident in rich societies where income gaps are expanding. Although the comparisons draw primarily on the US, the UK, and Southern European countries such as Spain and Portugal, the conclusions extend to many other countries.

In Chapter 3, I review the links and interactions between inequality and economic outcomes. We see how a poor distribution of income has been one of the causes of lack of quality education. Income gaps have also contributed to the consolidation of dual economies and insufficient investment in high-tech activities. The dynamic sectors have not changed much during the last century, in part because the wealthy had limited incentives to invest in more dynamic but risky sectors. At the other end, informal sectors with low productivity have expanded, providing bad jobs to millions of workers who then have not had enough resources to innovate. I also show how inequality may have been connected to low taxation and to unsustainable macroeconomic policies at different times in history, and how this contributed to financial crises—not unlike the experience in the US a decade ago.

Chapter 4 discusses the links between inequality and politics. I show how the winner-takes-all politics that characterizes the US today appeared much earlier in Latin America, where the wealthy have always exerted an outsized influence on democratic governments. At times, the Latin American elite has gone as far as supporting military coups and authoritarian governments.

Probably even more interesting for most readers will be the connection between inequality and populism—a rather problematic term that I use to refer to anti-system politicians who build direct connections to the electorate. Populist leaders have historically been a direct result of people's discontent with the political system and with the concentration of income and wealth. Some populists in Latin America improved the lives of large segments of the middle class and the poor—something President Trump is failing to do—but their positive impact often proved unsustainable. Politically, they eroded the party system, reduced the opportunities for informed policy debates, and weakened democratic institutions. Economically, populist governments often redistributed income in unsustainable ways, thus contributing to economic mismanagement. Will we witness some of the same problems in wealthy countries in the future?

Chapter 5 explores the social costs of inequality. I first consider the complex relationship between violence and inequality. While Latin America's record level of crime has many roots, I show how large income gaps between poor communities (where millions of young people feel marginalized) and the wealthy are a significant factor. In Latin America, inequality has also contributed to urban segregation and to the fragmentation of social services. Unfortunately, the wealthy seldom share hospitals and schools with the lower middle class and the poor, making social cohesion harder. The chapter also explores the ways in which ethnic and racial discrimination and income inequality reinforce each other. All these problems have contributed to a lack of social trust—the confidence that people have in their neighbors and public institutions. Inequality contributes to societies where every individual roots for him/herself and struggles to cooperate with others. In societies like this, the opportunities to create the kind of intra-class coalitions (between the poor and the middle class) required to expand redistributive social programs are severely hampered—a problem that is gradually becoming evident in other parts of the world as well.

Chapter 6 moves to the positive lessons that Latin America can offer. High inequality has contributed to the emergence of progressive ideas and social movements. From economic structuralism to the Catholic theology of liberation and from Mexico's Zapatistas to Chile's student movement, the region's dynamism can be an inspiration for activists across the world. The chapter also discusses the (moderate) improvement in income distribution that took place in Latin America in the 2000s. The story is well known among regional experts and policymakers but ignored in the rest of the world. Latin America's recent trajectory is rather paradoxical: one of the most unequal regions was improving precisely at a time when much of the rest of the world (from the US and the UK to China and India) was experiencing a growing concentration of income at the top.

After summarizing the main arguments of the book, the concluding chapter discusses what can be done to reverse course. What ideas could should guide our fight in the future? What policies should we promote? And what kind of political actors and social coalitions do we need to implement these policies and sustain political change? The chapter explicitly rejects simplistic or so-called revolutionary ideas; in fact, we already know much of what needs to be done. Countries must improve the distribution of human capital and wealth, redistribute power within the key markets, expand financial regulation and improve (or adopt for the first time) universal social programs. Of course, the implementation of such an ambitious policy agenda will only happen under the right political conditions. Deeper democracies, renewed progressive political parties, and stronger social movements are indispensable to win this fight.

Before discussing costs and solutions, let me first tell you a little bit more about the characteristics of inequality in Latin America: when it began, what we know about its evolution over time, and how bad it is today. This next chapter will examine the severity of the distributional problems in the region and show the relevance of Latin America for the rest of the world today and in the future.

Chapter 2

LATIN AMERICA: ALWAYS THE MOST UNEQUAL REGION?

Alexander von Humboldt was the archetypical scientific adventurer from the Romantic era. Almost 250 years ago, together with the French explorer Aimé Bonpland, he sailed to the Americas. Guided by his intense curiosity, he climbed the Chimborazo in Ecuador and discovered Venezuela's Casiquiare Canal, which links the Amazon and Orinoco rivers.[1]

Humboldt wrote extensively about his five years in the Americas, reflecting on the region's geography and on its people. He was particularly struck by high inequality. For example, he described Mexico as "the country of inequality. Nowhere does there exist such a fearful difference in the distribution of fortune, civilization, cultivation of the soil and population."[2]

If Humboldt could go back to Mexico today, he would still see sharp differences between rich and poor. In 2014, the wealth of the richest four Mexicans was equivalent to 9 percent of the country's annual production. Just using the yearly return from his wealth, Carlos Slim— the richest of all—could hire almost two million Mexicans at the minimum wage.[3] In the rest of the region, things are not very different: the wealthy everywhere maintain a privileged position. For example, each Latin American high net worth individual—a euphemism used by the financial industry to refer to people who own more than $1 million in assets, excluding their main house—has an average wealth of $14.5 million compared to $10.1 million in Africa and less than $4 million in the Middle East, North America, Asia Pacific, and Europe.[4]

This second chapter reviews Latin America's history of income distribution. I show how inequality has remained always high, despite significant variations across time and space. Latin America has repeatedly failed to sustain reductions in the income gap for long periods of time—contrary to what has happened in other parts of the world. This persistence of inequality over the long run makes the region's experience particularly relevant for current debates.

The Most Unequal Region of the World?

The Serbian economist Branko Milanović is one of the premier experts on inequality in the world. An amazing number cruncher and a creative thinker, he has succeeded in making the study of income distribution interesting and fun. In his books you can learn about almost anything, from Marx's contribution to the social sciences to life during the Roman Empire or the contemporary problems of global inequality. While at the World Bank, Milanović led an impressive effort to collect and compare hundreds of household surveys across the world. His data provided a better understanding of changes in global inequality—that is, the place of each human being in the world's income distribution—than before, and allowed researchers to compare the position of different countries. Figure 2.1 below is one of Milanović's most popular graphs, which I often discuss in my courses at Oxford. It locates Indian, Russian, American, Chinese, and Brazilian citizens on two axes: one measures their place in the national distribution of income, while the other locates them in the global distribution. The measure is not perfect: the data fails to account for the

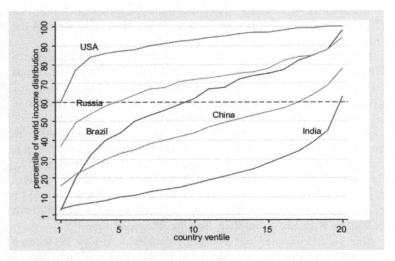

Figure 2.1 Brazil's unique pattern of distribution in the early 2000s. Note: The table places individuals within the income distribution of their country and the world. Income is measured at purchasing power parity dollars of 2002. Source: Milanović, B. (2012), "Global Income Inequality by the Numbers, in History and Now: An Overview," World Bank Policy Research Working Paper no. 6259.

richest people in each country, whose income—as I have already mentioned—is always underestimated in this kind of survey.

Notice Brazil's unique position: low-income Brazilians are among the poorest in the world while those at the top are almost as wealthy as in the US. Other data sources confirm Brazil's scandalous level of inequality: for example, the country's six richest men control as much wealth as the bottom half of the population. Even more staggering, each member of the richest 0.1 percent makes in a month the same as a worker receiving the minimum wage earns in 19 years.[5] Brazil's experience reflects a broader regional trend; in fact, in some countries, including Colombia, Guatemala, and Honduras, the situation may be even worse.

Of course, comparing inequality across the world is not easy: each country measures income distribution in a slightly different way, the quality of the data varies significantly, and the wealthy are not adequately captured in household surveys. Yet all the available information seems to confirm that Latin America is at the top of any ranking of inequality. For example, in a study of the Palma ratio—which, as we saw in Chapter 1, compares the income of the top 10 percent and the bottom 40 percent—12 of the 18 worst performing countries were Latin American, and no Latin American country was part of the group of more equitable developing countries.[6]

The Gini coefficient is an even more popular measure of inequality. It considers the income received by every individual in a society and goes from 0 (perfect equality) to 1 (total inequality). The Gini in Latin America is five percentage points higher than in other developing countries (see Figure 2.2): the contrast with Eastern Europe and Central Asia is particularly striking.

The unequal income distribution affects rich countries like Argentina and poor ones like Guatemala or Honduras, countries with a large indigenous population like Bolivia and more homogenous ones like Chile. As the General Secretary of the Economic Commission for Latin America and the Caribbean (ECLAC) puts it, "inequality is a historical and structural characteristic of the societies of Latin America and the Caribbean, which is evident in multiple vicious circles."[7]

Nevertheless, there are also significant differences within the region which we should remember in the rest of the book. Latin America includes 18 Spanish-speaking countries (including the Caribbean Islands of Cuba and the Dominican Republic) and Brazil. Their members have different levels of income (Uruguay's income per capita is more than seven times higher than Nicaragua's), export specialization (apparel and agriculture in Central America and the Caribbean, commodities in the rest), and histories. Some of these political and economic differences

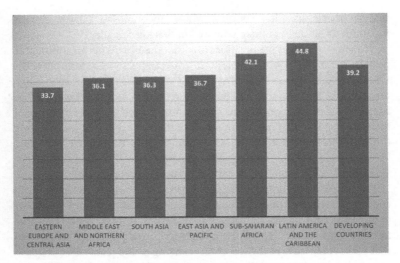

Figure 2.2 Gini coefficient for the distribution of household consumption per capita in developing countries, 2010. Source: Author's own, based on data from Alvarado, F., and L. Gasparini, "Recent Trends in Inequality and Poverty in Developing Countries," in A. Atkinson and F. Bourguignon (2015), *The Handbook of Income Distribution*, Amsterdam: Elsevier, pp. 697–805.

also translate into differences in income distribution: see Figure 2.3, which compares the Palma ratio and the share of the "middle class"— those in deciles five to nine—in 18 Latin American countries during the period 2000–16. Argentina and Uruguay stand out as the best countries in Latin America; they have historically benefited from a more diverse economy, a larger middle class, and a weaker elite. Other countries, such as El Salvador and Peru, were historically unequal but have improved in recent years because of a variety of political and economic factors including democratization (in both), the influence of the left (in El Salvador), and high economic growth (in Peru). In contrast, Brazil, Honduras, Colombia, Panama, and Guatemala remain at the top of the regional and global inequality rankings.

It's About the Rich, Stupid!

The reason why inequality is so large in Latin America is not that the poor are poorer than in other parts of the world, but that the rich are

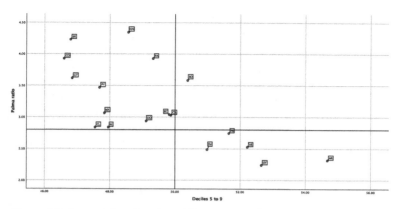

Figure 2.3 Recognizing diversity within an unequal region. Source: Author's own, based on data from the Socio-Economic Database for Latin America and the Caribbean (SCEDLAS).

richer. Take, for example, the case of Chile: there, poverty has declined rapidly in recent years and the income gap between the poor and the middle class is similar to that in more developed parts of the world. In fact, among the bottom 90 percent of the population, Chile is more equal than many OECD countries and social mobility—the probability that someone improves their social position compared to their parents— is higher.[8]

What distinguishes Chile from wealthier countries is the concentration of income at the very top. According to some estimates, the richest 1 percent in Chile control more than 30 percent of annual production, compared to 18 percent in the US—a very unequal country in its own right.[9] Clearly there are not one but two Chiles: in one, a small elite enjoys expensive houses, well-paying jobs, and the security that their children and grandchildren will maintain superb living standards. In the other Chile, the middle class and the poor face more economic uncertainty and can seldom influence political institutions or shape economic change.

Chile is by no means an exception in Latin America: according to *Breaking with History?*, the World Bank report on inequality I mentioned earlier, "Latin American distributions are mainly characterized by a higher income share among the rich relative to countries in other regions."[10] The Latin American rich control a shocking proportion of resources: for example, the wealth of all multimillionaires is 8.5 times greater than the annual expenditure on public health and almost five times higher than public investment in education.[11]

The differences in the lives of the wealthy and the poor in Latin America are extreme. Take the case of Mexico. There, Carlos Slim, one of the three wealthiest people in the world, owns so many pieces of art—including, for example, 380 Rodin sculptures—that he created one of the best art museums in Mexico to host them all.[12] In contrast, millions of Mexicans live in poverty, despite working long hours for the minimum wage. Indigenous people fare even worse: three out of four are poor and almost two in five live in extreme poverty.[13]

Inequality in Latin America is thus primarily about the concentration of income within a small elite—not even the top 10 percent but the top 1 and 0.1 percent. Who are they? In which sectors do they participate? Where does their wealth come from? Unfortunately, it is not easy to answer these questions: we have almost no quantitative information about these groups, who tend to be secretive and unwilling to collaborate with researchers. To understand their characteristics, one needs to rely on a variety of sources of different quality, including articles in national media, data from global media outlets, and country-level academic studies.

One of these sources is the list of world billionaires published annually by *Forbes*. According to its ranking, in 2018 there were 90 billionaires in Latin America, almost half of whom were located in Brazil (Table 2.1). Their combined wealth was equal to $412 billion, of which 77 percent was in the hands of Brazilian and Mexican nationals. The list included individuals from the largest seven economies in Latin America; the elites in other countries are also politically and economically powerful, but their overall wealth is constrained by the smaller size of their economies.

Travel to any of the best-known Latin American cities and this elite-driven inequality will become immediately evident. Take the case of São Paulo, the largest city in the region with more than 13 million people—33 million, if the entire metropolitan region is counted—a third of whom live in slum-like conditions. If you walk west from Ibirapuera Park—a vibrant combination of lawns, museums, a music hall, and Niemeyer-designed buildings—you arrive at Vila Nova Conceição. Combining upscale restaurants, government offices, and apartment buildings, Vila Nova is one of the most expensive neighborhoods in Latin America. You need $500,000 to buy a 100m² apartment or between $7 and 8m to purchase a four-bedroom duplex in one of the new building complexes.[14] From there, you can walk to neighboring Vila Olimpia, home of multinational companies like Unilever, Santander, and Facebook and well known for its bars and nightclubs.[15] The contrast between these

Table 2.1 Latin Americans in the list of world billionaires, 2018

Country	Number	Total wealth	Average wealth	Wealth (% GDP)
Argentina	9	15.6	1.7	2.4
Brazil	42	176.4	4.2	8.6
Chile	11	41.9	3.8	15.1
Colombia	4	20.8	5.2	6.7
Mexico	16	141.2	8.8	12.3
Peru	6	10.9	1.8	5.2
Venezuela	2	5.5	2.8	N/A

Note: The wealth data was downloaded in September 2018, while GDP is from 2017 and comes from the World Bank. Source: Author's calculation based on data downloaded from www.forbes.com in September 2018.

areas of São Paulo and the many favelas that surround the city could not be more striking.[16] There, you will find 1.2 million people struggling with high levels of crime and violence (as discussed in Chapter 5), poor infrastructure, low-quality housing, and no employment opportunities. Moving from São Paulo to Mexico City, Bogotá, or Caracas will only confirm Latin America's glaring contrasts.

Always Unequal?

Latin America's inequality is not new. Many experts locate its origin in colonial times. When Spaniards arrived in the Americas, they tried to replicate the social, economic, and legal system they had left behind in the Iberian Peninsula.[17] Their hope was to get rich quickly, while working as little as possible. To achieve this goal, the conquerors first instituted the *encomiendas*, which gave them ownership over large tracts of land as well as the right to tax indigenous people living there. A small elite of newcomers received a huge amount of resources from the Crown; for example, Hernán Cortés alone "controlled" more than 100,000 Indians. Indigenous people had to work for the *encomendero* and pay taxes in the form of corn, wheat, cloth, chickens, and many other goods to sustain the Spaniards' lavish standards of living.

The *encomienda* proved to be inefficient and unpopular and was eventually eliminated. Yet it was soon replaced by other exploitative systems such as the *repartimiento* and the *mita*. In theory these new systems gave indigenous people more rights (e.g. limits on how much they had to work), but in practice they represented new forms of forced labor. Indians still had to work for a member of the elite and pay high taxes. Conditions in the mines were particularly difficult: thousands of Indians struggled with 12-hour shifts hundreds of feet below the surface, poor-quality air, and daily abuses.

The colonial political system was extremely hierarchical. The descendants of the Spanish conquerors—either white or of mixed race—controlled local, regional, and national institutions and received more and better education than anyone else. Men occupied positions of power while women were treated as inferiors. The Spaniards' primary aim was to maintain an exclusionary economic system, while limiting the influence and power of indigenous groups and slaves. They lived in fear of a revolution from below: at the end of the eighteenth century, for example, the Caracas elite warned against the creation of army battalions made of people of color because they would "increase the arrogance of the pardos, and give them organization, chiefs, and arms to facilitate a revolution."[18]

According to many academics, this colonial system produced some of the highest levels of inequality in the world.[19] Ownership of land gave the elite enough influence and power to shape political institutions and policies exclusively in their favor.[20] Indigenous people, slaves, and, later, their descendants received extremely low wages and no public social benefits.

Some other academics have questioned this dominant story. For example, the economic historian Jeffrey Williamson believes that for centuries Latin America was not particularly unequal. According to his estimates, inequality in France in 1788 or in England in 1801 was actually higher than in Peru in 1856 or Brazil in 1872.[21] According to this perspective, Latin America did not become the most unequal region of the world until the twentieth century, after the first wave of globalization.

The contemporary relevance of this discussion on the origins of Latin America's inequality should not be exaggerated. Maybe the distribution of income was no worse in Latin America in the middle of the nineteenth century than in England during the Industrial Revolution; rapid economic transformation in Manchester, London, and other British cities did create wealthy winners and millions of losers, as Karl Marx eloquently explained. Yet it is clear that in Latin America institutions and policies were organized in favor of the powerful from early on: huge *latifundios*, underinvestment in primary education, and restrictive voting rights were the norm across the region.

The negative implications of this elitist model became particularly clear at the end of the nineteenth century. A series of technological innovations made international trade easier and cheaper, leading to the first wave of globalization. The construction of railways, the inauguration of long-distance steam service, and the introduction of refrigeration moved Latin America closer to the US and Europe: according to some estimates, transatlantic transport costs decreased by 45 percent between 1870 and 1913.[22] Latin American exports of beef, agricultural products, and minerals expanded quickly.

When the first wave of globalization met Latin America's traditional institutions, inequality accelerated. In Argentina, Brazil, Chile, and Uruguay the Gini coefficient increased by at least five percentage points between 1870 and 1920.[23] Rich landowners found new opportunities to make large amounts of money through exports. They benefited from the new trains connecting their regions to the main ports and from public efforts to further concentrate land in a few hands. Another world-renowned US historian, John Coatsworth, explains this dramatic transformation well: "modernization appears to have produced a massive new concentration of land ownership provoked, inter alia, by railroads that brought opportunities for commercial exploitation to once isolated regions; technological change (especially in sugar) that created economies of scale; the rapid development of large banana plantations in the tropics; and the sale of public lands in large blocks to land and survey companies and well-connected entrepreneurs."[24]

Latin America has remained the land of inequality since then—with the dire consequences that we will consider in the next chapters. It is true that income distribution improved in some periods thanks to economic growth and redistributive policies. The 1930s–1960s was a particularly positive period for countries such as Chile, Mexico, and Uruguay: industrialization, urbanization, and the expansion of social programs enlarged the middle class and reduced the income share of the rich. Yet progressive redistribution faced major obstacles, including a powerful elite and weak labor markets. Unluckier countries like Colombia and most of Central America never witnessed a significant reduction of the income gap.[25] The combination of a dual economy, weak political institutions, and a powerful economic elite—all inherited from the past—contributed to vicious circles of inequality. In contrast, during this same period, much of Europe, together with Australia, Canada, and New Zealand (as well as some developing countries such as China), experienced a "Great Leveling" as the income of the poor and the middle class grew much faster than that of the wealthy.

No Longer an Exception: Growing Inequality in Other Parts of the World

Of course, the Great Leveling is long gone, having finished abruptly in the late 1970s. Between the mid-1980s and the late 2000s, income distribution worsened in 17 OECD countries, while decreasing in just two (Turkey and Greece).[26] Outside the OECD, the expansion of inequality was also the norm: between 1990 and 2010 it increased by 11 percent in developing countries, according to the United Nations.[27] This negative trend has been particularly clear in the two Asian giants: China, one of the most equal countries in the world until the 1980s, is now one of the most unequal,[28] and India has a worse distribution of income today than at any time since data was first reported in 1922.[29]

This expansion of inequality across the world has been driven by the concentration of income at the top. The number of billionaires continues to expand rapidly, and the share of income and wealth controlled by the rich is staggering. In recent years, China has produced two new billionaires *per day* while in India—a country now ruled by billionaires according to the former *Financial Times* journalist James Crabtree—the top 1 percent owns 58 percent of total wealth—eight percentage points more than in the rest of the world.[30] In the US, the situation is not much different, as we saw in the introductory chapter.

Elite-driven inequality—a classic Latin American phenomenon—is now evident even in Northern Europe. According to the Swedish professor Jesper Roine, "Sweden is still a very equal society compared to most other countries. But it's true that gaps in income have grown, and Sweden is no longer as different as it once was in that sense."[31] The Nordic country now hosts 113,000 high net worth individuals—making the list of top 25 countries for the first time in 2017—and more than a dozen billionaires. In Norway, the number of high net worth individuals increased by 13 percent in 2017, more than in any other European country but Russia and the Netherlands.[32]

Will this growing concentration of income at the top just be a temporary phenomenon? Will we witness a new Great Leveling in years to come? Although providing a definite answer to these questions is almost impossible, the Latin American experience does not give us cause for optimism. We will see why in the next three chapters, where we will consider the economic, political, and social costs of inequality in Latin America and identify a series of vicious circles.

Chapter 3

THE ECONOMIC COSTS OF INEQUALITY

In 2013, Gregory Mankiw, a famous Harvard professor and former advisor to President George W. Bush, went to the rescue of the wealthy with an article titled "Defending the One Percent."[1] Inviting readers to reflect on the positive contributions that Steve Jobs, J.K. Rowling, and Steven Spielberg have made, he claimed that the rich were simply reaping the benefits of their unique contribution to society. In his view, inequality does not harm economic development and any attempt to reduce it through redistribution would be damaging.

In his fearless defense of the rich, Mankiw echoed a number of right-wing politicians and conservative economists for whom inequality can actually be positive. Their arguments include "high salaries are required to promote innovation," "giving more resources to the rich will increase savings and investment," and "it is good to have economies dominated by the most intelligent people." Of course, if these commentators were correct, unequal countries should have developed faster than more equal ones.

The Latin American experience disproves this claim. For decades, the region has grown significantly less than many developed and developing countries. In fact, in 2010 the ratio between the GDP per capita in Latin America and in rich countries was lower than a century earlier (27 percent vs. 35 percent). Year after year Latin American countries have failed to innovate and move away from exporting mining and agricultural products—a sharp contrast with South Korea's success in creating world-class high-tech companies such as Samsung.

Multiple reasons explain Latin America's failure but, as we will see in this chapter, inequality is one of the most significant. The combination of income concentration at the top and poverty at the bottom has created numerous obstacles to achieving economic development. In this chapter, I concentrate on four particularly significant problems—as reflected in Figure 3.1. The first two have to do with insufficient investment in education and innovation. The economic elite has historically lacked the incentives to promote high-quality education for all or to spend much on new technologies. If you are making vast sums in traditional sectors, why would you want to develop new ones? Meanwhile, a majority of the population have never been wealthy enough to spend massively on education and small and medium firms have not had enough profits to innovate.

Third, the economic elites have also used a variety of legal and illegal tricks to avoid paying the taxes they owe and to block progressive tax reforms. Unfortunately, governments without resources cannot fund much-needed investments in social programs and infrastructure.

Fourth, Latin America's experience reflects the link between income inequality and external crises. In some cases, high inequality has contributed to excessive borrowing, which is particularly problematic when the global economy deteriorates. In others, inequality has been an obstacle to implementing much-needed but costly macroeconomic policies at difficult times. The region's failure to react appropriately to changing international conditions in the 1970s, which resulted in one of the worst debt crises the world has seen during the 1980s, constitutes a great example.

Latin America's economic weaknesses have, in turn, contributed to even more inequality, leading to what economists call vicious circles. Inequality has led to economic stagnation which, in turn, has resulted in further income inequality, which has worsened the economy even more,

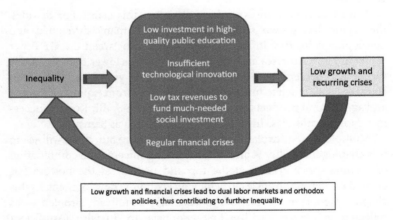

Figure 3.1 The economic costs of inequality, and its vicious circles. Source: Author's own.

in a never-ending spiral. The consolidation of dual labor markets (where good jobs are the exception) and orthodox spending policies have been at the heart of these negative processes.

Some readers will think that this painful story is irrelevant to other countries with higher economic growth and more economic dynamism. At the end of the chapter I will argue against this view. Latin America's problems, including uneven investment in education, difficulties in taxing the wealthy, economic crises, and informal labor markets, are increasingly evident in other parts of the world and seem more widespread and entrenched than ever.

A Historical Excursion

Let's start with the problems of education and innovation, beginning in the second half of the nineteenth century, a few decades after most Latin American countries gained independence. These were turbulent times for the continent: between the 1820s and the 1880s, there were more than thirty wars (both internal and external) in the region, with Argentina, Brazil, Chile, Cuba, Mexico, Peru, and Uruguay fighting at least two, and every other country experiencing periodic military coups.[2]

The result of this volatile period was the emergence of the so-called "oligarchic state" dominated by a small elite with support from the army.[3] In many countries, an authoritarian leader controlled political power, implementing policies that favored primary exporters. In other countries, electoral competition took place, but participation was limited to a small share of the population.

The exporting elite in power benefited from the rapid expansion of external markets during the first wave of globalization. Thanks to technological innovations in shipping and growing investment in railways, they began exporting beef to London, corn to the US, and copper to Germany. They formed a strong alliance with foreign companies, which have always been extremely influential in Latin America's history. Not surprisingly, the wealthy (with support from foreign actors) used their powerful position to push for pro-export public policies. This had three negative economic consequences. First, the concentration of land in a few hands intensified: the state took land from indigenous people and the Catholic Church and privatized common land, redistributing all to a small number of individuals and companies.

Second, in this environment the elite had no incentive to innovate. Exporting agricultural goods and/or various mining products was much more profitable than trying to produce manufactures. Between 1850 and 1912, primary exports grew by an annual average of 3.3 percent with a particularly fast expansion in Argentina (6.1 percent) and Uruguay (5.6 percent).[4] Meanwhile, the manufacturing sector struggled to become more productive. As the British economic historian Victor Bulmer-Thomas explained, artisans were simply "not part of the social political elite and lacked the bargaining power to influence public policy in their favour."[5]

Third, Latin American countries invested little in education. Why should they spend scarce resources on training workers that were only needed to produce coffee or sugar and mine copper, nitrates, and gold? For the dominant elite in the nineteenth and early twentieth century, a more educated citizenship would have only created problems, including more demands for democracy and redistribution.

By the beginning of the twentieth century—with a 75-year delay compared to Canada and the US—only Argentina, Chile, Costa Rica, and Uruguay had introduced mass primary education.[6] At that time, the literacy rate (i.e. the percentage of people above 10 years of age who could read and write) was only 17 percent in Bolivia, 15 percent in Brazil, 22 percent in Mexico, and 30 percent in Paraguay. In contrast, more than 90 percent of Canadians and were literate.[7]

Primary education did expand during the twentieth century, as countries modernized, learnt from their neighbors, and faced demands from an emerging urban middle class. Yet even then, inequality was a curse. Public schools, particularly in the rural sectors, remained poorly equipped and understaffed.[8] An American expert visiting El Salvador in the late 1940s aptly described the state of schools there—in a description that was equally valid for neighboring countries:

Very few Salvadoran schools are housed in buildings originally constructed for educational purposes. The great majority are found in former residences of the Spanish colonial type, in which the classrooms surround a patio that is used as a playground.... The classrooms are generally small, badly lighted, and poorly equipped. In 90 percent of them, there is little more than a blackboard, a map of El Salvador, and a few readers. The desks are mostly old, disfigured, and inadequate in number—frequently three and four pupils are found seated in a desk intended for two.[9]

Low-quality education led to high absenteeism as well as repetition and dropout rates. A 1952 report on Brazil's education system found that more than 40 percent of students dropped out of school without even passing the first grade and almost no student graduated on time. The situation was particularly worrisome in the poorest regions of the northeast, where, the report explained, "retardation in the primary schools reaches alarming proportions ... multiplying the first grades, crowding the classroom, and dividing the school periods into two, three, or even four sessions because there are not enough funds to build more schools."[10] In a recent study, the economic historian Ewout Frankema uses a sophisticated methodology to compare repetition rates across the world for the period 1960–2005. After discovering that Latin American countries performed very poorly, he concludes that "the quality of the educational systems that have been erected in 20th century LACs was far below international standards."[11]

None of this bothered the elite, since they had developed a parallel private system, particularly at the secondary school level. For example, two-thirds of the minority of Colombians who attended secondary school in the 1920s went to private institutions. Such situations continued unchanged for several decades. Additionally, the wealthy created exclusive universities where their children and those of the upper middle class received high-quality education and enhanced their social capital. For example, in Mexico, the *Instituto de Monterrey*— one of the 50 universities with the highest number of millionaire graduates in the world—was founded in the 1940s by Eugenio Garza Sada, owner of a large brewery, and other wealthy entrepreneurs from the region.[12] Around the same time, Raúl Baillères, founder of an economic empire now led by his billionaire son, together with a group of bankers and industrialists, created the *Instituto Tecnológico Autónomo de México* (ITAM) to train a new elite of economists and business people.[13]

The contrast with East Asia could not be more striking. In Latin America inequality contributed to underinvestment in education which, in turn, hampered the creation of a more dynamic economy. Countries such as South Korea, Taiwan, and Singapore—historically less unequal—have invested many resources in primary and secondary education since the middle of the twentieth century. A more skilled labor force helped them to promote the new economic sectors (from heavy industry to semiconductors) that were behind their economic miracle.[14]

The Problem of Education Today

"There are no fans, not enough chairs. The structure is in really bad shape, it needs to be re-painted, it needs fans as some rooms have them, others don't. The [chalk/white] boards also need improving. The kitchen needs improving, it's a total mess, really disgusting. There are animals in there that shouldn't be. There are cats, dogs," complained 19-year-old Gisele when describing her secondary school in Recife, Brazil. José Antonio, who attended a neighboring school, confirmed the bleak picture and linked it to the city's problems: "in Brazil, schools are very closed because of the violence. So you can't have schools that have open spaces, with trees, because, at night, outside of school time, vandals would come and destroy it. They would steal the equipment and everything in the school. Schools are very closed, grey, without colour, without life, exactly for this reason—to try to protect students from the outside world, which is very dangerous."[15] Gisele, José Antonio, and other young people paint a grim picture of demotivated and unprepared teachers, poor infrastructure, and insufficient hours of learning. Low-quality education in the context of difficult family lives leads many children to quit school or combine their education with demanding low-paying jobs or with motherhood.

These are not just exceptional cases. In her research on education and social policy in Brazil, my former student and now lecturer at the London School of Economics, Hayley Jones, demonstrates the extensive shortcomings of Brazil's public education system. After interviewing Gisele, José Antonio, and other young Brazilians, and collecting data from national and international institutions, Jones concluded that secondary education in poor areas of Brazil was not "making much contribution to human capital formation ... young people are [not] developing the knowledge, capacity, and skills needed to pull themselves and their families out of poverty."[16]

Similar problems are evident across the region. Insufficient class time and demotivated teachers still characterize public education in Latin America. As a result, despite significant improvements in recent years, the region's performance in international standardized tests remains weak. In 2012, students in the eight Latin American countries that participate in the Programme for International Student Assessment (PISA) performed significantly worse than their peers in other regions: 63 percent of all 15-year-old children who participated did not achieve the recommended level of math compared to just 23 percent in wealthy countries and 9 percent in Asia Pacific. The performance in writing was not much better: 45 percent of Latin Americans did not achieve the minimum required, compared to 18 percent in wealthy countries.[17] Other tests show similar limitations at the primary school level: in a UNESCO-led test implemented in 2006, a third of students did not achieve the required level of reading, while half did not have the minimum level of mathematics.[18]

Although multiple factors explain these shortcomings in quality, the concentration of income at the top is particularly important. On the one hand, the poor do not have enough income to attend private schools or enough political influence to demand better public schools in their neighborhoods. Most major social movements demanding better education—from the so-called *Pinguinos* in Chile to the Green March in the Dominican Republic—have been led by the middle class.

On the other hand, the elite has no incentives to promote better public education for all. Economically, the leading business groups do not require a highly trained labor force. In an excellent study on Latin America's economic model, Ben Schneider shows how Latin American companies tend to specialize in sectors that either require few workers or where low-educated workers are particularly important. For example, in Chile, copper mining during the 2000s accounted for 15 percent of total production but just 2 percent of the labor force.[19] In some of Brazil's leading business groups, such as Camargo Corrêa and Andrade Gutierrez, less than 15 percent of workers have college training.[20]

The children of the elite (and those in the upper middle class) usually attend private schools, which are strikingly different from those described by Gisele and José Antonio. The most exclusive schools across the region are either owned by the Catholic Church or have links to international (usually British or American) institutions. These schools provide not just a high-quality education, but also a network of personal and business contacts.[21] Since reviewing all elite schools country by country is impossible, I will give just three examples from the *Guardian*'s list of the best schools with a British curriculum in the world.[22] In São Paulo, St. Paul's School—whose 10,000 euro annual fee is higher than Brazil's average salary—prepares children to study "at top universities both in Brazil and abroad."[23] Newton College, which charges between US$8,000 and US$16,000, has an 11 hectare campus on the outskirts of Lima that includes a large theater, two swimming pools, and a sports center. Students also do fieldtrips in their geography and biology courses to a study center in the Amazon.[24] Talk about applied education! In Chile, the Grange School—one of the few English-based schools—has a hefty fee of US$10,000. Occupying 10 hectares in one of the most expensive neighborhoods in the capital Santiago, the school has educated large segments of the Chilean elite including several members of the Luksic family, one of the wealthiest in the country.

This educational apartheid has significant political consequences. Two education experts from the Inter-American Development Bank describe them well: "for the most part, the children of the politically influential people attend private primary and secondary schools. Thus they do not directly feel the deficiencies of the public school system, because their interests are not directly and immediately affected by the success or failure of public schools. This reduces the sense of urgency that might otherwise lead influential parents to press decision makers to make tough policy choices."[25]

Inequality Limits the Opportunities to Create More Dynamic Economies

Think for a second about a country where a small group of powerful individuals controls key economic sectors. These business owners can easily protect their large profits by influencing public policy. The managers and other skilled workers who work for them receive generous salaries and are thus happy with the status quo. Why would any of them want to innovate and invest in more complex and risky sectors? Additionally, the same country has a large number of poorly paid informal workers and entrepreneurs, who lack the resources, political connections, and access to finance to enter into new sectors. How can they become an engine of transformation even if they want to?

Actually, you do not need to imagine any of this; it is an accurate description of the connections between inequality and the lack of innovation and economic dynamism in Latin America today. Across the continent, a small number of business groups—owned by the wealthiest families—control most key economic sectors. In Chile, for example, just three families (the Luksic, Angelini, and Matte) owned all large publicly traded companies in the late 1990s.[26] In Argentina, 200 companies—many owned by large conglomerates—are responsible for more than a quarter of yearly output and almost three-quarters of all exports.[27] In Colombia, in the mid-2000s, half of the largest nonfinancial firms were in the hands of just five business groups and 90 percent belong to 23 groups.[28] During the same period, the five largest Mexican business groups controlled more than 10 percent of GDP.[29]

Business concentration is also evident at the sectoral level. A 2008 study published by the economist and business manager Huberto Campodónico found that significant sectors in Peru were in the hands of just a few companies. For example, the beer, telecommunication (fixed lines), and airline sectors as well as 81 percent of the milk business, 70 percent of cooking oil, and more than 60 percent of cement, iron, and steel were controlled by just two companies each.[30] A similar trend is also evident in Chile. In hardware stores, two companies (Easy and Sodimac) have become dominant players, contributing to the disappearance of almost 3,500 smaller firms that operated in the sector in the 1990s. Three pharmaceutical chains (Cruz Verde, Salcobrand, and FASA) are responsible for more than 90 percent of medicine sales. The list of sectors dominated by just two or three companies—many of which are part of larger conglomerates—also includes telecommunications (mobile and internet), cable, supermarkets, and electricity.[31]

This process of business concentration has not been "spontaneous" but can be directly linked to public policy. Since the late nineteenth century, family business groups have benefited from privileged access to state institutions to shape public policies in their favor. Large firms across the region have systematically pushed against competition policies that could eliminate monopolies or fine companies that collude to set excessively high prices. Once again, they have worked in tandem with multinationals, at times forming strategic alliances with them. As we will see later in the chapter, they have also opposed redistributive tax laws.

Close access to the state—made possible by high inequality—has thus helped large firms to sustain high profits. Examples of large family groups that benefited from state protection—even in the supposedly neoliberal era of the 1990s and 2000s—abound. Telefónica de México (TELMEX) is one of the most scandalous cases.[32] Owned by Slim since its privatization at the beginning of the 1990s, TELMEX has profited immensely from its monopolistic position and the state's lack of regulation. Instead of reducing the installation fee as required in the privatization agreement, TELMEX increased it by 85 percent. The company has repeatedly hiked the prices of local calls—where it does not face any competition—while reducing the prices for long-distance calls to ruin its competitors, in the kind of cross-subsidy that is forbidden by law.[33]

Powerful and protected business groups face limited incentives to innovate. It is much better for them to remain in their safe niches than to move into new sectors where competition from American, European, and Chinese firms is intense.[34] As a result, in Latin America the private sector is responsible for only one-third of total spending in research and development (R&D) compared to 50 percent in Asia and 70 percent in the OECD.[35] The Latin American private sector seldom introduces new products to the market: in fact, the probability of that happening is 20 percentage points lower in Latin America than in Eastern Europe and Central Asia.[36]

Large groups coexist with an ocean of self-employed workers and small firms where an estimated 60 percent of Latin Americans work.[37] As the Spanish professor Javier Vidal explains, most of these firms are characterized "by low productivity [and] difficulties with internationalizing their activities and incorporating technological innovations."[38] In Chile, for example, labor productivity (that is, the amount of output that each worker generates) in small firms is thirteen times lower than in large firms.[39]

Most small firms do not make any profit and have limited access to credit markets. Given their precarious situation, it is not surprising that most of these small and medium firms do little research. According to another World Bank study published in 2013, just 3 percent of small Latin American manufacturing firms innovate; the number of companies in other sectors is unlikely to be much higher.[40]

In summary, the large economic gap between a few powerful business groups with limited interest in innovation and a large number of small, unproductive firms with no resources to invest is behind Latin America's backward position. In 2011, spending in research and development was just 0.33 percent of GDP; in contrast, it was 1.1 percent in Asia and 2.0 percent in wealthy countries. The number of licenses and patents—which have increased rapidly in Asia in the last decade—is also extremely low.[41] Unfortunately, without innovation it is hard to sustain economic growth and a dynamic transformation of the economy.

The Difficulties of Taxing the Elite

In December 1999 Chileans elected the first Socialist president since a violent coup overthrew Salvador Allende 26 years before. An economist with a PhD from Duke University and an extensive career in government, Ricardo Lagos took power with the commitment to reduce inequality. Together with his Minister of Finance Nicolás Eyzaguirre, he promised to reform the healthcare system and expand corporate taxes. Eyzaguirre knew that he would face unjustified criticism: as he explained years later, "[critics] were trying to argue that the economy was going to stop, that investment was going to stall, that . . . small and medium enterprises were going to collapse . . . my team was a very serious team, in terms of knowledge of sound economic theory—the arguments were nonsense."[42]

When the government announced a modest increase in the corporate tax rate and a reduction of some loopholes, the business elite mobilized to stop the reform. They used their close links to right-wing political parties, their lobbying capacity, and their access to the press to weaken the proposal significantly. After a protracted negotiation, the government had to accept a minimal increase in the tax rate from 15 percent to 17 percent—well below the Latin American average of 30 percent. Years later, when another Socialist president, Michelle Bachelet, tried to implement a more comprehensive reform of all income taxes, the business elite was also successful in watering down the initial proposals.[43] As a result, and despite a moderate increase in the tax burden in the last two decades, Chile still struggles to tax wealthy individuals. Fiscal loopholes, which disproportionately benefit the elite, represent an estimated 4 percent of GDP, more than in any other OECD country except Mexico.[44] Taxes on natural resources such as aquaculture, fisheries, and forestry remain low, and tax rates for high-income groups are significantly below other countries.[45] The average effective tax rate for the richest 1 percent is around 16 percent, compared to 24 percent in the US and an even higher number in other OCDE countries.[46]

Chile's experience is by no means unique. Governments across Latin America have struggled to raise taxes, particularly on personal and corporate income. In a study published in 2009, I showed how most Latin American countries collected fewer taxes than one would expect given their level of income.[47] The contribution of property taxes—potentially an important income source, since houses and land cannot move somewhere else like entrepreneurs do—was then particularly disappointing. They represented only 0.3 percent of total revenues in the whole region and in five Latin American countries they generated no revenues at all.[48]

Things have not changed enough in recent years. Some academics and policymakers have celebrated the increase in tax revenues during the 2000s, linking it to the growing policy emphasis on equality. According to the Italian economist Andrea Cornia—who believes that Latin America "discovered" a new social democratic model in the 2000s—"tax policy underwent gradual but deep changes in much of the region. In a significant departure from the 1990s, tax policy during the 2000s often emphasized corporate income tax and reduced exemptions, extended the scope of presumptive taxation, cut regressive excises, and introduced indirect taxes on luxury items."[49]

Yet these researchers are too optimistic: the truth is that taxes in Latin America are still low and regressive and that much of the elite pays little.[50] Wealthy individuals have routinely used their political influence to keep taxes low. In eight Latin American countries the richest 10 percent of the population pay less than 5 percent of their income in income taxes, three times less than in the US and six times less than in Sweden.[51]

Every time there is an attempt at reform, the economic elite pressures the government to create new tax exemptions. This is particularly evident in some of the more dynamic sectors such as mining, *maquilas* (where clothes and electronics are assembled for exports), and tourism. The arguments to secure these benefits are always the same: "if we have to pay more taxes, we won't be able to compete with other countries," or "if you increase our taxes, investment and growth will suffer significantly." I still remember vividly a back-to-back trip I did to Costa Rica and the Dominican Republic years ago: when I arrived in Costa Rica, assembly producers and tourist operators were calling for more tax incentives to compete with the Dominican Republic. Of course, when I traveled to the Dominican Republic, they were doing the same ... but comparing themselves with Haiti. This is a never-ending and costly game: in some Latin American countries, tax subsidies are as high as 8 percent of GDP. In Nicaragua during the late 2000s, tax exemptions were 40 percent higher than the whole public health budget.[52]

Latin American states have also been unwilling to fight tax evasion and other fiscal crimes. Given the economic and political power of the elite in these unequal environments, governments across the region probably feel that it is a lost battle. Yet the result has been additional revenue losses: according to some estimates, tax evasion leads to a reduction of more than 50 percent of personal income tax revenue in several countries. In the case of the corporate tax, the loss ranges between 27 percent in Brazil and 65 percent in Costa Rica.[53] As a result of all these problems, the *Comisión Económica para América Latina y el Caribe* (Economic Commission for Latin America and the Caribbean, CEPAL) estimates that tax evasion was equivalent to US$320 billion or 6.5 percent of regional GDP in the late 2000s.[54]

Tax evasion has gone hand in hand with the massive use of unregulated tax havens. Leaked data on accounts at the Swiss subsidiary of the British bank HSBC—the so-called Swissleaks—revealed that Latin American residents have hidden deposits for US$52.6 billion—equivalent to one-quarter of total public investment in healthcare in the region.[55] The *Panama Papers*—leaked from the Panamanian law firm Mossack Fonseca by an anonymous source—identified thousands of wealthy individuals with offshore accounts, including politicians, artists, and powerful business people. In total, the Tax Justice Network estimates that Brazilians have more than US$519 billion hidden in offshore accounts (equivalent to 160 percent of Brazil's foreign debt), Mexicans have more than US$417 billion (equal to 224 percent of the country's foreign debt), and Venezuelans more than US$405 billion (a staggering 728 percent of their country's total foreign debt).[56]

Privileged access to the state in the context of high inequality explains the wealthy's success in avoiding taxes. In recent publications, Oxfam has identified some of the most common mechanisms the rich use to capture the state.[57] Let me mention here just a few. First, the elite's control of mass media—both newspapers and TV—has allowed them to shape public debate and build opposition against tax hikes. Multiple op-eds and TV programs repeat the same half truths about the negative impact of taxes on investment, the link between taxes and corruption, and the need to limit state regulation.

Second, the use of revolving doors is quite common in Latin America. Entrepreneurs and business managers spend their professional lives moving from the private to the public sector and back. A common excuse is that governments need the best possible experts, many of whom work in the private sector. Yet the problem is that when you put a powerful landowner in charge of the Ministry of Agriculture or a banker becomes the Minister of Finance, the chances of adopting progressive policies diminish substantially. Conflicts of interest are seldom properly regulated, and business associations tend to have better access to the government when it is occupied by their peers.

Third, as we saw in the case of Chile, the business elite often has close links to political parties, contributing to their campaigns and lobbying through formal and informal channels. Although most governments have advanced in the regulation of campaign financing, large corporations and powerful individuals still transfer millions of dollars to presidential and legislative candidates. The behavior of the Brazilian construction company Odebrecht in recent years constitutes a good illustration of this problem. According to company insiders, Odebrecht spent US$3.4 billion to fund electoral campaigns in Argentina, Chile, Colombia, Ecuador, Panama, Peru, the Dominican Republic, Mexico,

Venezuela, and, of course, its home country, Brazil.[58] Lobbying is also common across the region, affecting not only the executive and legislative branches but also the judiciary. In Guatemala, for example, the Constitutional Court has always been sympathetic to the arguments of the economic elites against taxation, often watering down the already weak tax legislation passed in Congress.[59]

High income concentration thus results in a powerful elite who succeed in avoiding taxes. At the other end of the spectrum, Latin American countries have large informal sectors made up of companies that struggle daily to survive, as we saw in the previous section. Around 40 percent of all Latin Americans work in informal activities that do not contribute directly to the state's coffers.[60] Governments are caught between a rock and a hard place: they struggle to tax the rich and cannot tax many other parts of the economy either.

Latin America's struggles to increase taxation have large economic costs. On the one hand, low taxes limit the resources available for healthcare, education, public infrastructure, and other vital activities. If tax revenues are just 10 or 15 percent of GDP, it is hard to build hospitals, hire enough doctors and teachers, support poor people in difficult times, and build enough roads. Yet this spending is indispensable to create more productive and dynamic societies and avoid painful external shocks, as the experiences of countries from Sweden to Mauritius demonstrate.

Social programs not only compensate for the negative effects of external shocks and economic adjustment, but also enhance competitiveness. Universal social policies promote human capital, expand aggregate demand, and improve social capital. They contribute to higher economic growth and the creation of more dynamic sectors—something Costa Rica has shown for years.[61]

On the other hand, underfunded states are more prone to economic crises and may be regularly forced to implement costly austerity policies. The reason for this problem is easy to understand: all governments face numerous demands for social services, subsidies, infrastructure, and even clientelist transfers to various supporters. If they do not have enough taxes, they either print more money—a common alternative before the 1980s—or increase public debt. Yet both of these responses are risky: when global economic conditions worsen, investors become less willing to lend to Latin America, triggering painful crises. Unfortunately, financial crises have significant distributional consequences.

Income Inequality and Financial Crises

During the second half of the 1970s, the global economy was flooded with cheap money. Successive spikes in oil prices left wealthy oligarchs in the Middle East with more money than they could spend, leading to a rapid increase in bank deposits across the world. US and European financial institutions were desperate to lend money and interest rates became lower than inflation, making borrowing very attractive.

Not surprisingly, in this environment money poured into Latin American countries, which were eager to invest in infrastructure, develop their manufacturing sectors, and promote economic growth. Between 1970 and 1982, Latin America's external debt multiplied by a factor of fifteen, going from US$21 billion to US$314 billion.[62] Everyone was happy: the state could expand government spending without tax hikes; the private sector launched new investment projects and expanded production for both the domestic market and exports; and citizens borrowed at low rates to increase their consumption capacity. Economic growth also picked up: the 1970s was one of the few decades in the recent past in which Latin American countries grew faster than rich economies.

Yet everything changed abruptly in 1982. On August 7 Mexico's Minister of Finance, Jesús Silva Herzog, announced a major devaluation of the peso—the second in six months—warning that "the international credit Mexico can obtain is limited, which makes it impossible to finance the current accounts deficit."[63] When Mexico's need to renegotiate its foreign debt became clear weeks later, a major debt crisis began in Latin America.

The crisis had terrible consequences for Latin America, triggering a "lost decade." Banks abruptly cut lending to the region and demanded full repayment of debts. Domestic and foreign investors moved their money away as quickly as they could, contributing to a further weakening of the economy. Governments across the region had to simultaneously deal with high inflation—between 1985 and 1990, the average rate of inflation was 584 percent in Argentina, 673 percent in Brazil, 824 percent in Peru, and more than 3000 percent in Nicaragua—insufficient resources, and growing social discontent. Poverty rates increased quickly, and Latin American economies stagnated: by 1990 all countries but Chile, Colombia, and the Dominican Republic were poorer than ten years before.[64]

The 1980s debt crisis was particularly painful but by no means an exception: crises have been recurrent in Latin America's history. Between

1970 and 1995, for example, the region suffered 50 percent more crises than East Asia or Europe and the Middle East.[65] In fact, Latin American economies are characterized by "stop and go": periods of growth—which often correspond to positive global conditions—end up suddenly, leading to banking or financial crises. Governments usually respond to these crises by adopting austerity policies, making things even worse.

What are common drivers of all these crises? According to the economist Dani Rodrik, income inequality is an important trigger. He explains how in difficult times, "deep social divisions provide an incentive to governments to delay needed adjustments and take on excessive levels of foreign debt, in the expectation than other groups can be made to pay for the eventual costs."[66] In unequal societies like those in Latin America, reaching agreement on economic adjustment between different social groups—which are far apart in terms of income and worldview—is almost impossible; there is too much distrust and not enough social cohesion. Confronted with such difficulties, governments prefer to maintain the status quo, hoping that the economic situation improves or postponing painful reforms until another administration is elected. Rodrik tests these arguments with a series of quantitative exercises, finding a positive correlation between income inequality and bad macroeconomic policies as well as between income inequality and economic growth collapses.[67]

Latin American economists have always been aware of this negative influence of inequality on macroeconomic management. Already in the 1950s, they developed an explanation of inflation based on the existence of struggles between different classes in unequal environments. To understand their argument, imagine that there is a severe drought in a country like Brazil that leads to an increase in food prices. Formal workers in the cities will demand higher wages to pay for food. In response to wage growth, large companies will increase their prices, which may lead to further demands for wage growth, resulting in a never-ending inflation spiral. In this kind of situation, governments can do little: if they try to control prices through austerity policies, they run the risk of triggering a recession. If they do nothing—often their preferred option—inflation skyrockets, triggering painful crises and lost decades like the 1980s.

From the Economy Back to Inequality

So far in this chapter I have focused on the negative impact of inequality on economic development in Latin America. By reducing spending in education and income from taxes, weakening incentives for innovation and triggering financial crises, income polarization has contributed to uneven economic growth for decades. Unfortunately, the story does not finish here. All the economic problems previously discussed can in turn contribute to even more inequality. In this way, Latin America has been forced to deal with painful vicious circles. I briefly mentioned one when explaining the negative impact of low taxes on income distribution. Here let me discuss another two.

The first has to do with the characteristics of the labor market in most Latin American countries. The lack of innovation and dynamism that I discussed earlier has contributed to the expansion of informal jobs and to sharp differences between good and bad jobs. Imagine walking around Mexico City or Lima or Quito; you will find many individuals in formal jobs: the clerk in the bank where you deposit your money or the director of the hotel where you are staying. Their job specifications and their level of productivity are almost the same as those of similar workers in wealthier countries. In contrast, you will see many people in the street cleaning shoes, selling food, and repairing phones or furniture informally. These jobs are not just informal but suffer from low productivity and are poorly paid.

Latin America's lack of economic dynamism means that the second type of job—which is even more common in rural areas—has always been the norm. Successive attempts to modernize the region's economies have never been totally successful. During the 1950s and 1960s, most Latin American governments protected their economies and promoted the growth of the manufacturing sector. While many new formal jobs were created, an even larger number of people migrated to the cities in search of a better life. Most were never hired in the formal sector, ending up in informal, poorly paid activities. In 1960, one in five workers outside the agricultural sector were self-employed in low productivity activities; the percentage was much higher in countries such as Bolivia (42 percent), Ecuador (37 percent), and Peru (31 percent).[68]

Of course, this kind of labor market dualism further contributed to income inequality. There was a clear hierarchy of jobs: self-employed workers and informal activities received low wages that were often insufficient to cover basic needs. The few lucky workers in high-productivity manufacturing or service activities received much higher wages. Company managers and business owners were obviously at the top of the pyramid. Social policy often worsened this segmentation of the labor market. Formal workers had access to social security, thus benefiting from high-quality healthcare and generous pensions. In contrast, informal workers lacked access to social rights. When they got sick, they either had to go to poorly staffed public hospitals or spend all their savings. When they aged, they had to continue working unless they had a generous son or—most commonly—daughter.

Things did not improve after 1985, when most Latin American countries implemented neoliberal reforms (liberalizing trade, reducing regulation, eliminating subsidies, and privatizing public companies and social programs) and embraced globalization. Quite the contrary: despite orthodox economists' expectations, informal employment increased during the 1990s as large firms fired workers and public employment decreased. Millions of workers were forced to accept poorly paid jobs with no social rights. Between 1990 and 1999, seven out of ten new jobs were created in the urban informal sector, while temporary employment expanded, social security coverage decreased (especially in small companies), and working without a written contract became commonplace.[69]

So inequality's first vicious circle has taken place through the labor markets: during the twentieth century, high inequality in Latin America contributed to insufficient innovation which, in turn, led to large gaps between good and bad jobs and even more inequality. Breaking this circle is hard and requires confronting all sorts of obstacles—some of which will be further discussed in the next chapter.

Financial crises also generate cycles of inequality through various channels. Currency devaluations (that is, the weakening of local money vis-à-vis major currencies), unemployment, and volatility tend to hit the poor particularly hard. Low-income families lack the tools to cope with higher prices, a paucity of job opportunities, and lower wages. In contrast, the wealthy often benefit from the weakening of the local currency—since they have savings in dollars abroad—and can find new jobs more easily.

Policy responses to the crises have made things worse. The British economist John Maynard Keynes famously recommended an expansion of government spending and a reduction in interest rates in recessionary times. In his view, if governments built roads, bridges, and schools, unemployment would decrease and people would regain confidence in the economy. Unfortunately, Keynes's recipe—which has worked more often than not—has seldom been followed in Latin America. Instead, in times of crisis most governments have reduced public investment, cut social programs, and increased interest rates—making the construction of factories more expensive. In doing so, they have contributed to unemployment, poverty increases, and a further worsening of the income gap. Pressures from international institutions like the IMF and the World Bank, lack of access to borrowing, and right-wing ideology explain these mistaken policy choices.

There are multiple examples of this second vicious circle in Latin America. I discussed one earlier, in the context of the 1982 debt crisis. During the 1980s more than 39 million Latin Americans fell into poverty and by 1989 almost one in three individuals were poor.[70] Additionally, the Gini coefficient increased in nine of the 13 countries for which data is available.[71]

The region responded to the crisis with the now famous (or infamous) Washington Consensus: a combination of short-term austerity measures and long-term market-friendly policies. Although I would need a whole book to evaluate these policies, many studies demonstrate that they contributed to further inequality. After carefully comparing the countries that adopted the Washington Consensus most enthusiastically with those that did not, the political scientists Evelyne Huber and Fred Solt concluded that "[Latin American] countries that had more drastic reform episodes increased their Gini index nine times more than countries that avoided them. There is no doubt, then, that higher levels of neoliberalism and more aggressive tactics of liberalization are associated with rising inequality."[72]

There are many other examples like this. In the late 1990s, a global crisis that began in East Asia soon spread to Latin America. Between 1997 and 1998, nine billion dollars left the region as panicked foreign investors looked for safer bets. Once again, the continent's economies were brought to a halt—experts and commentators talked now about a "lost half decade"—and poverty and inequality accelerated. As in previous decades, IMF-promoted austerity measures followed the initial shock. The Brazilian government, for example, introduced cuts in rural development, social protection, and environmental policy as well as food support.[73] As a result, most of the social gains of the 1990s were lost, making the costs of inequality evident once again.

From Latin America to the Rest of the World

"Countries around the world provide frightening examples of what happens to societies when they reach the level of inequality towards which we are moving. It is not a pretty picture," warned the Nobel Prize-winning economist, Joseph Stiglitz, in his bestselling book on the price of inequality in the US.[74] As I have shown in this chapter, Latin America provides a great example of this ugly picture. Persistent inequality has historically reduced the opportunities for economic development by leading to uneven investment in education and R&D, making taxation hard and triggering financial crises. In the previous section, I also discussed the historical segmentation of labor markets: a small number of well-paying jobs have coexisted with a much higher number of low-productivity, poorly paid ones.

In many ways, other parts of the world are already sharing this experience, becoming increasingly like Latin America. This is particularly evident in the case of taxes: the wealthy in a growing number of countries are abusing their influence to oppose income taxes. Both the conservative right and the center-left have bought the argument that taxes are costly for economic growth. In the US, the Republican Party has allied with the business elite to promote regressive tax reforms. Democrats have failed to systematically campaign against tax reductions, partly because they are increasingly dependent on funds from the wealthy.[75] Even in more equal countries, growing income concentration has gone hand in hand with lower public revenues: in Sweden taxes decreased by more than six percentage points as a percentage of GDP between 2000 and 2018.[76]

The segmentation of the labor market into good and bad jobs is also growing in Europe and the US. Full-time workers with high levels of education in sectors such as finance, healthcare, and ICT have experienced steady increases in their wages. At the same time, part-time and temporary jobs have expanded rapidly. In Germany, a high-ranking official of the Left Party explained in 2016 that "the economy is humming, but temporary employment is nevertheless at a record high" and complained about the creation of a "second class system." In fact, the number of temporary, poorly paid jobs there grew by a third between 2009 and 2014.[77] Most wealthy economies have witnessed a growing gap between permanent and temporary jobs, which has gone hand in hand with growing wage inequality.[78]

The expansion of the gig economy is a clear reflection of this trend. A growing number of workers no longer receive a regular wage but are paid for the "gigs" they do, from delivering food to driving people around. Uber (ride-hailing), Deliveroo (food delivery), Rover (pet walking), PeoplePerHour (short-term freelancing)—the number of companies and apps offering this kind of "job" opportunity is growing by the minute. More than a third of US workers participate in the gig economy, while in the UK an estimated five million people work in these activities.[79] The gig economy—together with the zero-hours contracts through which workers are paid by the hour—has often been praised as versatile and efficient. "The flexibility of the gig ... has real uses, whether that's being able to change hours from day to day, spend time with kids after school or look for other employment," argues Emram Mian, former director of the market-friendly Social Market Foundation.[80] In practice, however, they share many similarities with the Latin American informal sector: they are poorly paid, unstable, lack social rights, and are inequality-inducing.

The belief that inequality is contributing to financial crises has also extended across the developed world. Influential economists like Raghuram Rajan, former governor of the Indian Central Bank, have shown that income disparities were a major trigger of the 2008 Great Recession.[81] Stagnant wages forced millions of middle-class families to borrow in order to sustain their consumption patterns and purchase new homes. Banks and other financial actors were happy to lend them as much as needed, transforming their mortgages into increasingly complex financial products that they then sold to others. Unfortunately, just like in Latin America in 1982, the piling of debt eventually proved unsustainable, resulting in the worst global financial crisis since the Great Depression of the 1930s.

OECD countries are thus already experiencing some of the negative effects of inequality on the economy. And yet the Latin American experience shows that things could become much worse in the future. As inequality becomes socially embedded, problems are likely to deepen, leading to the multiplication of "Latin American replicas." The economic elite will have fewer and fewer incentives to innovate, preferring to protect their rents instead. The less spending on R&D there is, the harder it will be to develop more dynamic innovation systems—a problem likely to hit Southern Europe earlier than the US. In the case of schooling, insufficient public investment and a growing cost of private education could consolidate an unequal system, with a large number of young people receiving sub-par education. The lack of cross-class collaboration between the poor and the middle class—a growing problem in unequal societies—will reduce the chances of developing more dynamic education and redistribution policies even further. In a few decades, many countries around the world could be locked in the kind of vicious circle of high inequality and low dynamic growth that has affected Latin America for more than a century.

Chapter 4

THE POLITICAL COSTS OF INEQUALITY

In the morning of October 17, 1945, hundreds of demonstrators from various working-class neighborhoods on the outskirts of Buenos Aires gathered to protest against the arrest of Juan Domingo Perón—vice-president and secretary of labor of the military regime until a week before. The trade union-sponsored event soon morphed into a spontaneous protest, which marched toward the wealthy part of the city. Similar protests took place in other neighborhoods on October 17 and 18, including the city center. Protestors converged on the *Plaza de Mayo*—the historical square in front of the Presidential Palace—refusing to leave until Perón appeared.[1] The surprised military leadership was forced to reverse course and free him. In the evening of October 18, Perón emerged to address the enthusiastic crowd in front of the Presidential Palace.

The events of October 1945 in Argentina demonstrated Perón's popularity among a majority of workers. In the previous two years, he had improved labor legislation, building close ties with trade unions, and using state patronage to gain popular support. As Secretary of Labor, Perón reached the masses directly, speaking in a language they could understand. The October protests were followed by Perón's victory in the presidential elections of February 1946—launching a political experiment that would reshape Argentina's history and influence the rest of Latin America. Four years later, Evita Perón—then first lady and today an almost mythical figure—recalled the events of 1945 in a way that reveals much about the character of the movement:

> From these same balconies the leader began to appear like a sun, rescued by the people and for the people, without any more arms than his dear patriotic *descamisados*, forged in labor. This is the pure origin of our leader ... [17 October] was born in the factories.[2]

A direct relationship between a charismatic leader and the people, a certain disregard for stable institutions and political parties, and the promotion of anti-elite grievances characterized Peronism. A similar type of leadership—which many have called populist—is evident in Latin America across time and space: from Getúlio Vargas in Brazil in the 1940s to Hugo Chávez in Venezuela in the 2000s.

This chapter illustrates the way inequality has weakened the political system in Latin America (see Figure 4.1).[3] I show how political instability results from the interactions between powerful elites and a dissatisfied low-income majority. During democratic periods, the wealthy have succeeded in capturing the state, shaping the rules of the game and limiting social, economic, and political redistribution. Dissatisfied with this state of affairs, voters have often appealed to populist politicians who promise a radical break with the past. Populist politics, however, has often proved unstable, at times even culminating in elite-supported coups and authoritarian regimes.

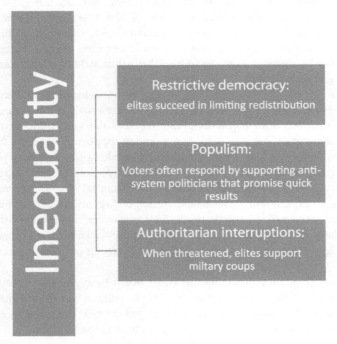

Figure 4.1 From inequality to unstable and exclusionary politics. Source: Author's own.

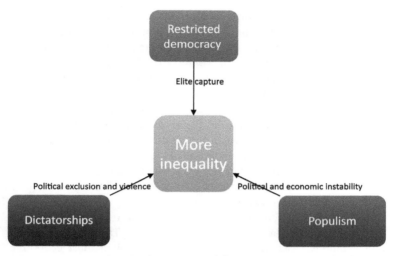

Figure 4.2 From politics back to restrictied democracy. Source: Author's own.

Inequality has thus contributed to weak, unresponsive and/or unstable political institutions which, in turn, lead to a further worsening of income distribution through several channels reflected in Figure 4.2. First, populist experiments have often resulted in economic crises with significant costs for the low-income majority. Second, right-wing authoritarian governments have consistently adopted regressive measures, thus benefiting the wealthy significantly. In Pinochet's Chile, for example, the Gini coefficient increased from less than 44 in the early 1970s to 59 in 1988.[4] Third, weak democracies have protected the wealthy and often failed to significantly expand economic and social rights.

This chapter is even more relevant for our understanding of today's world than the previous one. In recent years, we have witnessed the emergence of populist leaders in countries as different as the US and Hungary as a response to deep-seated inequalities. Unfortunately, these new leaders share many of the weaknesses of Latin American populists yet lack their commitment to redistribution.

The Uncomfortable Coexistence of Democracy and Elite Power

Contrary to a popular view of Latin America as a region of authoritarian *caudillos*, partial democracy has a long history there. During the second half of the nineteenth century, voting rights for men were introduced in thirteen countries.[5] By the first decades of the twentieth century, elections had become heavily disputed events in many countries. For example, in the 1930 presidential contest in Colombia, almost half of all adult males participated. The campaign was discussed in newspapers and cafes by voters and non-voters alike.[6] Women, who did not get the right to vote until decades later, participated in fundraisers and campaign events. According to the Colombian historian Eduardo Posada-Carbó, "elections were competitive, involving degrees of uncertainty, their outcome conditioned ... by much forthright and untrammeled electoral activity. An effective campaign, and an effective candidate, could make a difference."[7] In Argentina, Chile, and Uruguay electoral competition was even more intense.

Nevertheless, democracy was limited and restricted due, in large part, to high levels of socioeconomic inequality. The elite was at that time fabulously rich and powerful. They controlled most economic resources and social networks and had close ties to the military. The rest of the population, particularly in the less urbanized countries, depended directly on them. In 1950s Brazil, for example, more than half of the population lived in the countryside in primitive conditions. In such an environment, explains the historian Thomas Skidmore, "the way to survive was to find a powerful *patrão* (patron) to act as one's protector."[8]

The economic elite feared people's participation in politics; they were worried that poor voters would elect leaders who supported high income taxes and generous social programs. As a result, they did everything in their power to avoid real democracy. Until the beginning of the twentieth century, all countries constrained who could run for elections and who could vote. According to the Costa Rican Constitution, for example, the president had to be a citizen by birth, "secular," "active," and "the owner of property of a value not less than five hundred *colones* or with an annual income of not less than two hundred *colones*."[9] Across the region, the right to vote was only given to literate males who owned property.

Elections were seldom truly free, even in the most advanced Latin American countries. Argentinian voters were often forced to voice their voting preferences to polling booth officials, and secret voting was not introduced until 1912. In Chile, voters were in theory more protected, but irregularities were common in practice. In some areas of the country, for example, electoral authorities were in charge of placing the ballots in the boxes in full view of the public. During the 1840s, a market for votes was developed, with prices increasing or decreasing daily depending on how close the election was. Vote buying was so common that the newspaper *El Artesano* published a new commandment: "you will not give your vote for money." In Colombia, the military were an important source of votes for the government, who moved troops around during the electoral season to secure favorable results across the country.[10]

Pressures from the middle class and segments of the urban elite led to some improvements during the first decades of the twentieth century. A growing number of males were allowed to vote, regardless of their level of income. Secret voting was extended across the region and opposition parties were allowed to compete on a more level playing field. Yet many constraints and limitations remained. In Chile, the illiterate population was not allowed to vote until 1970, in Ecuador until 1978, and in Brazil until 1988. Meanwhile, women did not receive their voting rights in most countries until the 1940s and 50s.[11] In Bolivia and most of Central America, the response to demands from below was more repression instead of more democracy.

Economic historians Stanley Engerman and Kenneth Sokoloff have explored the links between income inequality and restrictions on democracy in a series of influential publications. They show how in the US and Canada—countries with better distribution of land and less powerful elites—universal and secret voting was introduced earlier than in Latin America, and the proportion of the population who voted increased faster. By 1940, participation rates in elections were twice as large in North America as in Argentina, Chile, and Uruguay—the most democratic countries in Latin America.[12]

Not surprisingly, this kind of restrictive democracy led to the political and social exclusion of millions of Latin Americans. This was most evident in the regulation of labor markets and in social policy—which the elite had incentives to keep as weak as possible for as long as possible. During the first part of the twentieth century, there was no regulation of working hours, minimum wages, or labor conditions. Even in Argentina and Chile, the conservative elite regarded social legislation as unnecessary at best. Police repression was the most common response to labor unrest across the region. In Chile, violent police responses to strikes resulted in hundreds of deaths in cities such as Valparaíso, Santiago and Antofagasta. The Iquique massacre was the worst: the army killed between 1,000 and 3,000 nitrate workers in a few hours.[13] All across Latin America conditions were particularly bleak for rural workers, who had a weaker mobilization capacity and faced threats from both the police and paramilitary groups hired by landowners.

Social policy also remained underdeveloped in most countries. In the previous chapter, we saw the region's historical problems with education. Public healthcare and pensions were no different. Lack of resources limited the quality and coverage of services, which were concentrated in a few urban areas. Public social spending was below 2 percent of GDP in all Latin American countries and few governments were concerned about it.[14] Low benefits meant low taxes—precisely what the elite wanted.

Starting in the 1910s, a few pioneering countries—among them Argentina, Chile, and Uruguay—introduced social insurance programs. Yet initially the only beneficiaries were the military and other public servants. Even when the programs were expanded in the 1930s and 1940s, large shares of the population—including those working in agriculture and in the informal sector, as well as women working at home—were excluded. Not surprisingly, most specialists refer to these early welfare systems as "truncated": only a privileged minority received quality services and generous transfers, and there were significant inequalities among beneficiaries. The military, for example, had access to better hospitals and to much more generous pensions than other professional groups.[15]

The First Wave of Populism as a Response to the Democratic Deficit

Tall, thin, and charismatic, Jânio Quadros won the 1960 presidential elections in Brazil promising political renewal. Replicating his successful campaigns for mayor and governor of São Paulo, he used a broom as his symbol and promised to sweep away all corrupt politicians. Devoid of a coherent ideology, he was elected mayor as a Christian Democrat, ran for governor with support from the National Labor and Socialist Parties, and was presidential candidate for the conservative National Democratic Union (UDN). Of course, like some well-known global leaders today he was more loyal to himself than to any political party: in the midst of the presidential campaign he quit the UDN to demonstrate his independence from politicians.[16]

Once in power, Quadros remained more worried about his image than about governing. He devoted more time to finding the best possible seating arrangements in his limousine than to securing agreements in Congress. He loved publicity stunts: in August 1961, for example, he gave Che Guevara—the world-renowned communist guerrilla leader and commando of the Cuban Revolution—Brazil's highest recognition for foreigners despite opposition from most of his supporters.

Quadros was an eccentric and not particularly successful example—he resigned after six months in office—of the kind of populist style that mushroomed in Latin America after 1930. Although the term is highly debated, most observers would agree that it refers to a political style in which a leader builds direct links to voters based on his/her own charisma, credibility, or popularity. Populist leaders are critical of traditional politicians and love to depict reality in black and white. They are the only good guys, protecting the people against the oligarchy and defending the nation against foreign threats.

Although populist leaders came with different ideologies and policy proposals, their emergence in Latin America was in all cases a response to the limits of elite-driven democracy discussed in the previous section. Populist leaders highlighted the hardship of the working class, while denouncing the power of the economic elites. In Brazil, for example, decades before Quadros promised a "war on the corrupt rich," Getúlio Vargas had expanded the rights of workers and fought to reduce the influence of the business elite.

Together with Argentina's Perón, Vargas is probably the best-known Latin American populist. Despite being "cold, reserved, cautious, impersonal"—according to the Brazilian writer Erico Veríssimo—Vargas transformed Brazil during his time in government.[17] Governor of Rio Grande do Sul—where he was born—and Finance Minister in his early forties, he became president in 1930 after a short revolution. During the following decade and a half, Vargas was interim president, led the approval of a new Constitution, staged a coup, and then promoted deep institutional reforms under what he called the "Estado Novo" or new state.[18]

Vargas was never particularly interested in strengthening formal democracy or protecting individual rights. Instead, he aimed to create new sources of power to counterbalance the deep-rooted influence of the rural oligarchies. Vargas concentrated his energies on strengthening state institutions, modernizing the economy, and improving the living conditions of urban workers. Feeding into the sense of exclusion of the working class, the Brazilian president used populist rhetoric to secure their support. He called himself the "father of the poor," promoting gradual change while simultaneously fighting against communism and the economic elite. His government legalized trade unions; created social security funds for some workers; and established an eight-hour working day and national minimum wages.

Vargas was forced to step down by the military in 1945 but won a free election five years later. In his return as democratic president, he maintained his commitment to urban workers and economic modernization. Unfortunately, growing corruption and deteriorating relations with the military weakened his government significantly. Vargas's end was tragic: he decided to commit suicide instead of meeting the army's request that he resign. His departing letter—which contributed to his status as a Brazilian hero—summarized all the populist features of his government and tells us much about the characteristics of Latin American politics at that time:

> Once more the forces and interests against the people are newly coordinated and raised against me ... They need to drown my voice and halt my actions so that I no longer continue to defend, as I always have defended, the people and principally the humble ... I offer my life to the holocaust. I choose this means to be with you always. When they humiliate you, you will feel my soul suffering at your side. When hunger beats at your door, you will feel in your chests the energy for the fight for yourselves and your children ... I was the slave of the people and today I free myself for eternal life. But this people to which I was a slave no longer will be a slave to anyone. My sacrifice will remain forever in your soul and my blood will be the price of your ransom.[19]

Vargas's influence can be partly explained by his ability to skillfully manage conflicts between different Brazilian states, between various segments of the elite (including landowners and new industrialists), and between various groups within the military. Yet his emergence and success primarily responded to the failings of previous governments to confront political and economic injustice. As cities expanded and the rural sector modernized, the urban working class aspired to a better life and more participation in society. Populism became a natural response to the uneven struggle between a dissatisfied but weak worker movement and a powerful and unresponsive economic elite.

The same drivers of populism are evident in other parts of Latin America. Argentina is another excellent example. Born at the end of the nineteenth century in a middle-class family, Juan Perón entered the military academy at sixteen and became military attaché in Italy during the government of Mussolini—a leader he always admired.[20]

Perón became head of the newly created Department of Labor after the 1943 military coup, and vice-president of the republic months later.

A crafty and ambitious politician, he soon realized that workers' discontent created a unique political opportunity. If trade unions were strengthened and labor conditions improved, a large number of Argentinians would happily support the military regime and, more importantly, would identify directly with him.

Perón followed this strategy enthusiastically: between 1943 and 1945, the Ministry of Labor promoted the creation of new trade unions; intervened in collective bargaining negotiations in favor of workers; implemented low-cost housing programs; and created the Institute of Social Security. Under Perón's watch, the government also passed a law establishing minimum wages as well as maximum hours.[21] His alliance with workers first protected him from his enemies within the government—as we saw at the beginning of the chapter—and in 1946 took him to the presidency, after winning the elections by more than ten percentage points.

As president, Perón deepened his pro-worker strategy. Agricultural employees were encouraged to unionize, and social security, training programs, and free higher education expanded. Perón found a key ally and supporter in his wife Evita. She became the idol of the *descamisados* or shirtless—the millions of impoverished workers supporting the Peronist regime. Through her foundation, Evita provided them with subsidized holidays, and built better union headquarters, hospitals, hotels, and low-cost houses. Before her death in 1952, Evita gave thousands of speeches denouncing injustice and praising the government (where she depicted Perón as "glorious," workers as "marvelous," and the oligarchy as "selfish") and met workers for hours—her working day did not finish until three or four in the morning.[22]

President Perón also became an enthusiastic supporter of modernization as a route to improving workers' living standards: "the future of the nation will be industrial or we will continue to be a semi colonial country," he proclaimed.[23] His government implemented an extensive program of nationalization, including the railroad and telephone companies, and created numerous incentives in favor of manufacturers and against private agricultural producers. Nevertheless, industrial policies were less coherent and effective than in neighboring countries like Brazil.

Perón's populist experience illustrates a potential tradeoff between socioeconomic redistribution and democracy in unequal contexts. His commitment to economic transformation and the reduction of inequality went hand in hand with a lack of enthusiasm for democratic institutions. He was always more interested in building direct ties to the "people" and concentrating power than in strengthening political parties and individual freedoms. In 1946 Perón dissolved the Labor Party (and other smaller parties that had supported his candidacy) and created the Unified Party of the Revolution, which later became the Peronist Party. His first administration prevented two opposition politicians from occupying their seats in the Senate; impeached the Supreme Court justices; harassed political opponents; and weakened freedom of expression and organization.[24]

As Perón's authoritarian tendencies intensified, the Argentinian democracy entered into the kind of death spiral that political scientists Steven Levitsky and Daniel Ziblatt describe in their book *How Democracies Die*.[25] A constitutional reform allowed the re-election of the president, strengthened presidential power, and modified electoral rules in Perón's favor. The 1951 presidential elections took place under a state of siege and with millions of pesos used to influence voters: not surprisingly, Perón won by a landslide and the opposition received less than 10 percent of the seats in Congress.[26] A cult of personality intensified quickly: streets, public squares, towns, and even two provinces were renamed in honor of Perón and his wife Evita. Independent social movements were discouraged, and trade unions were not allowed to strike without government's permission. Unfortunately, the opposition responded in kind, supporting four military coup attempts, the last of which succeeded in September 1955.

Populist experiments in other Latin American countries varied in terms of leaders (more or less charismatic) and the characteristics of policy reform (more or less radical), but they can all be understood in relation to prevailing income and power inequalities.[27] For example, we have the case of the "honest, clean-living, frugal, horse-riding, tree-loving, patriotic" Lázaro Cárdenas, general in the Mexican Revolution and president between 1934 and 1940.[28] He deepened the revolution, making the government more responsive to the interests of the majority. Cárdenas redistributed land, expanded labor rights, nationalized the oil industry, and promoted industrialization. Yet he also strengthened a one-party political system that never protected individual rights effectively.

In Ecuador, José María Velasco Ibarra was president five times in the space of 38 years but only once completed his term in office. A charismatic politician with a knack for great speeches— "give me a balcony and I will become president," he once boasted—Velasco Ibarra was first elected president with 80 percent of the vote in 1934.[29] His success was a response to demands for participation from the growing middle class of public servants and artisans and from a small but militant working class. Velasco Ibarra traveled the country, defending their rights and promoting street mobilization. A confrontational rhetoric was always more important for his success than ideological purity: in fact, he was at one time supported by the Conservative, Liberal, Communist, and Socialist parties.[30] As president, Velasco Ibarra promoted—not always successfully—land reform, higher wages, and better labor conditions, while simultaneously expanding public infrastructure, building schools and hospitals, and incentivizing the manufacturing sector. He saw himself as the representative of the people and, like other populists of this period, had no problem weakening democratic institutions when he saw fit. For example, he detained opposition leaders without any real justification in the early 1930s, and unilaterally abolished the Constitutions of 1935, 1946, and 1970, claiming that they were not truly democratic.[31]

Víctor Raúl Haya de la Torre, founder and long-time leader of Peru's most successful political party (the American Popular Revolutionary Alliance, APRA), constitutes the last example I want to discuss. The APRA emerged as a response to the transformation of the Peruvian economy: in the first part of the twentieth century, the number of urban working-class jobs almost doubled as people migrated from agriculture. From his student years, Haya de la Torre understood the needs of this growing group—who struggled with low salaries and tough working conditions in the context of high inequality—and worked to gain their support.[32] As *jefe máximo* (the ultimate boss) of the party and self-proclaimed "father of the workers," he organized street protests, promoted political and economic inclusion, and first ran for president in 1931. His influence and that of the party did not rely on a specific ideology or on institutional links to social movements, but on a direct, personal relationship with supporters. As a thinker and presidential candidate, Haya de la Torre called for land redistribution, economic inclusion, and modernization. As a victim of authoritarian regimes—he was forced to live in exile for many years—he supported democratic institutions more enthusiastically than other populist leaders. Yet for Haya de la Torre, social democracy was always more important than political democracy, and economic inclusion was more relevant than liberal institutions. This was particularly evident in a speech he gave in 1945 at a conference on the challenges of democracy:

> We need to respond to the universal call for democracy, with an answer that is particular to our country: not a French solution. Not

an American solution. We are going to respond with a Peruvian solution... We don't simply want political democracy, we want social democracy ... The new state does not incorporate men simply as citizens, it incorporates them because they have a role in collective life. It is a democracy that transforms citizens into workers ... Democracy is not simply a political right, democracy is not simply political architecture, but economic planning, public organization of the social function of production, distribution, and consumption.[33]

Overall, there is little doubt that populist leaders and movements in Latin America forced the elite to improve workers' rights and living conditions. The historian David Tamarin explained it eloquently in 1982 when talking about Argentina: "Peronist populism signaled something of a cultural revolution. As a vindication of native criollo culture and as a movement that propounded the dignity of the common worker and the deprofessionalization of politics, Peronist populism was a profoundly democratizing social force—perhaps, one should add, in spite of itself."[34] The new movements also expanded voting rights to new groups at a faster rate than in developed countries. Between the 1930s and the 1970s, the share of the population participating in elections increased across Latin America from 12 percent to 52 percent in Argentina, from 8 to 44 percent in Chile, from 3 to 25 percent in Ecuador, and from 20 to 61 percent in Uruguay.[35]

If populism contributed to inclusion and participation, why do I regard it as a political cost of inequality? The answer is simple: populist movements often triggered political instability and institutional volatility. Perón, Vargas, and the other populists loved conflict: politics was all about black and white, the "people" against the "oligarchs," and the "nation" against the "empire." While this was partly understandable in the context of income concentration, it left little room for debate and compromise.

Many populist leaders and movements viewed political institutions skeptically, considering them instruments in the grip of the elite. Although this was not an irrational assumption, their response was not always helpful. They often promoted new constitutions that concentrated too much power in the hands of the executive and created a plethora of new institutions from scratch. They over-promised in terms of what their governments could deliver (A new country! Equality for all!), while paying insufficient attention to how those results could be achieved over the long run.

Their common disregard for formal democracy was particularly problematic. Without freedom of the press, it was hard to secure public accountability and promote proper discussions of policies. As a result, corruption became a significant risk and policy design was not always effective. Meanwhile, strengthening independent, progressive social movements proved hard in the context of continuous attacks on the freedom of association. The disregard for formal democracy and individual rights was sooner or later used by the opposition as an excuse to support military coups—creating a vicious political circle.

Authoritarian Breaks as Extreme Elite Responses

On the morning of September 11, 1973—decades before another infamous September 11—Chileans woke up with the horrible feeling that something awful was happening. At 7 a.m., the Navy had bombed several television and radio stations in the port of Valparaíso, 124 km from the capital. Hours later tanks were marching through Santiago, toward the Presidential Palace. High-ranking military officials soon asked President Salvador Allende to surrender.

Allende, a doctor and socialist leader who had become Chile's president three years before, flatly refused. Instead, he took to the airwaves to call on all citizens to oppose the coup. In what became a symbolic speech of resistance, he warned against the risk of a military regime and called for hope:

> Workers of my country, I have faith in Chile and its destiny. Other men will overcome this dark and bitter moment when treason seeks to prevail. Go forward knowing that, sooner rather than later, the great avenues will open again, and free men will walk through them to construct a better society. Long live Chile! Long live the people! Long live the workers! These are my last words, and I am certain that my sacrifice will not be in vain, I am certain that, at the very least, it will be a moral lesson that will punish felony, cowardice, and treason.[36]

The air force responded to Allende's act of defiance by firing rockets at the Presidential Palace, which was soon in flames. The president's position was desperate: the military had abandoned him and people in Santiago were too afraid to take to the streets. Instead of running away or resigning, he committed suicide.

The coup—and the thousands of arrests of left-wing politicians and activists that followed—became a sad page in world history, destroying one of the oldest democracies in Latin America. Although led by the army, the violent intervention was encouraged and supported by the US administration and the economic elite. Since 1971 a group of businessmen had been meeting regularly to plot the demise of the socialist government. They resented his decision to nationalize banks and copper mines, democratize healthcare and education, expand land reform, and increase real wages. The so-called "Monday Club" included representatives of the Edward family—one of the richest in the country and owners of the leading newspaper *El Mercurio*—as well as the head of the association of Chilean manufacturers and several "Chicago boys"—the group of Chicago-trained economists that later designed the dictatorship's economic program.[37] This powerful group pressured the military to act and then celebrated the coup. On September 12, *El Mercurio* welcomed the new regime with the headline "Toward National Recovery."

Chile is by no means an exception. Across Latin America, when economic elites have been threatened by democratic governments, they have supported authoritarian "solutions." This was, for example, the most common response to the challenge from populist regimes: Vargas in 1954, Perón in 1955, Velasco Ibarra in 1935, 1947, 1961, and 1972; and several others were forced to leave office by elite-supported military coups. The political scientist Paul Drake summarizes the trend nicely: "the elites scrambled to co-opt or crush these movements. When the well-to-do feared that popular democracy jeopardized upper- and middle-class privileges, they imposed protected democracies or exclusionary authoritarianism. Some resorted to unusually barbaric dictatorships by the armed forces."[38]

The interruption of the Guatemalan democratic experiment in 1954 constitutes one of the most tragic examples. Since independence in the nineteenth century, Guatemalans had suffered one bloody dictatorship after another. The country had been ruled by the military for the benefit of a small landowning elite, while the rest of society had been excluded both politically and economically. In 1944, university students (emboldened by the successful overthrow of a military dictator in neighboring El Salvador) began a protest against their own authoritarian regime.[39] The government's subsequent decision to suppress constitutional guarantees intensified social mobilization, culminating in a successful general strike organized by students and trade unions on June 24. Five days later the dictator Jorge Ubico resigned and went into exile in the US.

After a long struggle between the military and the democratic opposition and within the military itself, free and fair elections finally took place in December 1944. The opposition leader Juan José Arévalo—until then a philosophy professor in Argentina—won by a landslide. Arévalo immediately launched an ambitious but pragmatic reform agenda. Subsidies and credit lines for peasants were introduced; public education and healthcare received a boost; a rather modest income tax was implemented; and worker rights were protected for the first time in Guatemalan history.[40] A new constitution extended voting rights to all adult citizens with the exception of illiterate women, and established a multiparty system, while simultaneously forbidding the Communist Party.

The reforms continued after the election of Jacobo Arbenz as president in December 1950. A military officer and former Minister of Defense, Arbenz was committed to a process of economic modernization that benefited a majority of the population. Following recommendations from a World Bank report, his administration focused on the promotion of agriculture and included measures to redistribute land and support small peasants.

Arévalo and Arbenz were not leftist radicals but committed democrats who tried to improve the distribution of income and opportunities without questioning the role of businesses. In his inaugural speech, President Arbenz enthusiastically proclaimed that "our political economy must be based on private initiative, the development of Guatemalan capital, in whose hands we must find the fundamental activities of the national economy."[41] Nevertheless, they had to deal with the constant and ruthless opposition from American companies (particularly the United Fruit Company) and the economic elite. Both presidents were accused of supporting communism and ruining the country. In 1944, for example, the landowners' association denounced the government for "exalting or exaggerating the rights of labor, without mentioning the responsibilities, kindling the most ruinous passions [. . . and thus destroying] social harmony, so necessary in order that the factors of production fulfil with success their noble goals of creating and increasing the national wealth."[42] Ten years later the business elite and the US administration encouraged a successful military plot that forced President Arbenz to resign.

Across Latin America, weak institutions and the elite's lukewarm support for electoral competition have led to regular shifts from democracy to authoritarian regimes and back. There were eight democracies in 1950, six in 1955, twelve in 1959, and five in 1976. In total, between 1950 and 1990 Latin America was responsible for nearly half of all the political regime changes in the world.[43]

The involuntary removal of presidents has become rare in the twenty-first century, but a few cases still highlight the ongoing threats to formal democracy in contexts of high inequality. In Honduras, President Manuel Zelaya was unceremoniously woken on June 28, 2009 by the military and—still in pajamas—put on a plane to Costa Rica. Even if his dismissal was supported by a majority in Congress and by the Supreme Court, the procedure was clearly illegal.[44] His sin? His political opponents accused him of trying to change the constitution to run for re-election. Yet there is another powerful explanation for his forced departure: the elite's worry about his economic agenda. As president, Zelaya had unexpectedly moved to the left, supporting the trade union movement, raising minimum wages by 60 percent, increasing social spending significantly, and allying with Venezuela's Hugo Chávez.[45] Feeling threatened by all these (re)distributive measures, the business elite enthusiastically supported the coup.

In Paraguay, President Lugo was also expelled from office through questionable means. Elected in 2008, Lugo was the first leftist president in Paraguayan history and the first from outside the dominant Colorado Party in 61 years. A former Catholic bishop, he promised to implement progressive policies, including new social programs and a tax reform. His central proposal was a much-needed land reform: with a Gini coefficient of 0.93, Paraguay had one of the most unequal land distributions in the world, which contributed to high levels of poverty.[46]

Lugo confronted fierce opposition from the landowning elite from the start. Just months after his election, the Paraguayan Rural Association (ARP) and the Association of Soya, Cereal, and Oilseed Producers (APS) organized a number of marches against the government and used the press to denounce Lugo's redistributive efforts. The leader of the APS, Claudia Ruser, went as far as accusing the president of links to communist guerrillas.[47] The relentless attack on Lugo during his time in office culminated with his removal in June 2012. Accused without any evidence of mismanaging an incident between the police and landless peasants that resulted in 17 deaths, he was impeached on June 21 and voted out of office just 24 hours later. He did not have time to mount a defense and was never properly questioned by the deputies. The irregularities of the process led many experts and most neighboring countries to describe it as a "parliamentary coup."[48]

Into the Present: The Limits of Democracy and a New Populist Response

Starting in 1978, Latin America's political system experienced an unstoppable democratic wave. Beginning with Ecuador in 1978 and concluding with Mexico in 2000, formal democracy extended across the region, and radically altered the political environment. As a result, while there were only three democracies in the region in 1977 (Costa Rica, Colombia, and Venezuela), all Latin American countries but Cuba were democracies 23 years later.

External pressures created positive conditions for this political change. Growing support for democracy in Europe, the US, and other powerful international actors made the maintenance of dictatorships harder. Demonstration effects were also useful: for example, the process of democratization in Argentina triggered similar pressures in Uruguay. Yet change was ultimately driven by domestic actors. Authoritarian regimes were unpopular from the very beginning: 66 percent of Chileans and 79 percent of Uruguayans were against military rule on the eve of their respective coups.[49] Social protests intensified during the 1980s: between 1983 and 1984, for example, Chilean workers organized more than 110 strikes against the regime. Brazilian metalworkers led by the young leader Luiz Inácio Lula da Silva—who would become president decades later—staged one protest after another demanding political liberalization.[50] In Peru, a general strike in July 1977—the first in the country since 1919—showcased the strength of trade unions and social movements. It also strengthened the hand of democratic political parties, contributing to the military decision to begin a transition.[51]

Pressures from below together with economic difficulties weakened the most radical groups within the authoritarian governments, providing a new impetus for negotiation. Across South America—at different speeds in different countries—military regimes progressively accepted the inevitability of democracy, no longer seeing it as a major threat. In Central America, the process was more painful: the transition to democracy was a direct result of long and bloody civil wars.

Why did the business elite consent to, and at times even support, democratization? Two reasons are particularly relevant. First, authoritarian regimes became less attractive. In some countries, such as Argentina, the elite became weary of the military regime's inept management of economic policy. In Mexico, the private sector stopped supporting the ruling Institutional Revolutionary Party (*Partido Revolucionario Institucional*, PRI) when it became more corrupt and incoherent. In Brazil, the loss of political influence led business groups to withdraw support for the authoritarian regime.[52] Finally, in El Salvador, the transition to democracy was partly driven by splits between conservative landowners and new internationalized business groups.[53]

Second, the business elite made sure that the new regimes would not harm their economic interest and political power. Chile's example is illustrative in this regard. The transition to democracy was organized in such a way as to protect the interests of the military hierarchy and the economic elite. New electoral rules guaranteed significant representation from conservative, pro-business parties, preventing a rapid move to the left. Non-elected seats in the Senate were allocated for representatives of the army and for Augusto Pinochet after he stepped down from the presidency. The business sector also devised formal and informal mechanisms to shape public policy, including control of the press and the major think tanks, influence on economic debates—totally dominated by free market ideas—and massive financial contributions to electoral campaigns.

Across the region, the expansion of neoliberal policies became a safeguard for the elite.[54] On the one hand, economic liberalization reduced the freedom of new governments to adopt radical policies. If a leftist president increased taxation or the minimum wage significantly, it had to deal with capital flight and other economic difficulties. On the other hand, the World Bank and other powerful international lenders forced countries to accept neoliberal policy packages. Some areas, such as monetary policy, also moved outside governments' purview, as central banks across the region became independent.

However, the limits of this kind of democracy and economic model were soon evident, leading to mounting social discontent in the late 1990s. The support for democracy plummeted across the region: between 1995 and 2001 it fell by 11 percentage points. By the latter year, support for democracy was below 40 percent in all countries. Most governments were seen as "highly elitist, autocratic, centralized, presidential, personalistic, clientelistic, incompetent and corrupt. They struggled to ... craft policies that would satisfy socioeconomic and regional vested interests and simultaneously achieve economic growth with equity," explains professor Paul Drake.[55]

Protests against the expansion of markets and the lack of true democracy gradually increased. In Bolivia, a movement against the privatization of water and gas led to the resignation of the neoliberal President Gonzalo Sánchez de Lozada—popularly known as "Goñi"— and strengthened the Movement toward Socialism (*Movimiento para el Socialismo*, MAS). In Ecuador, social protests organized by indigenous movements forced two presidents out of office in 1997 and 2001. In Argentina, the 2001 economic collapse led citizens to take to the streets, demanding "¡Que se vayan todos!" (all politicians leave).[56]

Soon enough, street protests translated into the election of left-of-center presidents in what was then called "the Pink Tide." Starting in 1998, progressive leaders were elected in Venezuela, Argentina, Brazil, Chile, Uruguay, Paraguay, Ecuador, Bolivia, and El Salvador. By the mid-2000s more than three-quarters of Latin Americans were under progressive rule.[57] The new presidents promised both political inclusion—expanding the rights of indigenous people and other discriminated groups—and economic redistribution.

Even if it contributed to the reduction of inequality—as I will discuss with more detail in Chapter 6—the Pink Tide was not without problems. In some cases, like Chile, leftist governments maintained cozy relations with the economic elite, leading to periodic protests and social discontent. Other countries, such as Venezuela and Bolivia, witnessed a return to the kind of populist politics that characterized the region in the middle of the twentieth century, with different results in each case.

In Venezuela, the resounding victory of Hugo Chávez in 1998 was a response to the exclusionary character of democratic institutions together with the unpopularity of neoliberal reforms. Low-income voters were tired of the two dominant political parties, which for 40 years had distributed oil rents among the middle class and the elite while excluding them. Most Venezuelans also opposed the neoliberal reforms introduced in the first half of the 1990s, which failed to halt the economic crisis. Low growth went together with a sharp deterioration of income distribution: between 1981 and 1997, the income share of the poorest 40 percent decreased by more than four percentage points (from 19.1 to 14.7 percent), while that of the top decile increased by more than ten (from 21.8 to 32.8 percent).[58]

Chávez criticized neoliberalism as "the way to hell" and committed to the creation "of a true democratic process, whose essence is no other than the roar and participation of the people."[59] His successive administrations expanded social policy, channeling oil income to new health initiatives and school programs from primary level all the way to university.[60] At the same time, like many other Latin American populist leaders before him, Chávez failed to strengthen public institutions: with the hope of reaching the poor quickly, many of his initiatives relied on parallel structures. He also fostered social polarization; his aim was to build close links to "the people" (*el pueblo*), while attacking the political opposition and the economic "oligarchy" relentlessly. Of course, some of his animosity toward the traditional elite was not entirely unjustified since they had tried to get rid of him through a failed military coup in 2002.

After Chávez died in 2013, his project unraveled. His successor, Nicolás Maduro, lacked the charisma and political skills required to maintain the populist project. He also had to deal with internal bottlenecks and a deteriorating international environment. The inefficiencies of the public oil company became increasingly glaring, contributing to a sharp drop in production. Oil prices decreased sharply, leaving the government without the resources required to fund social programs. Price controls led to hoarding and the creation of black markets but were unable to prevent hyperinflation. Meanwhile, US sanctions further worsened the country's economic prospects. Maduro's efforts to hang onto power led to a fatal weakening of democracy, intense political polarization, and growing social discontent. Chávez's efforts to improve income distribution and create a more inclusive society had ultimately backfired, illustrating once again the fatal costs of inequality in Latin America.

The Bolivian experience under President Evo Morales was much more positive, particularly in economic terms. A trade unionist and coca producer with Aymaran roots, Morales became leader of the MAS in 1998.[61] Members of the MAS participated in the uprising against neoliberal reforms, including the privatization of water in Cochabamba in 2000 and the decision to export natural gas three years later. A widespread desire for change led to Morales' resounding victory in the 2005 presidential elections. Despite (or perhaps because of) opposition from the US—whose ambassador had asked Bolivians to "open their eyes" and never vote for Morales three years before—and the economic elite, Morales received 52 percent of the vote. "Now we begin a new stage in Bolivia's history, where we will search for equality, justice and equity," proudly declared the first indigenous president in Bolivian history after his election.[62]

The Morales administration increased the state's participation in gas, expanded universal pensions and social services, and implemented investment projects in rural areas. New policies together with commodity-driven economic growth led to the halving of the poverty rate between 2006 and 2017 as well as a reduction in ten percentage points in the Gini coefficient. The government also promoted political inclusion, gender equality, and indigenous rights. Regarded as one of the most progressive in the world, the 2009 Constitution established gender parity in Congress and enhanced indigenous autonomy.[63] All these policies were undertaken without endangering macroeconomic stability: even the IMF—not a common supporter of progressive governments like this one—praised the Bolivian government in 2016 for "the sound macroeconomic management and poverty reduction during the past commodity boom."[64]

Despite his unquestionable achievements, the Morales period—like other populist experiments in the past—did not end well. In October 2019, he won his fourth presidential elections, but both the opposition and external actors such as the Organization of American States accused him of fraud. After two weeks of intense protests for and against the MAS government, Evo Morales, together with Vice-President Álvaro García Lineras and other members of the government, left the country and was granted political asylum in Mexico. They were replaced by an interim government led by the right-wing senator Jeanine Áñez, supported by large segments of the army. Áñez was supposed to quickly call elections but spent the first few months adopting controversial reforms against the previous government.

The ultimate fate of Evo Morales and the long-term future of the MAS are still unknown. Yet the 2019 crisis demonstrated—once again—both the risks of the populist political strategy and the power of the traditional elite. During more than 13 years in office, the Morales administration showed a certain disregard for liberal democracy. Staying in power for as long as possible was their primary aim: in the words of President Morales in 2016, "we aren't renters. As social movements, we have come to the presidential palace to stay for all our lives."[65] During its last years in office, the government weakened judicial independence and threatened journalists, opposition parties, and "unfriendly" thinktanks. Even more glaringly, the president ignored a 2016 referendum result that prevented him from running a fourth time. Not surprisingly, this enraged not only conservatives, but also more progressive segments of the opposition. At the same time, the traditional political and economic elites came to hate Morales and all he represented, and were looking for any opportunity to throw him out of the presidency.

In recent years, other Latin American countries have witnessed a return of conservative forces to power.[66] In Chile and Argentina, the shift from left to right may be part of a healthy political alternation—even if its impact on income distribution has been negative.[67] In other countries, the new right-wing governments should be seen as a revenge of the elite and the upper middle class against the left's redistributive efforts. In the previous section I already discussed the case of President Fernando Lugo in Paraguay, who was expelled by a questionable impeachment process and replaced by pro-elite leaders.

Brazil is another depressing example. For 13 years, the country was ruled by two presidents from the progressive Workers' Party (*Partido dos Trabalhadores*, PT). The election of both Lula (2003–10) and Dilma Rousseff (2011–16) was historical for different reasons: a trade unionist with little formal education, Lula was the first working-class president, while Rousseff was the first woman in high office. Under their watch, Brazil implemented new social policies—including the much-praised cash transfer *Bolsa Família*—increased the minimum wage, expanded race quotas, and promoted formal employment. As a result, more than 30 million people moved out of poverty and into the middle class. By contrast, the economic and social influence of the upper middle class decreased: wealthy Brazilians outside the super-rich—who continued doing very well—had a lower income share in 2014 than in 2002.[68]

While economic growth was high and the country was doing well, conservative groups could not do much against the PT. Lula left office with a 80 percent approval rate, transferring his unprecedented support to the less charismatic Dilma.[69] Yet when economic growth slowed down and a series of corruption scandals hit the PT, the attack was relentless. In 2016 Rousseff was impeached after being accused of creative accounting in the budget process—a trick that previous presidents had also used. Few opposition legislators made reference to these budgetary misdeeds during the impeachment process, voting instead to "save the country," "end communism," and "restore the foundations of Christianity." One particularly egregious Congressman, Jair Bolsonaro, dedicated his vote to the military official who had tortured Rousseff during the dictatorship.[70] Two years later former president Lula—who remained the most popular politician in the country—was convicted in a relatively small corruption case supported by rather weak evidence. Many national and international observers considered the case politically motivated and subsequent media reports questioned the behavior of the judge in charge.

In October 2018 Bolsonaro was elected president in an election where Lula—who was leading in the polls—was not allowed to run. Bolsonaro is a populist of a different kind: economically he is all in favor of protecting the wealthy and implementing neoliberal reforms. Politically, he uses a populist discourse, relying on social media to build direct links to the electorate and spread a divisive rhetoric. His "enemies" are the PT and also women ("I will not rape you because you do not deserve it," he told a PT Congresswoman), gay people ("I would be unable to love a homosexual son"), and blacks ("the afro-Brazilians do not do anything, they are not even good at reproduction").[71] He has also called for an aggressive strategy against criminal gangs, including massive use of lethal violence.

Various factors led to Bolsonaro's election, including anger toward the mainstream political class, which was involved in major corruption scandals, and concerns about insecurity. Yet there is little doubt that his election also represented a counter-revolution of the upper middle class and the rich, who wanted to recuperate Brazil for themselves. In fact, in the first round, Bolsonaro received up to 75 percent of the vote in middle- and high-income municipalities, but less than 25 percent in low-income ones.[72]

From Politics Back to Inequality

The Latin American experience illustrates the high political costs of inequality in the political sphere. The wealthy have always refused to support real democracy for fear of redistribution. In response, the poor have often searched for populist solutions that have failed to change power relations or strengthen democratic institutions over the long run. The problems, however, do not finish here: limited democracies, populism, and authoritarianism have in turn contributed to more inequality.

To illustrate this political vicious circle, let's begin by considering the negative distributional impact of Latin America's restricted democracy. In this system, the economic elite has many formal and informal mechanisms to influence political decisions. I already mentioned three of them in the last chapter. The role of an elite-controlled press in shaping political debates; the use of revolving doors between private and public sectors; and close ties to (mainly conservative) political parties have allowed the wealthy to shape policy debates time and again. Let me focus here on their direct contribution to electoral results.

Economic elites have exerted a significant influence on elections through their control of the press. The late Roberto Marinho and Emilio Azcárraga, then heads of the largest media conglomerates in Brazil (Globo) and Mexico (Televisa), famously boasted that they had no problem in using their television channels and newspapers to influence politicians. Newspaper and TV owners often charge subsidized publicity rates to their preferred politicians—who are seldom those with pro-redistribution agendas.[73] At times, media moguls are also politicians. For example, one of Bolivia's largest media companies, Unitel, is owned by a former senator opposed to Evo Morales. Sebastián Piñera, twice president in Chile and one of the country's richest men, remained part owner of Chilevisión until months after winning the elections. In Brazil, many regional politicians control local media as well.[74]

Electoral campaigns across the region are funded at least in part by private contributions. Although many business leaders often hedge their bets, they tend to be more sympathetic to conservative parties. Guatemala provides a great example: during the 2011 presidential elections, thanks primarily to business contributions, the conservative party outspent the left by a ratio of 12:1, unsurprisingly winning the election.[75] Even if public regulations have increased, electoral funding scandals are still common across the region, revealing the ongoing influence of the business elite.

More often than not, political institutions are simply too weak to withstand the power of the wealthy. The number of political parties in the region with the capacity to systematically advance a redistributive agenda is rather small: Uruguay's *Frente Amplio*, Brazil's PT, perhaps Chile's *Concertación*, and few others. In most countries, political parties are either short-lived, too weak, or uninterested in designing consistent electoral programs. As a result, it is hard for governments ever to promote the kind of economic policies that can truly transform the economy and redistribute income and opportunities.

Populist regimes' contribution to income distribution over the long run has also been problematic for at least three reasons. First, in their attempt to improve things, some populist governments have ended up triggering costly financial crises. Perón's first administration provides a good illustration of this problem. In his first years in office, real wages increased by 50 percent. Initially, this expansion did not create problems because international agricultural prices—and, as a result, Argentinian exports—were growing quickly as well. Yet when external conditions deteriorated in 1949, Argentina moved from a trade surplus to a deficit and the country's reserves were quickly depleted. Resources for industrialization also dried up as agriculture entered into crisis. Perón initially increased the money supply to keep the economy going, resulting in a 31 percent inflation rate in 1949. In the end, the attempt to redistribute income too quickly led to a crisis that forced a painful— and inequality-inducing—stabilization of the economy after 1950.[76]

The Brazilian progressive economist and former Minister of Finance Luiz Carlos Bresser-Pereira offers a compelling explanation of the "populist cycle." Initially, governments adopt expansionary policies, including a strong exchange rate (to make imports cheap), higher public expenditure, and higher wages. Not surprisingly, economic growth accelerates as consumption and investment increase. Unfortunately, the positive trend is short-lived. Little by little—or quite quickly, if there is also a negative external shock like the one Argentina suffered under

Perón—all economic indicators deteriorate: a trade deficit appears as imports grow faster than exports. The budget deficit increases as spending surpasses taxes. The money supply and inflation follow. All these problems consistently lead "to a severe crisis, sometimes accompanied by, at least, a change of ministers if not a coup d'état and inevitably ... a radical change in economic policy."[77] The impact of the crisis and of the neoliberal policies that follow on income distribution is often catastrophic.

Populist governments have particularly struggled to adapt to changing international conditions. Their focus on redistribution through public spending is hard to reconcile with negative shocks that reduce public revenues. This is not just a problem of the past. In contemporary Venezuela, when oil prices started dropping after years of expansion, the Maduro administration expanded its reliance on price controls and a multiple exchange rate system. It also funded public spending through monetary expansion, triggering a painful hyperinflation process: in 2018 prices increased by more than 1,000,000 percent.

Second, many populist leaders have shown little interest in building independent social movements. From Brazil under Vargas to Venezuela under Chávez, most governments of this kind have coopted trade unions and limit dissent. Labor and social organizations that have not followed the official line have been regarded as traitors. Yet without organized pressures from below, winning the fight against inequality is almost impossible.[78]

Third, the incessant polarization promoted by populists is hard to sustain over the long run. All these leaders have mastered the art of dividing the country between the "people" and the oligarchy, between a majority of supporters and a minority of enemies. Think about Hugo Chávez proclaiming "It is not me, it is the people" or Rafael Correa joyfully shouting "Ecuador voted for itself" after his 2009 electoral victory.[79] Although their strategy may at times have been justified (there is a sharp gulf between the winning elite and the rest in Latin America), it has consistently generated mistrust and conflict. How can dialogue and negotiations take place in this context? They cannot; instead, the opposition always responds by considering the president illegitimate. These spirals of volatility have often been negative for income distribution and have also contributed to authoritarian interruptions.

The effect of these authoritarian regimes on income distribution has been catastrophic. They have used a combination of political violence and economic reforms to weaken progressive movements and concentrate income in a few hands. The Chilean dictatorship (1973–89) killed more than 3,000 trade unionists and opposition party followers, and the Argentinian junta (1976–83) at least 30,000.[80] Repression and fear were used as instruments for social control: the goal was not only to eliminate challengers to the regime, but also to reduce labor costs and increase profits.

In most cases, the strategy was "successful": real wages stagnated, social programs diminished, and, as a result, income inequality accelerated. In Chile, for example, the income share of the highest decile increased from 34 percent in 1973 to 52 percent in 1987, while that of every other group diminished. As a Chilean magazine explained, the dictatorship did not just rob the poor to give money to the rich, it even robbed the rich to give money to the really, really rich—a reversed Robin Hood on steroids.[81]

In Brazil, the dictatorship focused on modernizing the country, contributing to the so-called "Brazilian miracle"—with rates of growth above 10 percent between 1968 and 1974. Yet it was a miracle for the rich and the upper middle class, not for the poor. Between 1960 and 1970, the income share of the poorest 50 percent decreased from 17.4 to 14.9 percent, while that of the wealthiest 10 percent increased by seven percentage points from 39.6 to 46.7 percent (meaning that in 1970 the top decile had three times more than half of the population!). In the 1980s, inequality continued growing, with the Gini going from 0.585 to 0.635.[82]

The regressive impact of coups is even evident in more contemporary times. Consider, for example, Honduras after the removal of Manuel Zelaya in 2009. The following months saw a rapid increase in repression. In a report titled "After the coup d'état: Violence, intimidation and impunity continue in Honduras," Human Rights Watch recorded 18 killings, hundreds of threats, and a systematic use of force against peaceful protests.[83] Once again, political repression led to economic inequality: while the income of the top 10 percent stagnated during Zelaya's government, it grew by 7 percent annually in 2010 and 2011. As a result, Honduras became one of the only two Latin American countries where the Gini coefficient increased during this period.[84]

Back to the Present

If we have learned one lesson in this chapter it is that sustaining well-functioning and stable democracies in unequal environments is extremely difficult. For more than a century, Latin America has swung between democracy, populism, and dictatorship. Conflicts over income distribution are fundamental to explaining these swings. Under democracy, in most countries, the elite succeeded in capturing the state and preventing significant redistribution. Populist leaders emerged as a response from a dissatisfied majority, who demanded more equity and political representation and higher standards of living. Populism often backfired, though, resulting in coups, economic crises, or both.

The experience of Latin America constitutes a sobering warning about what may yet come in other parts of the world. In countries as different as the US, the UK, India, and the Philippines, worsening income inequality has already contributed to discontent with politicians and institutions. A growing number of voters view political parties as unresponsive and corrupt, more interested in protecting the wealthy than in securing their wellbeing. These complaints are partly justified. In recent decades, mainstream political parties have gradually converged toward a technocratic consensus on a set of "correct" economic policies. The need to secure "market confidence," avoid high marginal taxes, keep monetary policy in the hands of independent central banks, and prioritize low fiscal deficits—at least until this year—has been embraced by left and right. Instead of discussing alternative economic options, political debates have often focused on social and cultural issues such as migration, the recognition of diversity, the value of gender equality, or the role of nationalism.

The French economist Thomas Piketty suggestively links this political convergence on economic ideas to transformations in the party system: the US and many European countries have moved, he argues, from class-based competition to competition between different elites.[85] In the 1950s and 1960s, left-wing parties were supported by unskilled, poorly paid workers, while most high-income, high-educated individuals voted for the right. Since the 2000s, left-wing parties have become an instrument of the "intellectual elite," while right-wing parties are primarily supported by high-income individuals (the "business elite"). Meanwhile, low-income voters no longer feel represented by mainstream political parties, searching for more radical alternatives instead.

The recent response to this lack of representation has been an upsurge of anti-system parties and leaders, from Donald Trump in the US to the National Front in France. Most of them are against globalization and migration, support nationalism, and promote a conservative social agenda on issues such as gender and sexuality. "The forgotten men and women of our country will be forgotten no longer," promised Donald Trump in his victory speech in 2016.[86]

These movements have many "populist" features. They use a divisive rhetoric that praises the value of the majority: "there is a revolt of the people against the elite," argued the French far-right candidate Marine Le Pen in the 2017 presidential elections.[87] They are in a continuous search for scapegoats: China, migrants, the non-white population. And, in many cases, they favor charismatic leaders who connect directly with voters: Trump, Le Pen, Orbán, and Erdogan are all better known than the parties they supposedly represent.

Current populist movements have also weakened formal democratic institutions—just like in Latin America. The recent bestseller *How Democracies Die* warns about the process of institutional weakening that is taking place in many countries, including the US. A growing number of the new political movements are rejecting the democratic rules of the game; denying the legitimacy of other politicians; tolerating violence; and threatening to curtail basic rights, including free speech.[88] Trump's presidency offers a litany of examples of this kind of behavior.

Yet unlike Latin American populists, the current movements represent conservative interests and have shown little support for redistributive policies. They are often against higher taxes, protection of union rights, universal social programs, and better minimum wages—all the policies required to improve the distribution of income. For example, Trump's signature policy proposal in the US was a tax reform that transferred millions of dollars to the top 1 percent. In Hungary, Viktor Orbán—while adopting some heterodox policies such as nationalization—set a single income tax rate of only 15 percent and increased the regressive value-added tax to 27 percent—the highest level in Europe.[89] As the former Chilean Minister of Finance, Andrés Velasco, warned in a critical op-ed, "from Trump in the US to Viktor Orbán in Hungary, from Matteo Salvini in Italy to Jair Bolsonaro in Brazil, and from Jarosław Kaczyński in Poland to Rodrigo Duterte in the Philippines ... their policies are likely to worsen, not improve, the distribution of income."[90]

The way they have tried to build social support is particularly worrying. Instead of criticizing the business elite, they have attacked various groups, including women—all these movements are profoundly misogynistic—and minorities. Migrants have been particularly targeted as terrorists, criminals, lazy, a threat to the country or to the welfare state, and responsible for low wages and growing inequality. This exclusionary discourse has been built around a false dichotomy between the people and the foreigner, making the latter (without evidence) responsible for the problems of the former. "Until we get ... youth unemployment down to zero, and people making high value-added jobs, I don't need any foreigners. And I'm not a racist. What I want is our citizens to get the jobs. Right now illegal immigration is used as nothing more than a scam to suppress workers' wages," explained Steve Bannon, one of the ideologues of far-right populism in the US who is now exporting its exclusionary ideology abroad.[91]

The discussion in this chapter highlights why we should be concerned about this kind of populist turn in the context of high inequality. If populists who aimed to reduce inequality failed in Latin America, what will happen with politicians like Trump, who weaken democracy while protecting the economic status quo? What will voters do when they realize that their economic situation is still not improving? What is the future of democracy in this context? Voters may be left feeling ignored, enraged, and cheated. As the chapter has shown, growing social dissatisfaction may only lead to instability, further harming income distribution, democracy, and peaceful coexistence at the same time.

Chapter 5

THE SOCIAL COSTS OF INEQUALITY

Hundreds of small, poorly maintained houses pile up in a disorganized manner. Many are unfinished and all have brass roofs that struggle to protect people from the rain. An impressive apartment building raises up across the street. It features individual swimming pools in each floor surrounded by two tennis courts, a large communal pool, and a beautifully trimmed garden. These are Paraisápolis and Morumbi, two different worlds, found side by side in the southeast of São Paulo.

The Brazilian photographer Tuca Vieira captured this contrasting reality in a 2004 picture that quickly became viral. In a 2017 interview, he explained how he hoped to reflect the "unjust and brutal difference between rich and poor, inherited from slavery, [which] is in the origin of many other problems—violence, below-par schooling, prejudice and many other issues."[1] A similar picture could have been taken in many other Latin American cities. From Mexico City to Buenos Aires, millions of people confront spatial disparities and social segregation. They regard their neighbors with suspicion, failing to discover what joins them together. They seldom talk to each other, share public spaces, or fight for the same objectives.

This chapter considers the social costs of inequality across Latin America and the resulting vicious circles (see Figure 5.1). I first explore the problem of violence. Today the region has the highest homicide rate in the world and the most violent cities. A record number of femicides also take place every year. Although this sorry state of affairs has many drivers, income inequality is one of the most important. "Inequality generates a feeling of injustice among disadvantaged people, who end up searching for compensation through other means," explains the World Bank economist Herman Winkler.[2]

I then discuss the impact of income inequality on spatial and social segregation. In recent decades, a growing number of affluent Latin Americans have moved to gated communities where they enjoy private playgrounds, private security, and other amenities. Their relationship

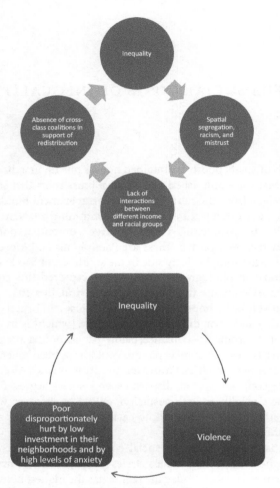

Figure 5.1 Two vicious social circles. Source: Author's own.

with the rest of the city and with other people is superficial and sporadic. Inequality thus creates different life experiences, expectations, and preferences. It also leads to fragmentation of social services: the wealthy, the middle class, and the poor seldom share the same hospitals and schools.

Large income gaps have also reduced trust in neighbors and institutions. In Latin America, every man and woman roots for him/

herself and struggles to cooperate with others. Latin Americans are also highly suspicious of political leaders, parties, and public institutions. Some examples are particularly extreme: only 19 percent of Venezuelans have confidence in the police—a lower number than in troubled countries like Afghanistan and Syria (32 percent in both cases).[3]

This chapter also explores the complex relationship between racism, ethnic discrimination, and inequality. Despite dominant ideologies of *mestizaje* and racial democracy—based on the belief that every Latin American is part of the same mixed race—Afro-descendants and indigenous people have lower education, fewer job opportunities, and higher poverty levels than the rest of the population. In most countries, the elite has often promoted racism and ethnic hatred as a way to perpetuate their power and influence, creating wedges between different segments of the poor and the middle class.

As I showed in earlier chapters, the problem is not only that inequality has social costs but also that these costs, in turn, lead to further inequality. In violent societies, low-income groups suffer disproportionately, both emotionally and financially. In segregated societies, there are large education gaps between rich and poor and few cross-class social networks. In mistrustful societies, the opportunities to build coalitions between the poor and the middle class—required to expand redistributive social programs—are severely hampered. In this way, structural inequality has perpetuated itself in Latin America through various social vicious circles. Other countries may be experiencing similar problems today and may struggle even more in the future.

The Most Violent Region in the World

According to Martin Daly, professor emeritus of psychology and neuroscience at the University of Ontario, inequality predicts murder rates "better than any other variable." Daly, author of *Killing the Competition: Economic Inequality and Homicide*, explains that "if your social reputation in that milieu is all you've got, you've got to defend it. Inequality makes these confrontations more fraught because there's much more at stake when there are winners and losers and you can see that you are on track to be one of the losers."[4]

Being both the most unequal and the most violent region in the world, Latin America is living proof of this relationship. Every hour 18 people die violently in the region—more than anywhere else in the world. Latin

America's homicide rate is three times higher than the global average (21.5 vs. 7.0 measured per 100,000 people) and 43 of the 50 most violent cities in the world are in Latin America.[5] It is not only murders: with 426 per 100,000 people—four times more than the world average—South America also leads the ranking of reported robberies.[6]

The relationship between inequality and homicide rates is also evident when comparing countries *within* Latin America. Figure 5.2 relates the Palma ratio (first discussed in Chapter 1) to the homicide rate in every Latin American country. Brazil, Colombia, Honduras, and Guatemala, the most unequal countries, are also the most violent; by contrast, some of the most equal countries, such as Argentina and Uruguay, are also the least violent. If we disregard the case of El Salvador—a clear outlier that combines a low Palma ratio with one of the highest homicide rates in the world—the relationship would be even stronger.

Those of you who have followed Latin America's recent trajectory may be doubtful. You may call attention to the fact that, in the 2000s, while inequality went down in most countries, violent crimes remained constant or increased.[7] Others will point to the multicausal origins of violence in the region, including the authoritarian past, the involvement of the army in politics, the 1980s debt crisis, neoliberal reforms, and the growth of transnational organized crime.

Overall, however, the evidence supporting the positive link between

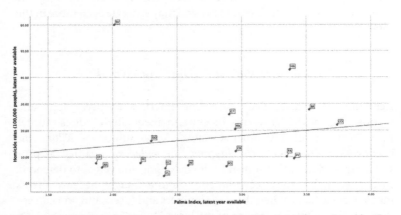

Figure 5.2 Relationship between inequality and violence at the regional level. Source: Author's own, based on data from Igarapé Institute (for homicide rates) and SCEDLAS (for inequality). Note: Data on inequality is for 2014 or the closest year before then; data on homicide rates is for 2017.

inequality and violence in Latin America is convincing. This link is particularly evident in the life of millions of young males who suffer the consequences of inequality and discrimination. In this demographic group, we find most of the victims and perpetrators of violence: in 2009, the homicide rate for men between 20 and 24 years old was 93 per 100,000—almost four times the average for the whole population.

Young people are acutely aware of their weak position in unequal societies and their lack of future prospects. In her study of four generations of Brazil's favelas—the poor and informal neighborhoods on the outskirts of cities like Rio de Janeiro and São Paulo—Janice Perlman talks about a paradoxical move from "the myth of marginality" to "the reality of marginality." When she began her interviews in the late 1960s, favela inhabitants had just moved from the countryside to the city and were still hopeful about their future. Three decades later, their children had higher incomes and better access to education and healthcare, but were frustrated by their lack of job prospects, the daily discrimination they suffered, and the pervasive threat of violence. Hope was replaced by disenchantment, and violence was used as a response to discontent.[8]

In Central America, social inequalities were behind the emergence of gangs in the 1980s and early 1990s. In *Adios Niño*, a fantastic description of the perils of life in Guatemalan gangs, Deborah Levenson collected views from gang members over several decades.[9] During the early 1990s, they framed their criminal acts in the language of class. For example, Berlin, a fashionable young man in a branded sweater, jeans, and white trainers, told Levenson: "I stole the sneakers from a *burgués* [a bourgeois], these pants from another, and that's how I get along, getting what I need to live." Other gang members had similar explanations:

> I've robbed everything! I am a professional thief, which is a bit more elegant than "delinquent" but I've always robbed from people who have money, robbing from the poor is evil (Caixo).

> Look, the only people I steal from are people with money, because robbing from an equal would not be right. I grabbed chains from the chicks at Monte María, Belga, and other private schools (Sivio).

Things changed in the late 1990s and 2000s when youth gangs become much more violent. Following the example of the *maras* in Los Angeles (Mara Salvatrucha and the 18th Street), they increasingly focused on fighting for space and killing each other. As one *marero* explained, "everyone sees themselves as soldiers serving *mi barrio* [my gang/my place] in a war without any Geneva Code."[10] In 2015—the most violent year in the country's history—18 Salvadorians were killed every day, most by the *maras*.[11] Homicide rates were also high in the other two countries of the so-called "Northern Triangle" (Honduras and Guatemala).

This transformation of gangs into *maras* is a complex phenomenon with multiple national and international roots. The US' decision to repatriate all felons without US citizenship to their country of origin was significant. In the early 2000s, 46,000 convicts and more than 160,000 undocumented immigrants were deported to El Salvador, Guatemala, and Honduras.[12] Most had been raised in the Los Angeles *maras* and immediately tried to reproduce the same structures in their "new" countries. Their job was made easier by the abundance of arms after long civil wars.

Yet income concentration has undoubtedly played a central role as well. During the 1990s, Central American countries experienced an elite-led neoliberal revolution that gave the private sector new opportunities to accumulate wealth. The elite became even more powerful and transnationalized than in the past.[13] The anthropologist Ellen Moodie vividly explains this sociopolitical change and its consequences in the Salvadorian case: "it was ARENA [the right-wing party representing the elite] that would radically restructure the economy. It was ARENA that would launch the 'liberation movement'—but for elites' unconstrained accumulation of capital, not the masses' rights to inclusion."[14] In this way, neoliberalism contributed to inequality and youth unemployment, feeding into the gangs' sense of exclusion. "Society isn't ours, it belongs to others, " explains William, a former *marero*; "when we join the gang, we look with indifference at the rest of the world."[15]

Outside Central America, marginality and exclusion are also behind youth violence. For example, the *Primeiro Comando da Capital* (PCC), initially a self-protection group for young prisoners in São Paulo and now a large criminal organization with more than 11,000 members, is a result of Brazil's racial and income gaps. "Poor black and brown men have been—and are—the subjects of the social processes that criminalize bodies and spaces ... This systemic violence is also the terrain from which the PCC builds its support," explains Cambridge professor Graham Denyer Willis.[16]

The threat that these violent groups represent has been adeptly used by elites to move political debates away from underdevelopment and injustice. In Central America, the *maras* have been framed as a common threat to all "good" citizens, from CEOs to informal workers. An ad from the Guatemalan National Civil Police followed this strategy to the letter:

Who are we? We are the majority, worker, business executive, housewife, athlete, chewing gum vendor, we are those who drive in the latest Mercedes Benz and those who take the bus or walk in the street. We are the people who do something constructive and positive for our country and our families and who every day confront the chaos and violence caused by *mareros*, those juvenile gangs. We are humble people, normal people who work to reach what is difficult but not impossible to achieve: PEACE.[17]

Instead of expanding education and creating well-paying jobs, governments across the region have opted for violent responses—what in Spanish is referred to as *mano dura* (the iron fist). Police killings, incarcerations without trial, and torture have become popular government responses. In this way, "inequality ... reproduces the victimization and criminalization of the poor, the disregard of their rights, and their lack of access to justice," explains Teresa Caldeira, one of the leading experts on violence and exclusion in Latin America.[18]

In São Paulo in the 2000s, police killed more people every two years than the Brazilian dictatorship did during its 20 years in power.[19] Renata Neder from Amnesty International in Brazil denounces the fact that "the black youth living in the periphery is a subject to kill. The favela is an enemy territory to be conquered. It is a logic of war ... If the police would stop killing, we would have between a 20 and a 25 percent reduction in homicides."[20]

In Central America, iron fist policies as a way to fight the gangs were first introduced in El Salvador in 2003. Initial measures included automatic imprisonment of any individual from the age of 12 with gang-related tattoos or other obvious gang signs. As a result, more than 20,000 gang members were arrested between July 2003 and August 2004.[21] Although these measures were later declared unconstitutional, El Salvador has continued its violent war on gangs, adding fuel to the fire of deaths. Guatemala and Honduras have adopted similar policies—with similarly poor results—at various times in recent years.

Incarceration is directly linked to inequality, as most Latin American prisoners come from low-income groups. Conditions in jail are harsh: inmates live in overcrowded buildings, eat low-quality food and face high levels of violence. Three of every four inmates in Chile, Mexico, and Peru are less safe in prison than outside—and the percentage is likely to be even higher in several Central American countries.[22] Prisons, which have become training grounds for new criminals, reproduce Latin America's class disparities. When I visited several jails in the Dominican Republic years ago, most inmates lived in the bathroom or in small rooms with many other inmates, while a few lucky ones (with either more money or better connections) stayed in double-occupancy rooms with their own TV.

This section on violence would be incomplete if I did not make reference to the prevalence of femicides in Latin America—a topic that deserves a book in its own right. In 2018, more than 3,500 Latin American women were killed because of their gender, and many more were kidnapped and raped.[23] El Salvador has been the world leader in femicides for quite some time: between 2007 and 2012, 14 women per 100,000 were killed there because of their gender.[24] Despite significant improvements in recent years, in 2018 the femicide rate was still seven per 100,000.[25] In just one Mexican city, Ciudad Juárez, more than 1,779 women have been killed in the last 25 years—most of them after suffering rape and torture on their way to and from work.[26] "The gender-based killing of women is the extreme on a continuum of violence that women in the region experience," explains CEPAL's leader Alicia Bárcenas. "The figures . . . show the depth of the patriarchal, discriminatory and violent cultural patterns that are present in the region."[27]

Femicides are thus part of a broader pattern of gender violence, which has been driven by a complex set of interconnected factors. Machismo, impunity, and state weakness are all important. Most governments still fail to take gender violence sufficiently seriously: in Brazil, for example, more than half of judges and policemen do not regard it as problematic. Inequality plays an important role through multiple channels. Indirectly, it contributes to state weakness—as we have seen at various points in this book. Directly, it leads to the creation of areas of poverty and exclusion where gender violence is more common. In turn, broader violence against women further contributes to inequality, by weakening their political strength and reducing opportunities for intra-gender social coalitions.[28]

Divided Lives, Private Spaces

In Lima, the neighborhoods of Las Casuarinas and Pamplona Alta are divided by a "wall of shame." On one side, $2m houses are surrounded by exquisitely landscaped lawns, multiple swimming pools, and a plethora of security guards. On the other, $300, 25-square-feet mini-houses made of scrap material are stacked together. In Las Casuarinas water can be seen everywhere from pools to gardens and fountains; in Pamplona Alta many residents cannot even drink from the tub.[29]

The 10 kilometers of concrete and wires separating Las Casuarinas and Pamplona constitutes a dramatic representation of the spatial effects of income inequality. In their search for protection and beauty, the wealthy build gated communities that only owners and visitors can enter. They use their growing resources to build a parallel universe, far away from the noise, dirt, and violence of the rest of the city. Living in one of these communities is both a sign of power and distinction and a tool to ignore other people's problems.

Gated communities—*barrios cerrados* in Spanish and *condominios fechados* in Portuguese—have sprawled across Latin America in recent decades. Luxury apartment buildings with their own gyms, swimming pools, and green areas have suddenly appeared across all major cities. In Brazil—home of the highest number of wealthy individuals in Latin America—the *condominios fechados* include all kinds of unique features, such as an individual pool in each apartment, bedrooms for three maids, waiting areas for drivers, and even rooms to store crystals and other precious objects.[30] Although they take different shapes and forms (from independent houses on the outskirts of Managua to modern skyscrapers in Buenos Aires or Rio de Janeiro), gated communities are all fortified and have become a different planet.

Of course, class segregation in Latin American cities is not new. For much of the twentieth century, the upper classes lived in well-equipped neighborhoods in city centers or in exclusive suburbs. They spent their weekends in *el club*: country clubs with golf courses, swimming pools, and fancy restaurants where they could socialize with each other, discuss business, and interact with high-ranking politicians. By contrast, low-income groups piled up in informal areas on the periphery of the main cities: many were recent immigrants from the rural sector, who built their own houses wherever they found a place. In São Paulo, for example, the population in newly opened areas on the outskirts of the city grew by 10 percent per year in the 1960s and 1970s in a spontaneous process led by private actors.[31] The state was absent from most of these new areas, failing to plan the space, build parks, and provide basic services such as electricity and sanitation.

What is unique about urban segregation today is the contradiction between how close people live and how far they are in practice. Most Latin American cities have become "islands of wealth in an ocean of poverty," but these islands are heavily protected with walls, cameras, and an army of private security. In a growing number of neighborhoods, you can find poor-quality housing for low-income individuals close to highly protected apartment towers and individual houses for the rich. In Buenos Aires, for example, during the 1990s, a growing number of gated communities appeared in southern parts of the city where the working class had traditionally been concentrated. Something similar is evident in Mexico City, where rich and poor live closer together than in the past—making inequality more apparent than ever before. Low-income groups are no longer concentrated in the west of the city alone but also live in other areas. The combination of spontaneous settlements, cheap land, and social housing has facilitated the move of thousands of households to neighborhoods previously controlled by the upper middle class and the wealthy. Yet close proximity has not translated into interpersonal interactions.

A series of interviews undertaken by the sociologists Cristina Bayón and Gonzalo Suriví illustrates this large gulf between social classes in Mexico.[32] For example, they talked with Andrés, a 26-year-old from Miguel Hidalgo (one of the wealthiest and most touristic neighborhoods in Mexico City), who explained how ignorant his friends are about other people:

> A very common comment among many professors at the university is, "Guys, you really have to go beyond La Herradura" or "Guys, you have to go beyond Interlomas to see the real Mexico," and I think they don't. Many people at the university have this vision of "I've never seen that Mexico" and even that it doesn't exist. I've heard a number of times, "Oh no, no way, it's not true." I remember some girls from the university saying, "I don't understand why everyone can't have a house in Mexico."[33]

Inequality-driven separation between groups contributes to discrimination. Another youngster from Miguel Hidalgo and a primary teacher who works in Chimalhuacán—a poor neighborhood—describe this problem vividly:

> You say to people, "Let's go there," and they think that just going there means they'll get mugged, raped, kidnapped, all of that; that's very true, people here are very scared. Fortunately, nothing has ever happened to me. One can't deny that there's a serious crime problem in Mexico, but not so much that just going there will be dangerous.

The guys here spend all their time in Tecamachalco, Huixquilucan, La Condesa, but don't go beyond.

They think Chimalhuacán is a mess, don't they? They think it's a conflict zone, one of drug addiction. They see it as the worst. [Where I live,] if I say "Let's go to Chimalhuacán," they tell me, "No, no, those places ... around there where you go, they kill people." "No, just imagine, I don't know why you work there, it's a violent area."[34]

Of course, urban segregation is a problem across the world from Chicago to London and Paris. Nevertheless, in many of these cities, there is still a larger middle class and more spaces for interaction. An upper-class Mexican student explains the difference between some of these cities and those in Latin America better than any statistic I could provide:

I lived for a time in Canada, and it wasn't the same. Something very funny happened to me once: I was studying English at a school, and one day a bunch of us were chatting outside the building and there was a guy sweeping the street ... That night we met him at the bar we went to and talked to him and everything! These things just don't happen here. I've never seen in this in Mexico—meeting the guy who sweeps the street in a bar, the same bar I go to with my friends.[35]

One final quotation further illustrates the link between income inequality and discrimination. Mariana, who lives in Santa Fe, another wealthy neighborhood, explains how people in her building behave with their employees:

The building where I live ... [is] a bubble ... Employees may not enter by the main gate, they have to use a special building; it's horrible. If they use the main elevator people get angry, but what is derogatory is that there is a side entrance for employees, like a secondary category of people. And yes, of course, they [my neighbors] are very humane ... and that is also something very characteristic of this population, being very humane ... So employees get special self-esteem workshops, against family violence, etc. And how is their self-esteem not supposed to be low if that's where it's being created[?][36]

Sadly, this is by no means unique to Mexico City. In some Brazilian gated communities, employees are searched when leaving the building after work. In most wealthy buildings across the region, there are separate elevators for different groups.

The combination of inequality, close proximity, and discrimination has other costs for low-income groups. The lack of social mobility is particularly glaring for them when they walk past the houses of the elite. They see their lack of status reflected in the faces of potential employers when they mention where they live. Current and former favela residents in Rio, for example, regarded living in a favela as the number one obstacle to social mobility. They are probably right: in fact, the benefits of education are much higher for the average *carioca* than for those living in a favela.[37] Something similar happens in Buenos Aires, where the chances that young people (18 to 24 years old) in informal settlements neither work nor study is 66 percent higher than for those living in richer neighborhoods.[38]

"As the spaces for the rich face inwards, the outside space is left for those who cannot afford to go in," Teresa Caldeira explains.[39] In many Latin American cities, there is little attention to public spaces where people from different classes, races, and ethnicities can mingle and interact. There is also insufficient investment in sidewalks where people can walk: I still remember how hard it was to take our daughter to her nursery when we spent a summer working in San José. We had to jump hole after hole with her stroller, crossing from one side to the other and walking on the road for long stretches. Public transportation is also uneven: even in the cities with the best transport infrastructure, such as Buenos Aires or Bogotá, buses are crowded and uncomfortable and everyone who can afford it drives their own car.

Income inequality does not only create spatial segregation, but also contributes to class separation in other areas. In general, and despite some improvements in the 2000s, upper middle-class and wealthy Latin Americans do not use public services, preferring to send their children to private schools and rely on private healthcare.[40] In Brazil, three out of five individuals in the top 20 percent had complementary private health insurance compared to just 5 percent in the bottom quintile. In Chile, around 60 percent of those using the (private) health insurance institutions belong to the wealthiest 20 percent—and the share among the elite is likely much higher. In poorer countries, the role of the private sector is even larger: in Guatemala, Honduras, Nicaragua, and Paraguay, private health spending is above 4 percent of GDP—similar or higher than what the public sector spends.

Unfortunately, many people within the middle class aspire to the same kind of health services. They respond to waiting lists and other shortcomings of the public sector by either buying private insurance or paying for private doctors from their own pocket. Even in countries with high-quality public health like Costa Rica, the middle class is relying on the market more and more when they need checkups or blood tests. As a result, "health is very unequal. There is one group that has access to the best healthcare and another that does not. These are like two countries," denounces the famous Argentinian neuroscientist Facundo Manes. This is unfortunate because, as he explains, "health in the world is not just about fighting sickness, but a key factor for social cohesion."[41]

The effects of inequality on Latin America's education systems are even worse. Around one in five Latin Americans attends a private school, significantly more than in other parts of the world. The children of the elite attend international schools or get educated abroad. Large segments of the middle class have also exited the public system in search of schools with better infrastructure and more teachers. In Brazil, Colombia, Costa Rica, and Uruguay, 30 percent of middle-class children in primary and secondary education go to a private school. In Peru (42 percent), Argentina (49 percent), and Chile (79 percent) the number is even higher. By contrast, the share of the emerging middle class— families making between US$4 and US$10 per day—who can afford to send their children to a private school is much lower: less than 10 percent in Brazil, Costa Rica, Mexico, and Uruguay.[42]

A well-functioning education system is an engine of social cohesion and justice: children from different races, origins, and income levels share the same classrooms, build lifelong ties, and learn to respect each other. A divided and unequal education system not only segregates but also fuels social divisions: the upper middle class and the wealthy join forces, forgetting about the rest. They benefit from the best laboratories, the best computers, and the best sport fields. More importantly, they spend time with children from similar families, visit their houses, and end up buying into an exclusionary view of society. Unfortunately, "the students from the poorest households are increasingly segregated from the rest of the population in public schools, with fewer interactions with children and young people from other social strata," according to a group of experts on inequality who conducted a study on Latin America's education systems.[43]

Living in gated communities and using private services are ultimately status symbols. Taking one's children to fashionable schools and using the most modern (private) hospitals are equivalent to becoming part of a country club. They are ways to demonstrate that the family "has arrived," joining the exclusive group of the "successful." They are also tools to strengthen families' social networks and protect their place in society—something particularly important in unequal environments. Sadly, this results in sharply divided societies, where income inequality creates both social apartheid and polarization.

Mistrust in Each Other and in Institutions

In 2013, the now president of Brazil, Jair Bolsonaro, proclaimed "we have to create ways so that the . . . ignorant and those without resources control their number of children. Because we control ours. The poor have no control."[44] He was echoing the popular view across Latin America that the poor are lazy, untrustworthy, violent, and love to have children. More than 45 percent of citizens in 12 of the 18 Latin American countries—including two of every three Argentinians—think that those receiving public social assistance support are just lazy.[45]

In a powerful TED talk, the Argentinian Mayra Arena debunks some of these myths about poor people like her. She explains how violent responses come from disappointment and rage and that the poor "have children because it is the only thing [they] can have . . . and each of them become a reason to wake up every day." Her talk is a call to build bridges and to mingle with people from other classes: "when a family with a house with a toilet [which she did not have] invites you to play . . . they teach you much more than to use the toilet. They teach you that life can be different . . . But I was not the only one learning. They also learned from me and my family."[46]

Yet mingling is precisely what does not happen in Latin America. High inequality leads to growing segmentation between those in gated communities and those in shanty towns, between those in elite private schools and those in rundown public ones, between those in rural, remote areas and those living in skyscrapers. In this way, inequality and segregation lead to mistrust as people become suspicious of the "other": the wealthy start seeing low-income groups as "lazy" and "criminals," while the poor regard the elite as "snobbish" and "abusive."

Indeed, personal mistrust is higher in Latin America than in most other parts of the world. According to data from *Latinobarómetro*—a Chilean-based nonprofit organization that carries out an annual survey of 20,000 Latin Americans—more than 60 percent of Brazilians, more than 50 percent of Bolivians and Peruvians, and more than 40 percent of Panamanians, Venezuelans, Dominicans, Mexicans, Salvadorians, and Guatemalans do not trust people in their own communities. The equivalent percentages for the US—not the most trustful country in the world—and Canada are only 20 and 11 percent respectively.[47]

Mistrust is high across all segments of society and has been increasing. For example, Perlman's study shows how people in the favelas have become more suspicious and less committed to the community. While in 1969 more than three-quarters of those she interviewed felt that the community was "very united" or "fairly united," 35 years later, 55 percent of the people believed that the community "lack[ed] unity." Her informants "feel trapped between the drug dealers and the policy and do not trust either one ... They feel the police do more harm and provide less help than the drug dealers, but they see both as disrespectful of life in the community."[48]

Skepticism about political institutions is even higher. Government, political parties, and the police compete with each other for the prize of "least trustworthy": only 35 percent of Latin Americans have at least some confidence in the police, 28 percent in electoral institutions, 24 percent in the courts, 22 percent in the government, 21 percent in Congress, and 13 percent in the party system. Some countries fare particularly bad: only 5 percent of Salvadorians and 6 percent of Brazilians trust political parties—probably only the party affiliates and a few more![49] Ask in the streets of Rio, Mexico City, or Buenos Aires and all you will hear is "the police is allied with organized crime" or "all politicians are corrupt." Mafalda, the clever six-year-old depicted in a popular Argentinian comic strip, reflects people's view on the state better than anyone. In a brilliant strip, Mafalda's mum asks her: "What are you guys playing?" Her friends enthusiastically respond: "The government." Her mum then warns them not to make a mess. Mafalda immediately reassures her: "Don't worry! *We are not going to do anything at all.*"[50]

Why do Latin Americans mistrust institutions so much? There are many reasons, including high levels of corruption and poor public service delivery. Yet inequalities in income and political opportunities are probably primary drivers. Most people resent their place in society and do not feel represented by political institutions; in fact, almost four out of five Latin Americans are convinced that governments rule for the benefit of the powerful and are uninterested in the preferences of voters—a much higher percentage than in other parts of the world.[51]

Unsurprisingly, low-income groups are particularly suspicious of public institutions such as the judicial system. In 2017, a group of US-based researchers organized a number of focus groups in Santiago (Chile) and Medellín (Colombia) to explore the links between inequality, trust, and the use of the judicial system. They found that the most discriminated groups (by race and/or class) thought that judges would always treat them unfairly. As a result, they often resorted to informal mechanisms to resolve conflicts and search for justice, including community meetings, non-government organizations, and, more worryingly, criminal gangs. On other occasions, these groups simply gave up and ran away from risky situations.[52]

Unfortunately, lack of faith in public institutions has also led many Latin Americans to look to the military for solutions. Despite the region's authoritarian past, the armed forces are the most trusted public actor in every country. Many people regard them as more professional than the police and less corrupt than most politicians. There is a (mythical?) belief that the army is apolitical and exclusively focused on the nation's welfare.

Building on this popularity, several Latin American governments increased the army's involvement in public policies in the 2000s. As we saw earlier in the chapter, this began with their participation in *mano dura* campaigns. Since 2017/18, the army's participation has expanded to many other policy areas. Brazil under Bolsonaro—a former army captain—constitutes the most extreme example. A few months after being elected, he warned that "democracy and freedom only exist when the armed forces want them to."[53] Six of the 22 people in his first cabinet were former high-ranking military officials. Other military men—they were, unfortunately, all men—led or oversaw other state companies and public institutions, including the oil giant Petrobras.[54]

In Mexico, the leftist President Andrés Manuel López Obrador moved from promising to "gradually take the armed forces out of the streets" during the electoral campaign to claiming that the army was "key to calm the country so there is peace and tranquility" more recently. During the first year of his presidency, the military led the fight against organized crime and participated in the protection of oil facilities and the construction of infrastructure projects.[55]

The army's participation in policymaking is bad news for both the health of democracy and the fight against inequality. "When the armed forces are linked to a government's political support, there is a greater risk of slipping into an authoritarian regime," warns the Brazilian political scientist Wagner de Melo.[56] Lack of transparency, weak protection of human rights, racial profiling, and political instability could easily increase in the region in the future. Growing involvement of the army in decision-making could also result in less attention to inequality and the redistribution of income.

Obviously, all the problems discussed in this chapter are interrelated. For example, social trust is closely linked to violence and people's perception of violence, and both, in turn, are related to income distribution. When people are afraid of crime, they have fewer opportunities to interact and can easily lose faith in other human beings. Think about this: two-thirds of Latin Americans rethought their weekend plans at least once during the last 12 months for fear of insecurity.[57] Most ended up staying at home instead of spending time with friends and colleagues.

Racism and Discrimination: Cause and Consequence of Inequality

Let's introduce one final (interrelated) problem: racism and discrimination. Discrimination against Afro-descendant and indigenous populations has contributed to income inequality and resulted from it. In fact, in some countries like Guatemala it is hard to distinguish between racial and income inequalities as they are one and the same.

Discrimination in Latin America has its roots in the process of colonization. As we saw in Chapter 2, after conquering Latin America, the Spanish created racist societies based on the oppression of indigenous people. Millions were killed or died because of sickness brought from Europe. Many others had to work long hours in fields and mines, and could not move without permission from white landowners. Africans soon accompanied indigenous people at the bottom of the social pyramid. Between five and ten million African slaves were brought to Latin America by force between the sixteenth and nineteenth century to work in sugar plantations, mines, and other labor-intensive industries. The scale of the slave trade was so large that by the early 1800s, more than 60 percent of all Brazilians, Panamanians, and Venezuelans were Afro-descendants.[58]

In the century after independence, the Latin American elites developed two different racial projects. They first tried to promote a whitening of their population. Building on the myth that Afro-descendant and indigenous people were lazy and ineffective, they looked for ways to expand the number of whites. Using arguments echoed recently by President Trump and others, several countries prohibited immigration of people from African origin. They simultaneously created incentives to bring European migrants, even if only a few countries—such as Argentina and Venezuela—succeeded in attracting them.[59] Discrimination was particularly intense in countries with a high number of indigenous people, who were regarded as economic tools more than political subjects. "The majority of the population will not be an active element of progress, but rather an instrument [of it]," wrote a member of the Guatemalan elite, referring to the Mayan majority.[60]

Starting at the beginning of the twentieth century, countries pushed for a new racial project: *mestizaje*. Elites across the region began promoting the idea that most people were of mixed race and that discrimination was non-existent. *Mestizaje* was an attempt to unify people in new national projects, contrasting the region's "racial harmony" with segregation in the US South. The Mexican philosopher, politician, and revolutionary, José Vasconcelos went so far as to talk about a "cosmic race" that would successfully combine all others: "In the Spanish America," he wrote in 1925, "... there will not be the race of a single color ... what will come from here is the final race, a synthesis or integrated race, made of the genius and blood of all peoples and, because of that, the most capable of true fraternity and a truly universal vision."[61]

In Brazil, sociologists talked about the country's success in creating a "racial democracy." In their view, mixing between slaves, indigenous people, and whites had resulted in growing harmony and tolerance. Novelists, musicians, and artists celebrated Brazil's unique sociocultural fusion and resulting racial understanding. Some even used it to explain the success of Brazilian footballers.[62]

There is little doubt that in Latin America there was more racial mixing than in the US, for example. Unfortunately, however, the project of *mestizaje* has often contributed to hiding discrimination and racism. It has allowed Latin American societies to avoid confronting the ugly truth that skin color *does* shape income levels. Even today, after three decades of democracy and (some) attention to ethnic and racial inequalities, Afro-descendants and indigenous people live in much worse conditions than others. In countries such as Bolivia, Guatemala, Honduras, or Nicaragua, three out of every five are poor. In Panama, the poverty rate of indigenous people is 90 percent compared to 30 percent for the rest of the population. In Brazil, per capita income for people of European descent is more than double that of Afro-descendants.[63] Even in relatively equitable Uruguay, the chance of being below the poverty line is more than twice as high for Afro-descendants as for the white population.[64]

There is also discrimination in access to social services. The literacy rate for Guatemala's indigenous women is 26 percentage points lower than for the non-indigenous. By contrast, the probability of dying during childbirth is twice as high.[65] Across the region, indigenous people and Afro-descendants attend worse schools and spend less time in education. In Mexico, often considered a "post-racial society" whose president defined *mestizaje* as "the future of humanity," those with white skin complete on average ten years of education compared to 6.5 years for those with browner skin. Skin color is more important than region, economic sector (urban vs. rural), or gender in explaining wealth and educational gaps.[66]

Racism and discrimination are evident in everyday life. Across Latin America, most commercials on newspapers and TV use white people to sell expensive products and indigenous or Afro-descendant models to depict poverty. Examples abound: a doll commercial in Peru featuring only blonde girls; another where a white model complains about the smell of her (Afro-Peruvian) roommate.[67] At times, the advertising industry perpetuates stereotypes even when trying to fight them: in 2019, the Mexican producer of the beer Indio launched a campaign titled Proudly Indian (*#OrgullosamenteIndio*) . . . which included white models only![68]

Some reactions to the success of *Roma*—the Oscar-winning Mexican film—show how deeply rooted discrimination is in parts of Latin America. The Netflix-funded movie, which depicts the life of an indigenous maid in 1970s Mexico, starred Yalitza Aparicio as the main character. The award-nominated actress comes from an indigenous family and had never acted before. Despite her international success, a group of Mexican actors opposed her nomination to Mexico's national film awards. In a private conversation with colleagues later made public, the Mexican actor Sergio Goyri used a racist term to refer to *Roma*'s star (*pinche India*) and downplayed her success.[69] Unfortunately, despite improvements in recent decades, it is still common to use "Indian" as a derogatory term or undervaluing the contribution of indigenous people and Afro-descendants to society.

Racial and ethnic discrimination are both costs of class-based inequality and also causes of it. According to Richard Wilkinson and Kate Pickett, authors of *The Spirit Level*, "in more unequal societies, more people are oriented towards dominance; in more egalitarian societies, more people are oriented towards inclusiveness and empathy."[70] When Latin Americans worry about their position in society, they search for other groups to exploit. Indigenous people and Afro-descendants are easy scapegoats: many people hold them responsible for insufficient modernization and economic development.

Powerful economic (and political) elites have continuously promoted discrimination as a way to maintain inequality. Guatemala provides one of the most dramatic examples.[71] After decades of a violent and costly civil war, the government and the guerrillas signed a peace accord in 1996. Three years later, the government organized a referendum to gather support for key elements of the accord, including higher taxes, some land redistribution, and the modernization of the state. Fearing redistribution and a stronger state, the business elite—one of the most conservative in the region—spent millions of dollars on the "no" campaign. They used scare tactics and scaremongering, warning about the threat of indigenous power and ethnic violence. Aiming to protect all their wealth, the elite advanced one racist argument after another: that Guatemala would become an indigenous state, that non-indigenous people would be marginalized, that the referendum would enhance the rights of a minority at the expense of everyone else. Sadly, their strategy was a total success: only 18.5 percent of the electorate went to the polls and the "no" vote prevailed by a margin of 55 percent to 45 percent.[72] More recently, in Bolivia, the interim government that ousted Evo Morales in 2019 (see Chapters 3 and 6) has been accused of using racist symbols and trying to create social divisions for their own benefit.[73]

From Violence, Social Segmentation, Mistrust, and Racism Back to Inequality

As in previous chapters, let's consider now the reverse relationship from social ills back to income distribution. Picking up on where we left it in the last section, let's begin with the negative distributional impacts of racism and discrimination. By dividing people across racial and ethnic lines, they both promote social divisions and polarization. Low-income groups no longer focus on the elite as the primary enemy; instead, white people worry about indigenous people and Afro-descendants and try to dominate them. Alberto Alesina and Ed Glaeser explain this negative process when discussing social policies in the US—another country mired by racial divisions:

> when there are significant numbers of minorities among the poor, then the majority of the population can be roused against transferring money to people who are different from themselves. Another way of thinking about racial or ethnic divisions is that the proponents of the welfare state generally attempt to draw distinctions between

economic *classes*. Racial, religious, and ethnic divisions distract from those distinctions and reduce the ability to forge a common *class*-based identity.[74]

In my own research on the differences in income distribution within Latin America, I find that, historically, having a small indigenous and Afro-descendant population has been a necessary condition for having lower inequality.[75] Fighting inequality in racially divided countries—affected by daily racism and discrimination—has so far proved difficult.

In countries like Guatemala and Bolivia the indigenous and non-indigenous poor have often seen each other with suspicion. Meanwhile, the middle class across the region has often understood that indigenous people are treated unfairly, but has still regarded them as uneducated and lacking culture. In Brazil, large segments of the middle class equate violence and crime with skin color; as a result, they have little interest to share schools and hospitals—and create political coalitions—with Afro-descendants.

Spatial segregation and fragmentation in social policy have also contributed to the perpetuation of inequality. If the children of the poor and the middle class do not play together or attend the same schools, how are they going to push for similar policies? If the middle classes go to private schools, why will they fight for better public schools? Across the region, the fragmentation of healthcare, pensions, and education has contributed to individualism and the segmentation of interests. Take the case of Argentina, where each of the 23 provinces manages its own public health system and, in parallel, 300 social insurance funds service the middle class. Every group enters the healthcare system through a different system and confronts different problems; for example, in the capital there are 7.3 hospital beds per 1,000 people compared to just 1.1 in the province of Misiones.[76]

Research undertaken by the Inter-American Development Bank (IDB) illustrates how the absence of social trust has also affected income distribution negatively. In 2018, IDB researchers asked a number of Latin Americans about their trust in institutions as well as their support for public education, policing, and income redistribution. They found that in all cases, low-trusting individuals were less likely to support equity-enhancing state interventions. These groups are likely to believe that children from other families will not put in the effort to learn and achieve good results. They often see the poor as cheaters and, as a result, do not support redistributive programs.[77] Unfortunately, this triggers another vicious circle: inequality leads to low trust which, in turn, prevents citizens from supporting redistributive policies, thus resulting in even more inequality.

The contrast between Latin America and the Nordic countries could not be more glaring. There, cross-class coalitions in support of redistribution have consistently contributed to equity. For many years, the poor and the middle class have jointly participated in trade unions and voted for social democratic parties that advance pro-equity policies. These social coalitions have been behind the push for high wages and generous social programs that redistribute income and opportunities from the wealthy to the rest of society. Instead of vicious circles, these countries have thus benefited from virtuous ones, as low inequality contributed to more collaboration between the middle class and the poor, leading in turn to more redistribution.

Let me finish this section by considering the impact of violence on the income gap. Most newspaper articles and many international reports present crime as a problem that affects everyone equally. Alarming headlines warn tourists not to visit a country because of its high homicide rate. Ratings agencies worry that crime will affect foreign investment and slow down the economy.

Yet the truth is that crime affects only a few neighborhoods. "Violence ... tends to be highly concentrated," explains Robert Muggah, founder of Brazil's Igarapé Institute. "The perception in many cities that everyone is equally at risk is flat-out wrong ... In Bogotá, just 2% of street addresses are where 98% of homicides occur."[78] Across Latin America half of all homicides take place in just 1.6 percent of the streets.[79] While most Latin Americans have never seen a homicide—even if they have read about thousands of them—poor individuals from marginal neighborhoods have witnessed many. The costs of violence in their lives is immense and takes place through many channels: anxiety, psychological insecurity, loss of supporting family members, and difficulties investing in education and economic opportunities.

The wealthy do not only suffer less crime, they also have more instruments to defend themselves. They spend millions of dollars on private security: the wealthier you are, the more protected with bodyguards and technology you can be. Latin America currently houses 16,000 private military and security companies, which employ an estimated 2.4 million workers.[80] In Brazil there are four private security guards for every police officer; in Guatemala the ratio is five to one; and in Honduras it is seven to one.[81]

The poor thus suffer from violence, while the wealthy successfully avoid it. As a result, the poor have more stress and are less productive, while their communities have less investment and fewer economic opportunities than wealthier ones. Inequality feeds into violence that triggers further inequality—in the last of the vicious circles discussed in this book.

From Latin America to the Rest of the World: Some Warning Signs

Inequality in Latin America has contributed to violence, segregation, mistrust, and ethnic and racial discrimination. These problems have, in turn, led to the perpetuation of unfair societies that struggle to reduce the gap between rich and poor. In this kind of environment, fighting structural inequality has become an unwinnable battle.

Similar problems are increasingly evident in other parts of the world, including many OECD countries. The US is probably the clearest example, as large income gaps between rich and poor contribute to various social malaises. Take the case of violence. Although the number of fatal crimes has decreased in the US in recent decades, it is still much higher than in most other developed countries. The US homicide rate is almost twice the OECD average, 11 times higher than in continental Europe, and 27 times higher than in Japan.[82] Income disparities are one of the forces behind this negative result: many homicides are perpetrated by young male Americans who face diminishing economic opportunities and feel that the economy is rigged in favor of the wealthy.[83] Income inequality is correlated with homicide rates at the state level and also explains why some neighborhoods suffer more property crimes than others.[84]

The US has also become one of the most segregated countries in the OECD. Walk through any American city—large or small—and you will find contrasting worlds: areas with dilapidated houses followed by streets with large, well-appointed homes. There are few parks and public spaces and, with the exception of parts of New York, Boston, and a few other metropolises, almost nobody uses them. Outside city centers, isolated suburbs with gated communities and independent houses extend for miles and miles. As the sociologist Robert Putman famously noted in the early 2000s—after two decades of growing inequality—Americans are now "bowling alone," living solitary lives and finding few opportunities to mix with other classes.[85] In this context, political polarization has intensified, making the creation of cross-class coalitions in support of redistribution harder than ever. Of course, racism does not help: discrimination based on ethnicity and race remains high, as recent episodes of police brutality have demonstrated, and has contributed to the weakening of redistributive welfare policies in recent decades.

Trust is also low in the US. It has decreased steadily as income concentration accelerated: the percentage of Americans who trust others went from 77 percent in 1964 to only 38 percent in 2014.[86] Lack of confidence in both neighbors and institutions was one of the factors behind Trump's surprising ascent to power: his supporters were suspicious of the media, the liberal elite, and people different from them. Reversing this trend may be harder—as the evidence in this chapter demonstrates.

Overall, there is little doubt that growing income concentration has made the US more similar to Latin America than most people care to admit. This was not always the case, as Richard Wilkinson, one of the academic leaders on inequality research, explains: "when the US was one of the more equal countries, its health was amongst the better, not quite at the top, but—in the top few. Now, it comes behind all the other developed countries. And it swapped places with Japan, which used to be one of the more unequal countries, had bad health, but then from the '50s through the '80s, they became more equal."[87]

The case of Europe is more complicated. There, welfare states are stronger and lessen the negative impacts of income distribution on society. European countries are more trusting, more cohesive, and less violent than those in the Americas. Yet growing inequality has triggered social tensions, which could accelerate in the future. Social fragmentation and discontent are on the rise and sustaining traditional cross-class coalitions in support of redistribution is increasingly challenging. From Spain to Italy and even Sweden, social segmentation is on the rise as middle-class families search for new ways to distinguish themselves from the poor.

Let me conclude this chapter with two snapshots that illustrate these emerging inequality-induced social problems in Europe. The first is the growth of xenophobia: more and more Europeans have revolted against refugees and migrants. Foreigners have been held responsible for low wage growth, job scarcity, decreasing social service quality, and the breakdown of cultural norms. Even if all these beliefs are wrong, migrants have still become a scapegoat for Europe's problems. Some segments of the political (and economic) elite are more than happy to drum up false charges against migrants, since it diverts people's attention away from income concentration.

Inequality is also contributing to social segregation: across Europe, new segments of the middle class are imitating the elite and opting for private services. School co-payments, private health insurance, and pension funds have become more popular as people embrace individualist values. Fearing a loss of status in an increasingly unequal environment, the middle class is searching for new ways to stand out. The expansion of private healthcare in Spain in the last decade is just one example of this broader trend. Today, one in four Spaniards complement their access to public healthcare with a private insurance. "The danger," warns professor Juan Oliva, former president of the Spanish Association of Health Economics, "is that we develop two speeds to access healthcare, a fast route for those with private insurance, and a slow one for those without. Public health is [still] a solid institution, but if more citizens abandon it, it will break and deteriorate."[88] Given the Latin American experience, this danger will no doubt accelerate in the future not only in Spain but in many other OECD countries unless we do more to close income gaps.

Chapter 6

LATIN AMERICA ALSO PROVIDES POSITIVE LESSONS

On a sunny October Sunday in 2018, Pope Francis canonized the Salvadorian Óscar Romero as a saint, praising him for "disregarding his own life to be close to the poor and his people."[1] Thousands of Salvadorians cheered enthusiastically. They had traveled all the way to Rome to celebrate the life of a priest who had denounced injustice and called for a peaceful transformation of El Salvador. They all saw the sanctification of Romero—now Saint Romero of the Americas—as a demonstration that a more equal and better world is possible.

A relatively conservative figure for most of his life, Romero experienced a dramatic transformation after becoming bishop of San Salvador in 1977. The assassination of his friend Father Rutilio Grande—along with a 72-year-old companion—and the upsurge in state-sponsored violence transformed him deeply. He became concerned by the conflict between the authoritarian regime and the leftist guerrillas, and the growing harassment of progressive priests.[2] Óscar Romero converted into a tireless defender of the poor and the persecuted. In his sermons and public events, he named those killed and called for an end to the military campaigns. He also embraced liberation theology—which highlights the central role of the poor—and sought advice from some of its leading figures.[3]

On March 24, 1980, Romero was assassinated by a death squad with links to the state while he was celebrating Mass. He had become too much of a threat to the government, the army, and the wealthy elite. The day before, in his regular Sunday homily at the cathedral, he had exhorted the military to end the violence: "In the name of God, in the name of this suffering people whose cries rise up to Heaven more urgently with each day that passes, I beseech you, I beg you, I order you to stop the repression!"[4]

Romero's life, assassination, and sanctification are a reminder of the prevalence of injustice but also a call for hope. His support for liberation theology, his denunciation of state violence, his demand for justice, and his commitment to the poor have inspired millions of people in Latin America and beyond.

This chapter discusses some of the positive lessons coming from the region. Latin Americans have confronted entrenched economic gaps through creative means. Their experience can provide inspiration for those fighting inequality in other parts of the world. In the following pages, I separate these positive experiences into three interconnected spheres—ideas, politics, and policies—and show how they are relevant for policymakers, activists, and students working in many other contexts.

Latin America has been a cradle of progressive ideas. From economists to theologians, critical thinkers have placed the exploitation of the region's majority at the heart of their analysis. Going beyond European theories such as Marxism, they have focused on the unique characteristics of developing countries, including their colonial past, dependence on external actors, strength of the elite, and uneven labor markets. Theologians have talked about "structural violence," educators about "oppression," and economists and sociologists about "dependency" and local and international elites.

Explaining all the innovative ideas coming from Latin America would require much more space than is available here, so I focus on just three major contributions. I start with structuralist economics and dependency, two perspectives that emphasize the link between international factors and domestic inequality. I then move to liberation theology, a progressive school within Catholicism, which places the poor at the center and focuses on fighting political, economic, and social injustice. The third (related) approach is the pedagogy of the oppressed proposed by the Brazilian Paulo Freire and his followers. Coming from different disciplines, all these ideas illustrate the creativity of Latin American thought and provide contemporary lessons. They signal, for example, the need to consider the interactions between key sectors of the economy, the elite these sectors create, and the opportunities for redistribution. They also call for a new politics and ethics of the poor, which understands that low-income groups are both victims and drivers of change.

In evaluating the impact of politics on inequality, it is important to go beyond formal institutions and consider the role of social movements. The region has been a breeding ground for progressive organizations fighting inequality and oppression. In the past, many were violent— leftist guerrillas were common across the region from the 1950s to the

1970s—and their impact was limited and contradictory. More recently, demonstrations against neoliberalism have contributed to shifts in the balance of power in countries such as Bolivia, Brazil, Chile, and Mexico. Latin America's social movements demonstrate the need for social actors to push for a more democratic future, use new technologies creatively, and build new links between society and political parties.

I end the chapter with a discussion of the improvement in income distribution during the 2000s—a unique period in Latin American history. At a time when much of the rest of the world was becoming more unequal, the Gini coefficient went down in 14 of 18 Latin American countries. The combination of increases in the minimum wage, interventions in the labor market, and redistributive social policies contributed positively to this outcome. Of course, other regions are different and will need context-specific policies, but the Latin American experience provides several useful ideas, including the positive role of social pensions and conditional cash transfers.

Before we begin, I should add a caveat: we should not exaggerate the impact of these ideas, social movements, and policies. Even if Latin America's innovations can inform current and future fights against inequality, their ultimate effect has always been limited. Income concentration has persisted because of the strengths of the political, economic, and social vicious circles discussed in previous chapters. Latin America's lessons still have more to do with the costs of a bad distribution of income than with its solutions.

Latin America as a Hotbed of Ideas

I have taught a course on the economics of Latin America every year since the beginning of my academic career. One of my favorite classes is the one on "structuralist economics." I love the fact that—contrary to mainstream economics—structuralism was proposed by Latin Americans to explain their own problems. Its success demonstrates the importance of developing indigenous ideas and policies. Yet its contemporary relevance goes beyond Latin America: many of its insights are useful to understand challenges in other parts of the world.

The initial structuralist ideas were proposed by the Argentinian economist Raúl Prebisch in the late 1940s. Born in Tucumán in 1901, Prebisch worked for the Argentinian government during the first stage of his career. He advised several ministers and co-founded the Argentinian Central Bank. During these years, he also became familiar with the work of John Maynard Keynes, the English economist who proposed a more active role for the state in economic management.

In 1949, Prebisch wrote a founding manifesto for the newly created CEPAL—a United Nations regional institution based in Santiago (Chile). The 58-page paper placed Latin America's problems in historical perspective, linked them to the region's place in the global economy, and proposed some policy solutions. The "Latin American manifesto" became the inspiration for everyone working at CEPAL.[5]

Structuralism developed a new way of thinking about the economy: more historical and more rooted in space than Anglo-Saxon economics. The lack of development in Latin America, Prebisch and his followers explain, resulted from its dependence on commodities and from its technological backwardness. Exporting mining and agricultural products was less advantageous than selling the kind of manufacturing goods produced in Europe and the US.

Structuralism provided a new interpretation of inequality. In their view, the only way to understand income distribution within each Latin American country was to consider the way the global economy was organized. Most technological innovations took place in countries like the UK, France, and the US—the "center"—and in many sectors simultaneously. These economies not only grew more but were also diversified and had many high-productivity sectors. Workers in all kinds of activities, from textiles to steam engines and from wine to steel-making, were highly productive and, as a result, relatively well paid. In contrast, countries in Latin America, Africa, and much of Asia—the "periphery"—were specialized in agricultural and mining products and relied on innovations from abroad. In the periphery, many economic activities—particularly within the manufacturing sector—were underdeveloped and most wealth was concentrated in the export sector. Most jobs were informal and poorly paid.

Here then is the main source of income inequality for structuralists: differences in productivity between various sectors, leading to large wage gaps. These differences generate a hierarchy of actors within any Latin American economy: at the top, the owners of the largest firms in leading sectors, and at the bottom, low-educated workers in subsistence agriculture and informal urban activities such as street vending. Unless countries diversify their economies, reduce the differences in productivity between sectors, and create more formal jobs, inequality will persist.

But this is not the end of the story. Income distribution is not just an economic problem having to do with leading sectors and informal jobs.

It is also directly connected to power and influence. As Prebisch himself explained, capitalism in the periphery "promotes the concentration of economic power and inequity. And the concentration of economic power leads to concentration of political power in the most favored strata."[6] The elite, which dominates the main economic activities, uses its capacity to shape prices, hire and fire workers, and influence politicians. The minority of workers who are part of a trade union also have some power to secure high wages. In contrast, informal, powerless workers have no bargaining capacity.

There is a striking difference between this explanation and the one provided by most mainstream economists. The latter often focus on the supply and demand of workers and capital available to explain income distribution. In their view, if a country has few capitalists but a lot of business opportunities, profits will be high. If educated workers are scarce compared to the number of skilled jobs available, they will receive high wages. If CEOs receive astronomic salaries it is because they have special talents and make a unique contribution to their companies. For many mainstream economists, inequality is a technical accident that has little to do with economic power or the characteristics of the economy. Even many progressive mainstream economists, who recognize the importance of political influence and the danger of monopolies, seldom pay attention to differences between economic sectors in the way structuralists do.

Structuralism was particularly influential during the 1950s and 1960s. Following their recommendation, many Latin American countries promoted the manufacturing sector by protecting the domestic market and offering cheap credit and other subsidies. Social spending also increased in several countries. Overall, the new policy model—often called state-led development or import-substitution industrialization—achieved many successes. Economic growth accelerated, new manufacturing activities (from apparel to automobiles) were developed, and inequality went down in several countries. Nevertheless, these benefits were lower than promised. Economic growth was volatile, dependence on mining and agricultural exports persisted, and concentration of income at the top remained high. As a result, social discontent accelerated, and political tensions intensified— as discussed in Chapter 4.

In this context, a new generation of Latin America thinkers proposed more radical ideas, giving rise to the dependency school. In their view, most changes within Latin America were driven by the interests of the US and some European countries and by the preferences of multinational firms. According to the most radical proponents of this approach, becoming fully independent from these external actors by, for example, promoting socialist revolutions was the only way to secure long-term development and improve income distribution.

Overall, I have always found the contribution of dependency thinkers less useful than that of structuralism. By making external forces responsible for Latin America's malaise, they hide the central role of the domestic elites. Calling for radical transformations of the global economy is important, but changes in the distribution of income must begin at home and be supported by domestic coalitions. By calling for radical breaks, the most radical *dependentistas* also downplayed the positive contribution that everyday politics can have.

Nevertheless, there is little doubt that the dependency school made a fundamental contribution to critical thinking. Latin Americans became thought leaders, providing perspectives that could never have emerged in Europe and the US. In this way, they also contributed to the creation of a fertile environment for progressive ideas and movements in other fields. One of these was liberation theology—the second major Latin American contribution to global thinking on equity I would like to discuss.

Liberation theology was a response of committed Catholic priests to the injustices and exploitation they observed in their everyday lives in the 1960s. Of course, this response was not sudden or isolated, but part of a broader progressive climate. In 1965, the Second Vatican Council—a special meeting of all bishops led by Pope Paul VI—had encouraged the Catholic Church to pay more attention to social issues. Three years later, the Latin American bishops gathered in Medellín (Colombia) made a loud proclamation in support of social justice: "we must favor every honest effort to promote the renewal and the elevation of the poor and of all those who live in conditions of human and social inferiority . . . we cannot have solidarity with systems and structures that hide and support serious and oppressive inequalities between classes and citizens of each country."[7]

That same year, the Peruvian priest and philosopher Gustavo Gutiérrez gave a lecture titled "Toward a Liberation Theology" that became the basis for his first book on the subject, *Liberation Theology: Perspectives*. Many others followed: Samuel Ruiz in Mexico, the Spaniards Ignacio Ellacuría and Jon Sobrino in El Salvador, Pere Casaldaliga and Leonardo Boff in Brazil, and Ernesto Cardenal in Nicaragua to name just a few.[8] Despite their differences—some put the emphasis on the role of indigenous people, others on the need for social change, some were more radical than others—they shared some common pillars.

They all placed poverty and injustice at the core of their thinking. Liberation theology popularized the term "option for the poor": a radical commitment to those at the bottom of the social pyramid.[9] Opting for the poor requires understanding how they live and what they need. It calls for a consideration of all dimensions of poverty, including lack of respect, discrimination, and insecurity. Catholics who truly opt for the poor must also live modestly—"a poor Church for the poor," proposed Óscar Romero—something hard to accept for the Latin American elites.

Of course, for liberation theologians, poverty has little to do with individual behavior but is a structural phenomenon and a social sin. "Poverty is for the Bible a scandalous state that goes against human dignity and is thus against God's will," wrote Gustavo Gutiérrez in his 1971 book.[10] Because poverty is a result of the way we organize our economy and our society, fighting against it demands radical changes at the local, national, and international levels. Liberation theology thus not only celebrates the poor, but also denounces the wealthy and the exploitation experienced by developing countries.

This way of approaching religion and society has had major implications on the way liberation theologians think and act. From the beginning, they engaged with social science. Liberating the poor could not be done by praying and providing spiritual support alone. It required improving people's everyday lives. To do so, theologians needed to understand how the national and global economies were organized and why conflict between different groups took place. Recognizing the existence of class struggles (permanent conflicts between capitalists and workers), liberation theologians embraced Marxism, studied history, and borrowed ideas from the dependency school. Their multidisciplinary approach has made their thinking particularly powerful.

They also went beyond words and embraced action from the start. From the 1960s to the early 1980s, thousands of priests and lay people created Basic Communities to work with the poor and publicly denounced poverty and inequality. The most radical followed the example of Camilo Torres—a priest who joined the Colombian guerrillas and died in battle in 1965—and supported leftist guerrilla movements.

Liberation theology has questioned the status quo tirelessly. For too long, they argued from the beginning, the Church had befriended the powerful, legitimizing their actions and implicitly supporting inequality and exploitation. Traditional Catholic thinking focused excessively on spiritual matters: having faith in God and following all Catholic principles was more important than fighting everyday injustices. The Church was also too hierarchical: priests possessed all the power and set all the rules, thus creating insufficient space for laymen and laywomen's initiatives.

Not surprisingly, the Catholic hierarchy was not happy with these criticisms. In 1984, the Congregation for the Doctrine of the Faith—the Vatican institution in charge of preserving and protecting "true" Catholic thinking—published a blistering attack on liberation theology. Signed by the German Cardinal Joseph Ratzinger—later Pope Benedict XVI—"Instruction on Certain Aspects of the 'Theology of Liberation'" warned against "the deviations, and risks of deviation, damaging to the faith and to Christian living, that are brought about by certain forms of liberation theology."[11] The document went further, denouncing liberation theology for embracing violence, focusing almost exclusively on the "class struggle," ignoring the spiritual dimensions of religion, and lacking rigor. At the same time, the Vatican punished several theologians, silencing Leonardo Boff for a year and suspending Ernesto Cardenal and other priests for their participation in the Nicaraguan Revolution.[12]

These attacks weakened liberation theology significantly. Nevertheless, its relevance in the fight against inequality has remained. Catholics and non-Catholics alike can learn from its defense of the poor and criticisms of the establishment; the creative link between spiritual growth and daily actions; and its support for nonviolent resistance against injustice. Additionally, liberation theology has always built fruitful conversations with thinkers in other disciplines, influencing— and being influenced—by them.

Paulo Freire is probably one of the best known. Freire's ideas on education constitute the last Latin American contribution I want to discuss in this section. Freire was born in 1921 in the Brazilian northeast, the poorest region of the country. His family struggled financially during his youth and, as a result, he was at one point four years behind in school. Nevertheless, he ended up studying law at university. After graduating, he worked as a secondary school teacher and later at a nonprofit that supported workers and their families. Freire quickly understood the disconnect between the way education was organized and the actual lives of working families.[13] During the 1950s, he finished his PhD and led several successful literacy projects, shaping Brazilian public policy in this area. After the 1964 military coup, Freire was imprisoned and forced into exile. He moved to Chile, where he worked in the agrarian reform, and later became a visiting professor at Harvard and a special educational advisor for the World Congress of Churches in Geneva.

Bold and with a long beard for most of his adult life, Freire had the looks of a progressive and committed intellectual. He wrote his first book, *Education as the Practice of Freedom,* in 1967 and his most famous, *Pedagogy of the Oppressed,* in 1968. The book, published in English and Spanish in 1970, did not come out in Brazil until 1974 because of the military junta's opposition. Thanks to these books and his subsequent policy work in Africa and Brazil, Paulo Freire became one of the most influential educators of the twentieth century. His progressive thinking influenced teachers and shaped curriculums across the world, effectively linking the role of education with the fight against inequality and oppression.

Freire's starting point is the distinction between oppressed and oppressors. In any capitalist society, most people struggle with low income, insecurity, and discrimination. The whole system is organized in favor of a small minority. Their power is not just economic but also ideological. They can force most citizens to accept society as it is—not as it should be—and to embrace dominant narratives about merit, productivity, and the justice of the market.

Formal and informal education, Freire argued, reproduces oppression and limits dissent. He warned against the "banking concept of education," which is based on the idea that the primary goal of students is to accumulate knowledge. "Instead of communicating, the teacher issues communiques and makes deposits which the students patiently receive, memorize, and repeat," Freire explained in *Pedagogy of the Oppressed.*[14] According to this model, students should focus on memorizing the multiplication tables, the capitals of the world, and all kinds of historical facts—but should not be encouraged to question why this is useful or important.

This kind of education has many drawbacks. It emphasizes "technical" knowledge devoid of its social context and political implications. Banking education also teaches children and teenagers to submit to the authority of "leaders" and avoid critical thinking. It makes low-income people—young and old—see themselves as ignorant, undervaluing the knowledge they already have. In *Letters to Cristina,* a beautiful autobiographical book written as a series of letters to his niece, Freire criticized "elitist, authoritarian schools" because they "do not take into account, in their curricular organization and their treatment of program content, the knowledge that is generated by social classes that are subjugated and exploited."[15] Learning becomes a boring exercise, which ends up discouraging many students—something Hayley Jones observed decades later in the study on Brazil discussed in Chapter 3.

In contrast, Freire proposed an education focused on liberation—borrowing from the language of liberation theologians. In his view, education should promote critical thinking, encouraging students to ask questions and find deeper meanings. Teachers must promote a process of discovery; students should be able to question reality and search for more creative ways to organize the world. Progressive educators should also rely on the knowledge and experience that students already have. For example, instead of focusing on formal grammar when teaching writing skills, they could build on children's vocabulary. In making this proposal, Freire considered his own experience. One of his best teachers, he explained with affection, "would ask me to write in a straight line all the words I knew. Afterwards, I was supposed to form sentences with these words and later we discussed the meaning of each sentence I had created. This is how, little by little, I began to know my verbs, tenses, and moods . . . My teacher's fundamental preoccupation was not with making me memorize grammatical definitions . . . I was always invited to learn and never reduced to an empty vessel to be filled with knowledge."[16]

A liberating education should be built on dialogue. Students should participate in the process at every step of the way: when designing the curriculum, when learning new concepts, and when doing problem-solving exercises. The process of dialogue should help to break the barriers between teacher and pupil, promoting a less authoritarian and more democratic relationship. The good teacher should always link theory and practice, allow students to question her/him and promote joint discovery. How different is this approach from the way most schools are organized even today!

The end goal of education in contexts of oppression and inequality is to free students from dominant thinking, encouraging them to change the world. Freire often called for a transformative education that simultaneously encouraged respect. "The ideal is to promote the transformation of rebellious consciousness into revolutionary consciousness. To be radical without becoming sectarian. To be strategic without becoming cynical. To be skillful without becoming opportunistic. To be ethical without becoming puritanical," he eloquently explained to his niece.[17]

Despite the inherent problems with all the theories discussed here—e.g. a limited attention to race and gender, too much focus on external factors, excessive influence of Marxism—they remain relevant today.

Together they constitute useful alternatives to the dominant thinking coming from Europe and the US. They do not try to be abstract representations of "capitalism," "knowledge," or "markets," but reflections of specific realities and their contradictions. Because they are embedded in Latin America's history, they unsurprisingly put a lot of emphasis on inequality, exclusion, and exploitation.

Even if rooted in a particular context, they also have universal relevance. Increasing inequality, growing elite power, and constant exploitation of the poor make structuralism in economics, liberation theology in Christian thought, and Freire's pedagogical proposals as useful as ever. They can inspire new thinking and new actions across the world. Let me provide just one example of this influence. The Poor People's Campaign—a religious-based social movement in the US that is fighting inequality and promoting social and economic rights—has borrowed many ideas from liberation theology. Led by William Barber and Liz Theoharis, the campaign regards conservative policies as unjust and the lack of attention to the poor as immoral. They are "trying to articulate a kind of American-style liberation theology for the Trump era—one that's relentlessly focused on inequality and white supremacy," according to a recent profile of the progressive movement and its members.[18]

The Originality of Latin America's Social Movements

In April 2019, the *New Statesman*—a British progressive magazine founded more than a century ago—highlighted the role of US and UK millennials in spearheading a global socialist rebirth. "It makes sense"— explained one of the key supporters of the progressive leftist Democrat Alexandra Ocasio-Cortez—"that the two countries that fell to neoliberalism first may be the furthest along in organizing . . . resistance to it." In the same article, a co-founder of Momentum, a leftist group associated with the British Labour Party, explained that activists on both sides of the Atlantic faced a similar challenge: "how to harness the power of ordinary people against opponents with more money and establishment power."[19]

The *New Statesman*'s article constitutes an illuminating example of the Anglo-Saxon tendency to regard themselves as the center of the world. "This piece is actually nothing short of scandalous," tweeted the Norwegian professor Alf Gunvald Nilsen; "the fact of the matter is that when it comes to both suffering the brunt of neoliberalism and organizing resistance to it, the global South has been at the frontlines."[20] I agree: for more than three decades, Latin American social movements have struggled against the unregulated expansion of markets, forging regional alliances in the process. From the Zapatistas in Mexico to the MAS in Bolivia, Latin Americans provide powerful lessons that progressive activists and policymakers in the US and Europe should consider closely.

Before I discuss some of these contemporary movements and explain their originality and creativity, let me go back a few decades. Modern resistance to inequality and exploitation did not begin in the 1990s, but decades earlier.[21] Starting in the 1960s, a significant wave of violent opposition to the establishment spread throughout Latin America. The success of the Cuban Revolution in 1959 after three years of intense fighting inspired revolutionary movements in many countries. Hoping to follow the lead of Fidel Castro, Ernesto "Che" Guevara, and their comrades, young leftists from Venezuela to Guatemala founded rural and urban guerrilla groups.[22]

Most of these early movements were weak and short-lived. In Argentina, several attempts to organize guerrillas, first in Tucumán and later in Salta and Jujuy, were foiled by the army. Efforts in Brazil, the Dominican Republic, and Uruguay met with similar fates. Others were better organized but still unsuccessful.[23] In Venezuela, the *Fuerzas Armadas de Liberación Nacional* (National Liberation Armed Forces, FALN) were active for a decade, attracting students from the Central University of Caracas, boycotting elections, and organizing military campaigns in several regions. Yet they never succeeded in gaining support from a majority of the population and gradually became irrelevant. Overall, most Latin American guerrillas during the 1960s were too optimistic and rather naive. They failed to grasp the strength of the state apparatus and the army's willingness to respond with force.

During the 1970s, a second wave of insurgency began in Central America.[24] Students, intellectuals, and middle-class professionals joined forces with peasants in opposition to inequality, exclusion, and authoritarianism. In Nicaragua, the *Frente Sandinista de Liberación Nacional* (Sandinista National Liberation Front, FSLN) overthrew the bloody and unpopular dictatorship of the Somoza family in 1979 after a decade-long struggle. The Sandinista victory encouraged the Salvadorian and Guatemalan guerrillas to intensify their violent opposition to the authoritarian regimes. The 1980s was a period of civil wars in the three countries. In El Salvador and Guatemala, the US-supported army fought against the revolutionary forces. In Nicaragua, a US-funded counterrevolutionary movement opposed the FSLN's effort to consolidate a socialist state.

The Central American conflict had devastating social and human costs. In Nicaragua, 30,000 people died during the 1980s and the economy experienced a major crisis—with inflation reaching 33,602 percent in 1989. In El Salvador, there were more than 13,000 extrajudicial executions, 5,500 forced disappearances, and 4,400 torture cases. According to the Truth Commission, 85 percent of these atrocities were committed by the government and paramilitary groups. The Guatemalan conflict was even more tragic: 250,000 people—mostly indigenous peasants—were killed during the three decades of the civil war, a third of them in the seven years between 1980 and 1987. The civil wars ended with peace accords that secured democratic transitions and open spaces for peaceful mobilization but did little to reduce socioeconomic inequalities.[25]

This may seem like a digression from the promised discussion of contemporary social movements; but the experience of Latin America's guerrillas provides valuable lessons for those fighting inequalities across the world today. Three are particularly important. First, many of these movements constituted desperate responses to political and economic inequality. A growing number of people saw guerrilla activity as the only viable means of defending their rights and promoting more open and inclusive societies. We should never forget that the lack of political responses to people's demands and aspirations will often trigger violence. Second, during the 1960s and 1970s, the Cuban Revolution and other liberation movements provided young Latin Americans with a utopia, a vision of how to build better societies. Even if many of these ideas later proved naive and counterproductive, they still point to the usefulness of powerful reference points. It is easier to fight for justice when we have a dream to reach. Third, and more painfully, Latin America's past also shows that the costs of violence almost always outweigh its benefits. Even in those countries, such as El Salvador, where the uprisings contributed to social changes, the costs were immense. Generations of Latin Americans are still dealing with the trauma of torture and deaths.

Let us now return to the present. Latin America is rich in social movements that have contributed to the fight against inequality by focusing on specific problems such as indigenous rights, land reform, and opposition to neoliberalism. In the next pages, I discuss four examples to illustrate this richness, but many others could be mentioned. We will begin with a Brazilian case. With more than 1.5 million members, the *Movimiento dos Trabalhadores Rurais Sem Terra* (the Rural Landless Movement, MST) is by far the largest social movement in Latin America. The MST was founded in 1984 by activists from trade unions, leftist political parties, and the Catholic and Lutheran churches.[26] Inspired by liberation theology and other progressive ideologies, they wanted to reduce land inequality and provide income opportunities for the rural poor.

Land invasions have always been the movement's main tactic. Their planning takes place over several weeks. MST activists first recruit families among small landholders, rural workers, and the rural unemployed. At the same time, they identify large unused agricultural properties that are good targets for occupation. When they are ready, the recruits—which range from 50 to thousands of families depending on the size of the occupation—drive together in cars, trucks, and buses and occupy the chosen estate. A camp with wooden houses is then built and the occupation campaign begins.[27] "The camp is the movement's struggle – through occupying, people break away from cultural norms, society and tradition and come together in the fight for land," explained Irma Brunetto, an MST activist, in 2014.[28] Relying on the constitutional provision that allows for expropriation of unused land, the goal is to force the government to redistribute the occupied land among participating families.

The occupation of private land is an effective mechanism to mobilize the base, pressure the landowning elite, and get public institutions in trouble. These activities create public relations nightmares: when MST activists are evicted from the occupying land, they re-camp in neighboring roads and stay for months. During this time, the MST litigates in court, requesting ownership rights over the unused land. "The MST often wins"—explains the sociologist John Hammond—because "occupations usually lead to expropriation [... and] occupiers living in nearby encampment can exert a moral force. Though an occupation is a militant act requiring ideological commitment and willingness to undertake significant risks, the MST nevertheless assumes and benefits from a public posture embracing moderation and legality."[29]

Since its foundation, the MST has undertaken thousands of occupations—more than 7,000 between 1987 and 2006 alone—that have benefited more than 350,000 families directly and many more indirectly.[30] At the same time, the MST has worked tirelessly to improve local communities' standards of living. Its members mobilize to secure schools, roads, credit, and better housing after each occupation. They have also helped the new small landowners to achieve sustainability. The goal has always been to replace "modern" production methods that are intensive in pesticides and use expensive crops with more sustainable, environmentally friendly ones.[31] To do so, families often work together; in fact, MST members have already created 100 producer and credit cooperatives and 96 small agro-industries.[32] One of the most successful, BioNatur—founded more than two decades ago in Rio Grande do Sul— produces 100 tons annually of more than 200 different organic crop varieties.[33]

The MST has succeeded in linking its local operations to a national agenda. Since its inception, the movement built close links to the PT and other left-wing political parties. At the same time, it has pressured successive administrations to implement land reform. In 1997, months after the slaughter of 19 activists by the military police, the MST organized a national march to Brasilia. Thousands of people walked for 64 days from three different parts of the country in defense of land reform. They all converged on the Brazilian Congress, where the final rally gathered almost 100,000 people.[34] Allied politicians have not been spared from the movement's pressures. For example, when Dilma Rousseff refused to meet with them for three years, the MST organized a march with 15,000 members to the Presidential Palace. President Rousseff was then forced to welcome the MST's national coordinating committee to her office and to respond to some of its demands.

The movement is not concerned solely with land; it has also put forward broader proposals for equitable development. It has denounced the social and human costs of neoliberal policies and called for more generous social programs. Education has played a particularly important role in the MST strategy. Almost since its foundation, the movement has run a network of primary and secondary schools that have used pedagogical techniques inspired by Paulo Freire. There are now 1,800 schools, which have already educated more than 250,000 students. In 2005, the MST also created its own university, the Escola Nacional Florestan Fernandes, near São Paulo, which has already trained thousands of Latin American and African social activists as well as local members.[35]

The MST's decentralized, equitable, and democratic internal organization constitutes another strength. Its building blocks are the *nucleos de base*: groups of ten families located in the occupation camps that elect two representatives to the encampment meetings. Representatives from each camp attend regional meetings that elect members for each state coordinating body, which, in turn, elects national representatives. Each of these coordinating groups make decisions collectively, avoiding the emergence of overly powerful leaders. The search for gender equality has also been noteworthy. After years of struggle by women members, the MST finally committed to gender parity in its representative bodies and now pays significant attention to gender issues.[36]

The MST's work has never been easy. Between 1985 and 2006, an estimated 1,465 activists and peasants were killed—and only 10 percent of the perpetrators were brought to justice.[37] Some Brazilian presidents have treated the MST as a criminal organization and police assaults have often resulted in activists' deaths. The attack from the current administration has been particularly virulent: "activists of the MST, your time has come. Your work is criminal, and I believe that it is also terrorist," proclaimed Bolsonaro during the 2018 electoral campaign. Later, as president, he celebrated the reduction in the number of land occupations. "The MST is weaker now because of [our policy of] facilitating the bearing of arms," he boasted.[38] Yet the MST continues to inspire millions of activists in Brazil and abroad. The movement provides a great example of what activists can do to fight inequality. They should combine mobilization at the local level with national campaigns; help people improve their living standards while making them politically active; focus on a single issue but linking it to a broader agenda; invest in training and capacity to educate a new generation of female and male leaders; and promote leaders who support the community without taking personal credit.

Mexico's *Ejercito Zapatista de Liberación Nacional* (National Liberation Zapatista Army, EZLN)—the second movement I want to discuss—has been particularly successful at managing public relations, securing transnational support, and denouncing non-economic sources of inequality. On New Year's Eve 1993, several groups of armed indigenous Mexicans, covering their faces with masks, descended to San Cristóbal de las Casas, Ocasingo, and other municipalities in the state of Chiapas. Occupying squares, public buildings, and even a prison, they declared war against the central government. "They don't care that we have nothing, absolutely nothing, not even a roof over our heads, no land, no work, no healthcare, no food nor education ... ENOUGH IS ENOUGH," the EZLN explained in a statement that has come to be known as the First Declaration of the Lacandon Jungle.[39] The uprising came as a total surprise to the political class and the economic elite. At a time when they were trying to build a "modern" and "prosperous" facade (Mexico had just signed the North American Free Trade

Agreement with the US and Canada, and was about to become a member of the OECD), a group of well-organized activists came from out of nowhere to show the world the real Mexico.

The EZLN was led by Subcomandante Marcos, a tall and enigmatic figure who covered his face with a ski mask while smoking a pipe. He was joined by a small group of equally mysterious individuals, some of them white, others of indigenous descent and all with covered faces. During the following weeks, the EZLN commandos fought two different battles. On the military front, they were severely outnumbered and outgunned: they were fighting with old rifles and wooden sticks against a modern army sent from Mexico City. In contrast, they mastered the public relations game. Using communiqués that linked their cause to previous struggles and benefiting from close contacts with friendly journalists, they gradually reshaped the public discourse on democracy, equitable development, and ethnicity.

Support for the Zapatistas poured in from across the globe. In Mexico, social movements and left-wing political activists marched to demand a ceasefire, organized concerts to raise funds, participated in a National Democratic Convention proposed by the EZLN, and supported the peace talks. Academics and the press began paying more attention to ethnicity, racism, and rural development. Internationally, the uprising inspired activists, academics, and progressive political parties in the US and Europe. Relying on information from the internet—which had become widely available just one year before—they created an informal transnational supporting network. Marches, teach-ins, and lobbying campaigns were organized; op-eds were written in some of the world's largest newspapers; and many foreigners traveled to Chiapas to offer their help and support.[40] Foreigners were attracted by the high level of inequality and also inspired by Subcomandante Marcos's combination of radicalism and poetic skills. "Freedom is like the morning. There are people who wait sleeping for its arrival, but there are others who stay awake and walk during the night to achieve it. I say that the Zapatistas are addicted to insomnia," he proclaimed in 1996. And three years later, he insisted: "we call everyone not to dream but to do something simpler and more definitive: we call them to wake up."[41]

After the first weeks of the uprising, a ceasefire was agreed, and peace talks began. However, negotiations did not go anywhere, while the army intensified its presence in Chiapas. In subsequent years, the EZLN changed its strategy, from land invasions in 1995, to marches and gatherings supporting indigenous rights during peace talks in 1996, to roadblocks and building occupations during the electoral campaigns of

1997 and 2000.[42] In this way, the EZLN morphed into a social movement with local and international agendas. Locally, the Zapatistas created autonomous municipalities. Totally independent from government influence, these communities developed unique methods to choose their leaders and organize service delivery. Rejecting traditional politics, they made decisions through participatory assemblies and rotating leaders. Governance relied on ancient customs, so-called *usos y costumbres*. Equality between men and women was promoted, even if advances in practice were slower than expected. An independent system of education was gradually developed, starting from the training of community-based educators and following with the creation of schools.[43] Internationally, the EZLN continued organizing global gatherings to discuss the problems of the Mexican democracy and to propose alternative development models.

When I asked my friend Salvador Martí, a first-rate researcher on social movements and ethnicity, why he thought the EZLN was important, he told me: "it contributed to democratizing the political regime and provided citizenship rights and pride to the Mexican indigenous population." Yet its global relevance goes well beyond its impact on Mexican politics. The EZLN experience highlights the importance of shaping discourses, building links with global movements, and connecting the local, regional, and transnational dimensions. We can also learn from the EZLN's ability to place indigenous rights within a broader agenda of equality and development. The movement has also been able to capture the imagination of millions of activists in Mexico and abroad, something those fighting inequality should always try to do.

Both the EZLN and the MST have focused on the interests and needs of the rural poor. In contrast, Chile's student movement—another illustrative case of Latin America's creativity—is a middle-class and urban social movement. It is worth discussing it next because of its many strengths, including the use of new mobilization tools; its ability to gain support from a majority of the population; and its policy and political influence.

The return of democracy to Chile in 1990 led to the election of a center-left coalition. The *Concertación*, which included the Christian Democrats and the Socialists, governed the country without interruption for two decades. Despite keeping much of Pinochet's neoliberal economic model unchanged, successive *Concertación* administrations still benefited from social movements' support. Progressive activists did not want to make too much noise, fearing, at least initially, a breakdown of democracy. Most came from the same generation as the politicians in power and had little appetite to oppose them. Social movements supported a gradualist reform agenda and were keen to build constructive relations with government officials.

To the surprise of both old activists and *Concertación* officials, everything changed in 2006.[44] In April, hundreds of students in their traditional black and white uniforms took to the streets. Initially protesting against the high cost of public transportation and the poor quality of school infrastructure, the *Pingüino* movement—so-called because of the color of the uniforms—soon questioned the whole education system. "Stop postponing our future," students shouted, demanding the reduction of inequalities between public schools and subsidized private ones.

Initial protests in a small number of schools were followed by a massive rally on May 30. In contrast with smaller marches in previous years, the *Pingüino* movement received ample media attention and popular support. According to polls conducted in April and May, almost nine out of ten Chileans agreed with the students' demands. The success of the mobilizations forced the socialist President Michelle Bachelet to respond. In a televised live address, she accepted most of the movement's short-term demands and committed to create an Advisory Commission on the Quality of Education. The Commission evaluated the General Education Law and proposed long-term changes.

Even if the ultimate reforms were less significant than initially expected, the *Pingüino* movement turned Chilean students into a major political force. The 2006 protests were a training ground for a new generation of political and social leaders, also inspiring thousands of students to fight for social change. They were also the precursor for an even larger round of protests five years later. In 2011, college students mobilized first in Santiago and later in the rest of the country to demand cheaper funding and a larger participation of the state in the education system. "Education is a right," "worthy education," "against profits," "for free and high-quality education" were some of the slogans they wrote on colorful posters.[45] The protests spread like wildfire from a small number of public universities to the rest of the higher education system as well as to secondary schools. Neither police repression nor early concessions could stop the movement: by late June, students had occupied around 600 schools and were organizing huge marches almost daily.[46] As in 2006, students benefited from high social support: in August, despite five months of disruptions, 80 percent of Chileans saw the movement favorably. In contrast, President Piñera's approval rating had dropped below 30 percent. That month, nearly a million Chileans—forming a cross-class alliance of low- and middle-income families—gathered in the capital to support the students.[47]

The 2011 protests constituted a turning point in Chile's recent history. The student movement succeeded in changing the discourse on education, convincing most Chileans to regard it as a social right. They also forced successive administrations to implement meaningful changes. The conservative Piñera government reduced interest rates on student loans and increased the regulation of private universities. Scholarships for low-income students were also expanded. The subsequent left-wing government pursued a more radical reform agenda. On her return to the presidency, Michelle Bachelet passed a tax reform and a series of education laws, including the Law of Higher Education and the Law for Inclusion. Chile's education moved in the right direction: the new laws required the transformation of for-profit schools into nonprofits, reduced inequalities between secondary schools, and guaranteed free university education for students in the lower 60 percent of the income distribution. Public early-years education was also strengthened. Overall, Bachelet's reforms contributed to reducing Chile's education inequalities—even if further changes are urgently required.[48]

Why was the Chilean student movement so successful? What can activists in other regions learn from this experience? There are at least five significant lessons to consider. First, students did not accept the status quo, preferring to dream big instead. In contrast to their parents, they were never limited by the baggage of the dictatorship and the transition to democracy. They were also unwilling to accept the basic tenets of the neoliberal model still dominant in the country, and in other parts of Latin America. "For each person that says that this is not the way," explained a video from a student journalist while showing a picture of former Chilean presidents who criticized the movement, "100,000 students repeat, 'yes, we can!'"[49]

Second, the movement leaders in 2006 and 2011 built support gradually and strategically. Initial demands focused on bread-and-butter issues: the cost of public transportation, the quality of infrastructure in specific schools, delays in the payment of scholarships, and problems with the issuing of student cards. As more and more students joined the protests, more ambitious objectives were introduced. The sequence of events was thus important: initial mobilization led to the emergence of multiple assemblies where students discussed their problems and strategized their next steps. It was in these assemblies that free education, state involvement, and the reduction of inequality emerged as primary demands.

Third, the movement succeeded in both creating cross-class coalitions and protecting their independence from political parties. Their leaders came from a variety of ideologies and represented different political interests. In 2006 the movement made an effort to integrate all kinds of schools: from Santiago and from the provinces, from upper middle-class neighborhoods and from lower-income ones. Equally, in 2011, the student confederation included the country's leading Santiago universities but also newer and lesser-known ones from across the country. The student movement made an effort to enhance democracy and encourage participation. Local assemblies became discussion centers and oversaw the work of the leaders. They organized sit-ins and joined forces in the preparation of the various rallies. The student movement "got their strength from the floor that supported it," explained a participant in 2007.[50]

Of course, this does not mean that the movement was apolitical. Quite the contrary: the ultimate goal of many participants—particularly in 2011—was to make the political and economic systems more responsive to all Chileans. Many saw these protests as just one step in the long-term battle for Chile's soul. Several of the movement's leaders later became politicians, helping to transform the country's party system. For example, Giorgio Jackson, president of the student federation in the Catholic University of Chile in 2010–11, became a deputy in 2014 and was one of the founders of the left-wing coalition *Frente Amplio* (Broad Front). Camila Vallejo, president of the student federation of the University of Chile during the same period, became a deputy for the Communist Party and is now one of its most popular members.

Fourth, the way they presented their demands was particularly refreshing. "It was their innovative framing ... that gave them their greatest strength," explains the Chilean political science and social movement expert, Eduardo Silva; "Students held the inequalities of Chile's market-driven education system up as a mirror for the inequalities of Chilean market society."[51] The general public could immediately see the relevance of the students' claims, linking them to their own struggles. Inequality ceased to be an abstract concept mentioned by politicians, becoming an everyday problem connected to the cost and quality of education. Students also offered an alternative narrative to the dominant neoliberal one. Popular concepts such as merit, consumption, and individualism were gradually replaced by social rights, citizens, and freedom in people's imaginations.

Finally, student protests were creative and used new technologies effectively. They combined traditional strategies such as marches, school occupations, and assemblies with more innovative ones. On June 24, 2011, for example, thousands of students danced together a "Thriller for Education" in front of the Presidential Palace. Inspired by Michael Jackson's famous song, they wore zombie costumes to denounce their own deaths as a result of the high cost of their loans.[52] Flash-mobs, mass races, kiss-ins, and street dances were organized across the country and later played in news clips and Twitter feeds across the world.[53] They combined a serious political message with some fun, making the whole movement more attractive and less threatening.

Let me now move to Bolivia and conclude the section with a short discussion of the MAS, one of the most successful movements-turned-political-parties in the world. Bolivian social movements have traditionally been more active than those in neighboring countries. After a national revolution in 1952, peasant associations, mining unions, and other organizations mobilized to demand benefits from the state. Successive governments often responded by increasing wages and other perks for specific groups without doing enough for the rest of society.

The *cocaleros* in Cochabamba—one of Bolivia's two coca-producing centers—gradually became one of the best-organized groups. Starting in the 1960s and accelerating in the 1980s, they built a multilevel social movement. At the bottom, a handful of families in different neighborhoods created *sindicatos* to organize the distribution of land and some basic infrastructure. Each group of around ten *sindicatos* later constituted a *central* to better interact with the local government and with NGOs. The *cocaleros* also created *federaciones*: groups of at least three *centrales* that operated at the provincial level. Overall, *sindicatos*, *centrales*, and *federaciones* played multiple roles in people's lives: from coordinating the construction of schools to helping secure land titles; from collecting extra money for teachers to organizing football tournaments and community parties.[54]

In the late 1980s, a combination of forces converged to make the *cocalero* movement more political.[55] Thousands of tin miners, who had lost their jobs after the neoliberal restructuring of the Bolivian Mining Corporation, moved to the coca-producing area of Chapare. They brought with them a history of unionism and political mobilization as well as a visceral opposition to neoliberalism. At the same time, the Bolivian government passed a law that constrained coca production. The *cocaleros* saw the US-sponsored war on drugs as an attack on their livelihood as well as on their culture. They opposed eradication bitterly: "We spent months on end with *bloqueos* [road blockades], fighting for our rights ... we faced the army, we faced the helicopters which shot at us from the sky ... but we managed to resist the eradication of coca," remembered Leonilda Zurita, a leading activist and subsequent senior figure of the MAS.[56] The *cocaleros* of Cochabamba were also members of the *Confederación Sindical Única de Trabajadores Campesinos de Bolivia* (Unified Syndical Confederation of Rural Workers of Bolivia, CSUTCB), a leading rural trade union confederation founded in 1979. Dominated by indigenous people from different regions, the CSUTCB gradually became a key player in the fight against neoliberalism.

The war on drugs led some movement leaders to call for the creation of a "political instrument." They argued that *cocaleros* could not protect their way of life without being present in decision-making institutions. Among the proponents of the idea was Evo Morales (later Bolivian president), who had migrated to Chapare with his family in 1981 and soon became a social leader. After several years of discussion—most *cocaleros* viewed political parties and the state with suspicion—the movement finally agreed to participate in formal politics. In its 1995 Congress, the CSUTCB created the *Asamblea por la Soberanía de los Pueblos* (Assembly for the Sovereignty of the Peoples, ASP). After the Electoral Commission refused to recognize the ASP as a party, its members ran under the banner of the small *Izquierda Unida* (United Left) in subsequent elections. In 1995, IU-ASP won ten municipalities and two years later it gained four seats in Congress.[57]

After an internal split in 1998, Cochabamba's confederation of *cocaleros* led by Evo Morales created the *Instrumento Político por la Soberanía de los Pueblos* (Political Instrument for the Sovereignty of the Peoples, IPSP). Again, facing legal difficulties with running in the municipal elections, they borrowed the name of a recognized but tiny party, the MAS. In the 1999 municipal elections, the MAS-IPSP received 70 percent of the votes in several subregions of Cochabamba but just 3.3 percent nationwide.[58] Obviously, the challenge then was to increase the political movement's national appeal. To do so, the MAS incorporated left-leaning intellectuals and expanded its presence in urban centers such as El Alto and La Paz, working to attract middle-class voters.[59] Its strategy succeeded: in the 2002 presidential and legislative elections, Evo Morales received 21 percent of the vote—just 1.6 percentage points less than the winner, Sánchez de Lozada—and the MAS won 27 seats in Congress. Yet the MAS was still the political arm of a social movement more than a real party. While peasants and *cocaleros* were considered "organic members," urban sympathizers were called "invitees."[60]

During the period 2000–2005, the MAS benefited from the growing opposition to neoliberal reforms. Led by a range of social movements—some linked to the MAS—hundreds of thousands of Bolivians protested against privatization and liberalization. In the most intense months of the struggle, daily marches and blockades were organized in Cochabamba, El Alto, and other Bolivian cities. Repressive responses only encouraged Bolivians to redouble their efforts, ultimately forcing the resignation of two presidents. Evo Morales successfully capitalized on this discontent: running as an anti-neoliberal outsider, he won a resounding victory in the 2005 presidential elections.

Morales's rise to power represented the victory of the *cocalero* and peasant movements. In the following months, he remained leader of the main *cocalero* confederation. He traveled to Cochabamba and other regions often and tried to participate in as many assemblies as possible. Even if most of the ministers in the first administration were intellectuals and NGO managers, grassroots activists remained ecstatic. "We are not from the MAS, the MAS is ours" summarizes well how they felt about the government and about the chances for a more equitable future.[61] Many of the policies that followed—from the nationalization of gas to the new constitution; from enhanced indigenous autonomy to more generous social programs—were exactly what they expected. Together with high economic growth, they contributed to a sustained reduction of income inequality.

Between 2005 and 2019, the MAS arguably became the world's most successful movement-based party in power. Despite many challenges and contradictions, it has maintained its loose structure and its tight links to social movements. "The party's grass-roots social base wields significant influence over the selection of candidates for elective office and in the policy-making sphere," argues Santiago Anria, author of one of the best academic studies on the MAS. At the local level, government officials still meet regularly with activists, participating in day-long assemblies and other consultative gatherings. *Sindicatos, centrales,* and *federaciones* remain training grounds for future progressive political leaders. At the national level, allied social movements are still able to mobilize against unpopular measures, from subsidy cuts to tax hikes.[62] More than once, the government has been forced to reverse course, leading Morales to remind everyone that he "rules by obeying."[63]

Why did the MAS succeed where others failed? There are at least three reasons, which progressive parties and movements in other countries would do well to remember. First, the *cocaleros* and peasant movements have remained well organized and closely rooted to their communities. Through assemblies and other meetings at the local, regional, and national levels, both political and social leaders are accountable to all the members. Second, the MAS is still a loose party, which has avoided the kind of centralization experienced in many progressive parties. There are few paid officials, marketing experts, and other professionals. Third, activism in Bolivia remains intense: Bolivians are used to taking their demands to the streets and are unlikely to stop even with their allies in power.

Of course, as we discussed in Chapter 4, the government of the MAS did not finish as planned. After being accused of electoral fraud—with inconclusive and controversial evidence—in the first round of the 2019 elections, Evo Morales resigned and sought asylum in Mexico. At the time of writing, Bolivia is planning new presidential elections for late 2020 and Morales will not be allowed to run. Although this is a major setback for the MAS, there is little doubt that the movement will recuperate from the current crisis. Even if its new candidate does not win, the party will remain powerful and will sustain close links to social movements in the urban and, especially, rural sectors.

Policies: Lessons from an Unexpected Reduction of Inequality in the 2000s

Most of the world witnessed a worsening of income distribution in the 2000s.[64] The exception? Latin America. Reversing a long-term negative trend, almost every country in the region saw a reduction of inequality. Academics, policymakers, and journalists across the globe took note: "in the past 10 years, South America never had it so good. The continent surfed a global commodity price boom, helped by abundant global capital ... Uniquely, social inequality shrank across the continent," explained the *Financial Times* in 2014.[65] Several books considering the lessons from the Latin American success were written and even the International Monetary Fund (IMF) praised the region.[66]

How was this reversal possible? Some of it was just luck: the increase in the global prices of copper, gas, oil, and other primary exports left Latin American governments with millions of unexpected dollars in their coffers. Suddenly they could implement redistributive programs without having to raise taxes or confront the economic elite. Borrowing internationally also became cheap, benefiting even those countries in Central America that are not rich in natural resources.

Yet luck is seldom enough. In fact, in previous booms, Latin American governments had failed to improve income distribution, further concentrating wealth and opportunities in a few hands. In contrast, this time around they were willing and able to implement some progressive policies in favor of low-income groups. They included higher spending in education, labor market interventions, and more ambitious social programs than before.

Starting in the early 1990s, Latin American governments expanded education coverage in primary and, to a lesser extent, secondary education. This expansion benefited the poor disproportionately, leading to a reduction of inequalities in school attainment. The Gini coefficient of years of education decreased by five percentage points in Brazil between 1998 and 2007, by seven percentage points in Mexico between 1996 and 2006, and by four percentage points in Peru between 2001 and 2007.[67] As a result, "the well-educated no longer commanded such disproportionally large incomes as before; and low-skilled workers, reduced in number, made more than in the past," according to the Inter-American Development Bank in 2017.[68] Nevertheless, as we discussed in Chapter 3, large differences in the quality of education received by different groups remained.

The changes in the labor market were probably more important. Progressive governments across the region understood that informal jobs pay less, come with fewer social rights, and weaken trade unions. Positive economic conditions provided them with a unique window of opportunity to move low-income individuals from the informal to the formal sector. Some governments invested more resources in labor inspectors; others cut red tape and introduced simpler taxes. In Brazil, for example, several laws simplified the process of registration and tax payments for small and medium-sized firms, while simultaneously creating incentives for the formalization of domestic workers. Argentina and Uruguay also expanded labor rights for domestic workers—a pro-women trend later followed by other countries—and created tax incentives to promote formalization. Across the region, the share of formal jobs increased from 39 to 49 percent during the 2000s.[69]

Simultaneously, minimum wages were expanded in most countries. Between 2000 and 2013, the real minimum wage more than doubled in Brazil, Honduras, Nicaragua, and Honduras, while also growing significantly in Bolivia and Ecuador.[70] Higher minimum wages contributed to reducing inequality without affecting total employment—contrary to what many mainstream economists would expect. According to a study by the Argentinian economist Roxana Maurizio, the growth of the minimum wage was responsible for an estimated 86 percent of the reduction in wage inequality in Brazil, 27 percent in Argentina, and 12 percent in Uruguay during the 2000s.[71]

Changes in social policy were the last component of the pro-equity policy mix. Latin America become a pioneer in a new kind of anti-poverty program: conditional cash transfers (CCTs). First introduced in Brazil and Mexico in the late 1990s, CCTs provide a small income to poor families who take their children to school and to health checkups. CCTs were quickly embraced by Latin American politicians and global institutions. Politicians liked their popularity among poor voters, their small cost compared to other programs, and the fact that they did not give "free" money but came with conditions. International institutions like the World Bank came to believe that CCTs would reduce poverty not only in the short run, but—by increasing the demand for education—also in the long run.

By 2013, 129 million poor people—one in four Latin Americans— were receiving a CCT.[72] The most successful programs had a small but significant impact on income distribution: for example, Brazil's Bolsa Família was responsible for 10 percent of the reduction in the Gini coefficient.[73] Yet their overall effect should not be exaggerated. CCTs were often too small to move people out of poverty permanently. In most cases, they failed to contribute to better labor market opportunities for young people: as a result, they never delivered on the promise of eliminating long-term poverty.

Other social programs were more important for redistribution. Many Latin American countries embraced universalism—the provision of social benefits for the whole population—as an aspirational policy goal. Some created new programs to provide free healthcare and basic pensions for the poor. Others reformed their pre-existing systems to make them more equitable and better able to serve *all* citizens. The region became a cradle of innovation in this area at a time when other regions such as Europe were struggling to protect social rights. Bolivia created one of the few universal pensions in the world; Uruguay unified private and public health services so as to provide the same benefits for all; Colombia— thanks to the active involvement of its Constitutional Court—took significant steps toward creating a universal healthcare system.

Why were Latin American countries able to implement pro-equity policies this time when they had failed in the past? The answer has a lot to do with democracy.[74] Starting in the late 1980s, a wave of democratization engulfed the region as authoritarian regimes fell in one country after another. Despite their many shortcomings (discussed in Chapter 4), the new democracies forced politicians to pay more attention to poor voters.

The consolidation of democracy also gave progressive parties more influence. From El Salvador all the way to Uruguay, leftist presidents placed equity at the top of their policy agenda. They implemented some of the most ambitious social reforms and generally presided over larger improvements in income distribution than their conservative neighbors.[75] More importantly, they jointly contributed to a gradual shift in dominant discourses: by the late 2000s, no Latin American politician in their right mind could praise neoliberalism or fail to recognize the costs of inequality.

Democracy also contributed to the reduction of inequality by giving new space to social movements. People took to the streets to demand new policies and pressured governments—and society more generally—to recognize the rights of excluded populations such as indigenous people and rural workers. Social movements also sparked a discourse shift away from neoliberalism: "through sustained networking and resistance, which secured redistribution and recognition, many Latin Americans have come to expect more of their governments," explains the academic Alice Evans.[76]

The changes in the 2000s were significant and unexpected. They went against a global tide, generating useful policy lessons. Nevertheless, their long-term significance should not be exaggerated. Latin America remains the most unequal region in the world. There is also growing evidence that income (re)distribution took place primarily between some segments of the middle class and the poor, while leaving the very rich untouched. Take, for example, the case of Brazil. Between 2002 and 2014, the real income of both the poorest 50 percent and the richest 0.01 percent increased by more than 35 percent. In contrast, the real income of many upper middle-class Brazilians actually went down.[77]

The redistributive power of public policies still needs to increase significantly. Progressive income taxes in Latin America are still lower than in rich countries and tax revenues are insufficient to cover states' needs. Across the region, the wealthy and the middle class have access to much better health and education services and higher pensions than the poor. Some governments rely too heavily on CCTs as their main anti-poverty intervention and most countries have failed to modernize their economies sufficiently. The success of the 2000s has also proved unsustainable. The end of the commodity boom and the victory of conservative leaders like Bolsonaro are already reversing past distributional gains. Ultimately, overcoming Latin America's history of inequality and breaking with powerful vicious circles will require much than ten good years.

Chapter 7

AND NOW WHAT? HOW TO FIGHT INEQUALITY IN LATIN AMERICA AND BEYOND

Every successful book dealing with global challenges offers some catchy policy solution. Liberalize and deregulate markets, strengthen the role of a mission-oriented state, create a universal basic income, break down powerful corporations, increase education, give money to the poor. We are all avid for new ideas to confront economic stagnation, climate change, and world poverty.

I should thus finish this book with some revolutionary proposal that promises to overcome inequality *fast*. Ideally, I would also link my ideas to the COVID-19 pandemic we are suffering at the time of writing, and convince you that the world will change for the better quickly. Unfortunately, I cannot. The truth is that reducing inequality substantially—particularly inequality at the top—is hard. It is a slow process that will take at least a generation if not more. The elite will not give up their current privileges easily. They have more political power and economic resources than the rest of us combined and are more than happy to use them. Also, no policy instrument or political process will resolve the problem by itself: neither higher taxes nor more regulated labor markets or stronger unions alone will be enough. We need all of these things and more *simultaneously*. We must also avoid one-size-fits-all solutions: each country should concentrate on those elements of the policy menu that are most urgent based on their historical trajectories, economic structure, and institutional setting.

This chapter puts together a long-term policy agenda, drawing on existing research on developed and developing countries. In so doing, I reject simplistic dichotomies between pre-distribution (i.e. transforming market institutions) and redistribution (i.e. taxing some to provide money to others); between job-oriented policies and social programs. The proposed measures would radically transform the distribution of income over the long run by redistributing assets, reducing the influence of the wealthy on key markets, and introducing more ambitious industrial and social policies.

Making policy recommendations, however, is the easy part. It is much harder to place them within a coherent narrative of what we want to achieve. In recent decades, progressives have lacked an appealing description of the kind of society we want to build. We have failed to develop an alternative to the neoliberal "dream" of individual pursuits, meritocratic-based success, and market-led societies. Maybe the COVID-19 pandemic has created a small window of opportunity to develop this new narrative now, considering the growing role of the state in many countries and the recognition that wellbeing is not an individual but a global challenge.

Continuing the conversation I started in the last chapter, I also call for attention to political requirements. The best policy recommendations without the right politics will be useless. The last part of this chapter thus deals with the political requirements. I highlight the central role that stronger democracies and reformed progressive parties must play in the fight against inequality. I also call for the strengthening of social movements, drawing on the Latin American experience discussed in the previous chapter. Although with less detail, this chapter also discusses an alternative narrative to the dominant one, building on our joint humanity. We are first and foremost social beings whose welfare is directly dependent on that of others—something 2020 has clearly demonstrated. We are also ethical beings and should thus reject excessive inequality as morally wrong.

The Latin American Experience Demonstrates how Difficult the Fight Against Inequality is

Before moving toward the discussion of policies and politics, however, let me first restate the argument of the book once again, reviewing lessons and warnings that Latin America provides for others. For decades if not centuries, the region experienced the kind of income concentration that is now common in other parts of the world. From Mexico to Chile, the wealthy amassed a large share of output, controlled most of the land, and owned all large companies. This book has shown how high inequality generated significant costs, which have proven almost impossible to overcome. It has contributed to a stagnant economy, dysfunctional politics, and multiple social challenges—of the kind many other countries are suffering now or could suffer even more in the future.

During the nineteenth and most of the twentieth century, access to education was beyond reach for a large share of the region's population. The wealthy had no interest in funding primary and secondary schools which they were not going to use. They pressured Latin American governments to allocate resources to universities that only they would attend. By contrast, the poor majority could not afford to send their children to school—particularly when they became old enough to work instead. While education coverage has expanded rapidly in recent decades, sizable quality gaps persist.

Inequality also disincentivized spending on research and development. If wealthy families were already making hefty profits in traditional sectors—from mining to trade—why would they invest in high-tech activities? Why should they try to compete with the US and China, when they could focus on other sectors where they faced almost no competition? Small and medium-sized firms potentially had more incentives to innovate and enter into new sectors, but they lacked the money to do so.

Latin American elites have also succeeded in keeping taxes low and regressive. In country after country, they have used their economic power and political influence to stop significant tax reforms. As a result, most Latin American countries collect fewer taxes than expected, given their level of development. Even those countries with high tax revenues, such as Argentina and Brazil, rely disproportionally on (regressive) consumption taxes. What was a Latin American problem for decades has now become a world challenge: taxing the wealthy is today harder than ever before almost anywhere, from the US to Sweden. Chapter 3 also discussed how inequality contributed to financial crises—a negative relationship that can now be observed in other parts of the world as well.

Politically, inequality in Latin America has contributed to volatility, with a succession of weak democracies, populist governments, and bloody dictatorships. Chapter 4 showed how the elite's political power and the poor's search for recognition drove these cycles of political instability. In both the late nineteenth century and the late twentieth century, the wealthy consented to the introduction of limited democracies: elections could be used to appoint political leaders, as long as redistribution of income and influence would remain limited. Restrictions on voting rights and social mobilization in the nineteenth century, and neoliberal ideas and institutions a century later, conspired against the reduction of inequality.

Not surprisingly, many Latin Americans got tired of these arrangements. Rejecting traditional political parties, they supported populist leaders and movements such as Perón in Argentina, Velasco Ibarra in Ecuador, and, more recently, Chávez in Venezuela. Populists built direct links to the masses and promised quick redistribution. They expanded social rights, but simultaneously contributed to economic crises and political polarization. Their governments were often interrupted by elite-backed military coups, which worsened political and economic inequality. Overall, Latin America's political lesson is clear: in unequal environments, democracies tend to work poorly, forcing voters to search for more redistributive but somewhat problematic populist solutions.

Finally, inequality has also resulted in significant social costs. Chapter 5 focused on the links between income distribution, violence, segmentation, and lack of trust. Latin America is not just the most unequal region, but also the most violent. Social injustice "generates social disintegration, violence, bitterness, resentment and lack of confidence in institutions," explains Ricardo Fuentes-Nieva, director of Oxfam Mexico.[1] Youth gangs, homicides (including femicides), and property thefts have become a common response to unemployment, marginality, and powerlessness.

Inequality (and violence) are also major drivers of segmentation: physical walls separate the houses of the wealthy from the rest of society. Rich families also send their children to exclusive schools and attend private hospitals where they seldom meet individuals from other classes. As a result, there is little communication and understanding between different groups. Not surprisingly, Latin America has become the most distrustful region in the world: only four in ten Brazilians trust their neighbors compared to nine in ten Canadians. Chapter 5 also explored the disturbing relationship between inequality and racism: across the region, powerful elites have used racist (and sexist) discourses to divide the poor (between black and white, indigenous and mestizos) and protect their privileges.

As problematic as all these costs are, Latin America's experience offers an even more concerning lesson. Inequality tends to perpetuate itself through a number of vicious circles. Insufficient spending on R&D and innovation in high-quality education have contributed to dual labor markets. A few productive companies coexist with a sea of unproductive small and medium firms—thus perpetuating income concentration. Profits and high-paying jobs are located in a few sectors, while a majority of the population receive subsistence wages. Also, inequality contributes to financial crises, which, in turn, often lead to widening income gaps.

Politically, restricted democracies, populism, and dictatorships all contribute to the perpetuation of inequality. In restricted or limited democratic systems, social spending is low and benefits a small number of middle- and upper-class individuals exclusively. Populist governments distribute more income in the short run. Yet they often implement unsustainable economic policies that eventually trigger financial crises. Right-wing dictatorships are particularly harmful, often leading to regressive redistribution from the poor to the rich.

Violence, segregation, and lack of trust make cross-class coalitions almost impossible. The middle class is often suspicious of the poor—seeing them as "lazy," "ignorant," and "violent"—while the poor feel mistreated and misunderstood. The resulting miscommunication breeds an individualist culture and prevents collaboration. Building redistributive welfare systems in this kind of environment is almost impossible; most countries are left with regressive and inefficient policies instead.

Can Latin America reduce inequality steadily even in the presence of these costly vicious circles? Can other countries prevent their consolidation? What needs to be done in terms of policies and politics? These are precisely the hard questions I tackle in the rest of the chapter.

The Many Policies Available to Reduce Inequality

Before considering policies to reduce inequality, we first need to understand how the distribution of income takes place. Think about your own life: what are the factors that influence your income? Economists usually consider three.

Factor 1: the wealth and education you have—often called endowments. Some people have a lot of property, stocks, and other financial assets. Others have no savings at all. Large landowners coexist with individuals with no land. Some people enter the labor market after years of study, while other workers have not even finished primary education.

Factor 2: the income you make from your job and all your assets. Introductory economics books use the concepts of supply and demand in different markets to explain this. For example, your wage depends on how many people with a similar level of education to yours there are. If your skills are in high demand and there are few people like you, your wage will be relatively high. By contrast, if you do not have unique skills, you will face competition from many others. If you own land in a highly sought-after area of a city, you can rent it at a higher price than if it is in an unpopular one.

The dominant perspective has an almost magical view of markets. There is an "invisible hand"—to use Adam Smith's famous expression— that sets wages, rents, and prices without interference. In practice, however, markets are influenced by power relations. In labor markets, large corporations use all the tools at their disposal to keep wages low. They threaten to fire troublesome workers, hire subcontracting firms, and pressure the state to weaken labor rights. In land markets, large landowners force small owners to sell their land at low prices. In financial markets, large investors often impose conditions on smaller ones. Improving income distribution in this area thus requires two kinds of intervention. On the one hand, it demands a power shift in key markets through competition policy and labor market and financial regulation. On the other hand, countries should also implement industrial policies to create more and better jobs.

Factor 3: the redistribution of income through taxes and social spending. Your final income will depend not only on your wages and the return of your savings, but also on how many taxes you pay and which social benefits you receive. In most but by no means all countries, taxes and social spending together contribute to reducing the income gap between rich and poor.

Reducing inequality is not only about changing market rules—what the American political scientist Jacob Hacker has called pre-distribution—or about implementing more social policies.[2] It requires changes at every step of the process, including improving the allocation of wealth and education, changing the way markets operate, and redistributing more income, more effectively. Efforts in one area will often have a positive impact in another. For example, strengthening trade union rights is likely to expand wages in relation to profits, while also increasing demands for social spending.

Let's now review the most significant measures at every step of the process—while remembering that these tools should be applied differently in each country depending on its level of development and institutional strength.

Changing the distribution of endowments

Land reform has historically been one of the most important instruments to improve income distribution. Most equal countries in the world successfully weakened the power and influence of large landowners at some point in their history. Take the cases of Taiwan and South Korea.[3] Between 1945 and 1955 both expropriated large quantities of land from the rural elite, while expanding the number of small and medium-sized landowners. In South Korea, many wealthy families lost up to 90 percent of their land as holdings above 3 hectares were outlawed. By contrast, most tenant farmers—who had previously rented their land—became owners and received ample state support. As a result, productivity increased in the rural sector while the traditional elite was severely weakened. In Taiwan, the government transferred to tenants all the land controlled by Japanese nationals as well as a lot of previously rented land. The *Economist*—normally a staunch critic of state intervention— praised all these measures: "income inequality shrank thanks to the new [small] farmer-capitalists . . . Farming was the start of Taiwan's economic miracle."[4]

Latin America—and much of Africa—has failed to improve land distribution over the long run. Efforts to transfer land to the poor were particularly intense during the 1950s and 1960s. At that time, even the US supported these efforts as part of the Alliance for Progress. Yet land reform did not generally threaten the interests of large landowners, who were often able to reverse the reforms. Land redistribution was seldom accompanied by support for small producers, who, as a result, often ended up selling their land back to the wealthy. Today Latin America's Gini coefficient for land distribution is 0.79—higher than anywhere else in the world.[5]

"While the environment has changed considerably since the days when it first emerged as an important policy issue," explains the World Bank economist Klaus Deininger, "land reform remains an important policy tool to address inequality of opportunity in many situations."[6] Governments in developing countries should commit to the real transfer of land from the wealthy to the poor accompanied by investment in infrastructure, education, and other support for small producers. The role of land (re)distribution is less significant in OECD countries given the relatively low importance of agriculture.

By contrast, improving the distribution of human capital—a rather ugly term used to refer to each person's level of knowledge and skills— and wealth is universally relevant. Let me leave the discussion of education for later, when I tackle the role of social policy, and focus here on financial wealth instead.

Across the world, wealth inequality is even higher than income inequality. In the UK, for example, the Gini coefficient for wealth distribution is almost twice that of income distribution (0.62 vs. 0.32).[7]

In the US, the richest 5 percent own two-thirds of total wealth, while a third of Americans do not have any liquid savings.[8] In Latin America, at least 75 percent of all the wealth is in the hands of just 10 percent of the population. Lack of savings—together with limited access to cheap credit—leaves millions of people without the opportunity to invest in their children's education, create new businesses, or confront personal crises. The rich can live off their savings and investments—and still become richer thanks to high rates of return.

Fighting wealth inequality requires first a change in tax policy. Wealth is increasingly undertaxed. Inheritance taxes—which are particularly important to secure equality of opportunities—have been eliminated in many countries, from Australia and Norway to Russia and India. Since the 1960s, their contribution to total tax revenues has declined by 60 percent in OECD countries, despite their positive role in promoting equality of opportunity. Property taxes have also received insufficient attention: in Latin America they represent less than 1 percent of total revenues.[9]

There are complementary options to increase taxes on wealth. Governments should take inheritance taxes more seriously and "sell" them better to the public. They are not "death taxes"—a popular description among American conservatives—but "equal opportunity" taxes. While primarily focused on large fortunes and liquid assets, inheritance taxes should also be imposed on expensive houses and company shares. They could easily be (re)designed in ways that do not force heirs to break out their parents' companies or sell the family house: for example, they could be collected in installments over a period of months or even years.

Property ownership should be taxed more. Countries across the world should consider the introduction of land value taxes, which are based on the price of the land as if it was fully exploited. For example, a piece of unused land in a prime location would be charged similarly to one with apartment buildings. Land value taxes—which have been supported by both right and left, from the market-friendly *Financial Times* to socialists such as Jeremy Corbyn—have several advantages. They can hardly be avoided since land cannot be moved. They can encourage effective use of land, preventing speculation. They can be simultaneously used to combat rural land inequality—a huge problem in Latin America—and capture rents from gentrification in large cities. Their implementation would also force governments to improve their land registries.[10]

Wealth taxes are receiving increasing attention in both academic and policy circles. US Senator Elizabeth Warren made taxing large fortunes a central element of her 2020 presidential campaign. Her proposal, prepared by the economists Emmanuel Saez and Gabriel Zucman, would levy a 2 percent tax on those with net assets between US$50 million and 1 billion. The tax rate would increase to 3 percent for wealth above US$1 billion. The proposal also included an exit tax equal to 40 percent of total wealth for those who choose to leave the country—thus preventing easy tax evasion. Wealth taxes already exist in countries including Sweden, Denmark, and Spain; they have worked best when complemented with measures to avoid tax evasion.[11]

In his bestselling book *Capital in the 21st Century*, Thomas Piketty made an even more ambitious proposal: a progressive annual tax on global wealth. The "Piketty tax" would be levied on the wealth of all individuals, regardless of where it is located. It would also include progressive rates: at one point, he proposed a 0 percent rate for net assets below 1 million euros, 1 percent between 1 and 5 million, and so on, up to a rate between 5 and 10 percent for assets above 1 billion euros. Its global character would help to reduce tax evasion, discourage tax competition, increase international transparency, encourage sharing of banking information, and enhance collaboration between tax agencies across the world. Is this kind of tax likely to be implemented any time soon? No, but it sets an aspirational goal and helps to shape global policy debates. As Piketty explains, "even if nothing resembling this ideal is put into practice in the foreseeable future, it can serve as a worth-while reference point."[12]

Taxes are by no means the only way to improve the distribution of wealth. In addition to reducing the wealth of the rich, countries could try to increase that of low-income groups. One of the most creative and ambitious proposals is the creation of social funds and child bonds. A recent report from the UK Commission on Economic Justice proposed the creation of a Citizen's Wealth Fund that would then support a one-off dividend for every youngster in Great Britain. This kind of proposal is partly inspired by Alaska's Permanent Fund, which relies on oil rents. Others have suggested giving every child an initial endowment which could then be spent on education or other investment projects. All these proposals have a similar goal: to promote equality of opportunity and reduce the large gaps between individuals from birth.[13]

Shifting power in key markets

In almost every market some players are more powerful than others: firms are more influential than workers, large corporations more powerful than small ones. Subcontracting arrangements, short-term contracts, and pressure on small suppliers are just some of the instruments powerful businesses use to keep costs down and maximize profits. State intervention is key to reducing market power asymmetries, thus contributing to a better distribution of income. In this section, I focus on two policy areas: competition policy and labor market regulation (including the strengthening of trade unions).

Think about some of the leading sectors such as digital technology, food and beverages, clothing, and pharmaceuticals. In each case, a few corporations control a large share of total sales. At the global level, just two companies produce almost all large commercial aircraft; four companies, half of all cars; two companies, 95 percent of microprocessors; one company, half of all carbonated soft drinks; and another company, 70 percent of all razors.[14] In Latin America, a single family may own a leading supermarket, be a shareholder in the most popular beer producer, own newspapers, and have interests in mining.

According to American law professors Jonathan Baker and Steven Salop, governments should allocate more resources to promote competition and be more aggressive in demanding compensation.[15] In doing so, improving income distribution should become a primary goal: competition agencies could focus their energy on cases that can benefit low-income groups disproportionately. For example, regulating price abuses in the food sector should take priority over preventing price fixing in private schools. Governments could also focus on the poor when proposing solutions to the lack of competition. For example, they could allow mergers between pharmaceutical companies only if they commit to reducing the price of popular medicines, or could demand more investment from broadband providers in rural areas and poor neighborhoods.

Competition agencies across the world must also actively confront the growing power of leading tech companies. In the UK, for example, 74 percent of social networks' market share is in the hands of Facebook, Amazon controls 80 percent of online book sales, and almost all internet searches are done by Google.[16] Tech companies are using their market influence to prevent competition, monopolize the use of private data, and generate huge income for their owners. Whether breaking them down—as suggested by some American politicians—or just limiting their most egregious behavior, something needs to be done urgently at both the national and international levels.

Let's now move to the labor market. In recent decades, policymakers across the world have embraced radical liberalization measures: the reduction of firing costs, the elimination of minimum wages, and the weakening of other protections. Conservative icons such as Ronald Reagan and Margaret Thatcher used all the power in their hands to weaken trade unions. This anti-labor attack played a major role in the rapid growth of inequality in the Anglo-Saxon world. In Latin America trade unions have generally been small and weak, often defending the rights of their (few) members over those of the majority.[17]

Reversing this trend should be at the center of any progressive agenda. We already saw in the last chapter how minimum wages can make a positive contribution to equity. They often pull low salaries up, helping many workers move out of poverty. Contrary to what neoliberal economists claim, their negative impact on employment creation is negligible—as case after case from Brazil to the US demonstrates. "There's just no evidence that raising the minimum wage costs jobs," explains the Nobel Prize-winning economist, Paul Krugman—instead they lead to "better morale, lower turnover, increased productivity."[18]

Governments should also consider what to do with wages at the top, which in recent decades have skyrocketed. In the US, after decades of double-digit growth, half of the CEOs from the 200 biggest corporations make over US$336,000 *per week*. In the UK, the typical annual salary of the leader of a large corporation has moved from 20 times that of the average worker in the 1980s to 160 times in 2012. These income gaps have also expanded in other European countries, albeit not so dramatically. It is of course, not a problem of OECD countries alone: in Brazil during the 2000s, high-level executives in São Paulo earned more than their counterparts in New York or London, despite much lower wages overall.[19]

Most proposals in this area have focused on the relationship between maximum wages and other wages. A referendum in Switzerland proposed fixing the relationship between the highest and lowest wage in every company. The plan was ultimately rejected, but only because it established an excessively ambitious ratio of 1 to 12. More credible ratios (say, 1 to 20) are likely to receive much more support across the world in the future. "One neat idea is to link the maximum wage to the minimum wage, which would give CEOs an incentive to argue for higher minimum wages!" suggests the Oxford economist Simon Wren-Lewis.[20] Some worry that this kind of policy could reduce incentives to create new companies and generate new wealth. However, this was not a problem decades ago, when wage inequality was much lower and capital investments as high as today.

Finding ways to strengthen trade unions is probably the most important tool to rebalance power in labor markets. This will not be an easy task; the decline in unionization rates across the world is partly a result of the crises in manufacturing jobs and the expansion of the gig economy. Nevertheless, much can be done. First, governments could create incentives to facilitate the presence of trade unions in every company. For example, unionized companies could be favored in public contracts. The right to unionize should be recognized across the world, as demanded by International Labour Organization (ILO) conventions. Second, workers' membership could be encouraged. Workers could be automatically enrolled in a union unless they chose to opt out. Union fees could also be deducted from the payroll before taxes. Third, governments should promote collective bargaining agreements between companies and trade unions, particularly at the national level.

Strengthening unions is not a responsibility of public policy alone. In many countries, trade unions are unpopular and have failed to reach large segments of the population. Trade unions need to become more effective at explaining their role and more democratic in the ways they operate. They should always consider the health of the whole economy and not simply the interests of their members when making demands— something already happening in the Scandinavian countries. In parts of the world with large informal sectors, they should find more creative ways to reach informal workers, building closer links to social movements.

Creating more and better jobs

Regulating wages and promoting trade unions will be useless without enough good jobs. Unfortunately, jobs may be in short supply in the future: "Machines are turning into workers" warns Martin Ford, author of *The Rise of the Robots*. "Virtually every industry in existence is likely to become less labor-intensive as new technology is assimilated."[21] In the US, according to the most pessimistic projections, almost half of all occupations have at least a 70 percent chance of disappearing because of automatization.[22] Across the world, 46 percent of all jobs are likely to be automated or change significantly in the next few years.[23]

At times, this dystopian vision is presented as an unstoppable force. "The unfortunate reality is that a great many people will do everything right ... yet will still fail to find a solid foothold in the new economy," explains Ford.[24] Yet the reality is much more complex: the destruction of jobs will coincide with the creation of new ones, some sectors will expand more than others, technological innovation and human creativity will remain important.

How can we not simply adapt to the future but change it? How can we guarantee that good jobs dominate? History tells us that an active state that interacts constructively with the private sector is particularly important. Most examples of successful economic transformation—Scandinavia, South Korea, Taiwan, China—relied on what economists call industrial policy.[25] Even in the US, often (wrongly!) considered a free market paradise, the state drove most significant innovations—as convincingly shown by Mariana Mazzucato in *The Entrepreneurial State*.[26]

Industrial policies—better called sectoral policies since they often involve services—refer to any public intervention intended to favor desirable economic sectors that would not emerge without support.[27] They include tax incentives, subsidies, trade protection, discrimination in public contracts, and many other tools used in favor of specific activities—thus "picking winners." Contrary to what some neoliberal observers want us to believe, sectoral policies are not trying to curtail private activities. Quite the contrary: most often their aim is to encourage companies to move away from their comfort zone into new sectors, providing them with cheap inputs and useful knowledge.

Sectoral policies are primarily about developing new, high-tech sectors. The way to do this will be different depending on the level of development. Countries at the technological frontier such as Germany, Japan, or the US should focus on discovering new technologies and introducing new products. What do we need to create driverless cars? Artificial intelligence? More effective ways of delivering health services? How can we develop green technologies? Governments should also expand research and development, targeting activities that meet the most urgent social needs and can benefit the largest number of sectors.

In the global South industrial policy should primarily concentrate on copying and adapting already existing technologies. Governments in Latin America, Asia, and Africa should identify profitable activities that they can undertake effectively, from software development to business services, learn how global leaders produce those goods and services, and try to imitate them. This process will at times involve attracting high-tech foreign companies but will most often require developing successful domestic firms.

Unfortunately, starting in the 1990s, regulations promoted by the wealthiest countries have created many obstacles for industrial policy. Protecting specific sectors from global competition, subsidizing new activities, and offering exclusive support to domestic firms is no longer allowed.[28] Nevertheless, some countries—such as Singapore and South

Korea—have found ways around these limiting rules, and global regulations may become more favorable to interventionist policies in the future.

Promoting high-tech activities through sectoral policies can accelerate economic growth, strengthen technological capabilities, create new jobs, and even move countries toward a green economy. However, if one of the primary goals is to improve the distribution of income, this is not enough. In fact, in some instances, the development of high-tech sectors could easily contribute to inequality. Take the Costa Rican case. In the mid-1990s, the Central American country launched an ambitious campaign to modernize its economy through foreign investment in high-tech. In 1996, the government succeeded in attracting Intel, which opened its first semiconductor assembly in Latin America. Other IT and medical equipment companies followed, and by the early 2000s Costa Rica had become a high-tech hub in the Americas. The move contributed to export upgrading and to economic growth but did little for equality. High-skilled workers and some entrepreneurs in new economic sectors benefited, while many more were left behind. This gap between winners from industrial policy and those left behind is not unique to Costa Rica but has been a problem in other countries, such as Ireland.[29]

To prevent inequality, states should thus support high-tech activities and low-productivity sectors at the same time. The Venezuelan innovation expert Carlota Pérez refers to "a two-pronged approach to development: top-down and bottom-up," while I use the analogy of an airplane with two engines.[30] While one engine provides incentives for technological advancement, the other creates learning opportunities for low-income groups. While one focuses on capital-intensive sectors with high productivity, the other concentrates on encouraging labor-intensive activities. Governments should also find ways to support small-company upgrading in areas such as management and accounting.

A shift in the role of financial markets

During the 1950s and 1960s—the golden age of equality, particularly in developed countries—financial markets' main role was to support the production of goods and services. Wall Street existed to make Main Street's life easier. Banks focused on lending to productive companies and could not invest in the stock market. Financial instruments such as options and derivatives were heavily regulated. Hedge funds were small and had limited influence on the daily workings of companies. Capital flows between countries were heavily controlled and exchange rates were fixed. In developing countries, interest-rate ceilings and mandatory allocation of credit to specific sectors were quite common.

Starting in the 1970s, things began to change dramatically. Transformations at the national and international levels shifted the balance of power between the financial sector and the rest of the economy. Commercial and investment banks joined forces: the same institution could now lend money and invest in shares at the same time. Regulation of banks, controls of interest rates, and limits on derivatives were all gradually eliminated in one country after another. Hedge funds multiplied and the volumes of financial assets exchanged daily skyrocketed. International capital flows also grew exponentially: the ratio between the volume of currency exchange every day and the volume of world trade went from 2 to 1 in 1973 to 10 to 1 in 1980 and 70 to 1 in 1992.[31] Latin American countries were at the forefront of some of these changes, enthusiastically embracing financial liberalization.

The consequences were revolutionary. Banks became more interested in what happened in the stock market than in lending to productive companies. In all sectors of the economy, short-term profits became more important than long-term success. Working in a hedge fund was now more rewarding—at least in financial terms!—than becoming a doctor or a researcher. Developing countries began focusing on the attraction of short-term financial flows as a tool to accelerate growth quickly, without worrying much about instability.

The impact of this process of financialization on inequality across the world cannot be overstated. "The success or failure of the financial sector has had serious effects on the rest of the economy and most of its returns have gone to the wealthy driving inequality," argues a contributor to the market-friendly *Forbes* magazine.[32] Four channels have been particularly important. First, by pressuring companies to produce short-term profits, financial markets have contributed to periodic firings, growing flexibility in labor arrangements, and low wage growth. Second, high wages in the financial market have been one of the drivers of inequality at the top. For example, financial deregulation contributed to a 20 percent increase in the pre-tax earnings of the wealthiest 10 percent in the UK and a 10 percent growth in Japan.[33] Third, the expansion of financial investment opportunities accelerated the income gains of wealthy savers. As Thomas Piketty has convincingly shown, having wealth became much more profitable than having a good job. Fourth, financial deregulation contributed to financial crises in Latin

America (e.g. Mexico in 1994, Argentina in 2001), Asia (South Korea, Thailand, and others in 1997), and, more recently, in the US and Europe. As we already saw in Chapter 3, the long-term consequences of these crises on inequality are devastating.

Regulating financial markets is thus more urgent than ever. It requires multiple measures in different areas. Let me offer here just a few examples. Commercial and financial banking should be split, and the participation of banks in financial markets limited. Governments should strengthen public development banks that provide access to cheap, long-term credit to small and medium-sized firms. The use of derivatives and other speculative financial assets should be properly regulated. Developing countries should be allowed to impose capital controls, particularly in moments of crisis. I realize this may sound like a shopping list! Yet all the proposals share a common objective: to limit the profits of the financial sector and to put financial institutions at the service of the real economy again.

Redistributing income more effectively through universal policies

Academics love to talk about their own research and mine—done in collaboration with my friend Juliana Martínez Franzoni—is on universal social policy. I would happily spend pages and pages explaining why I think redistribution through universal programs is important. But don't worry, I will be short.[34]

These days only diehard neoliberals would argue in favor of eliminating all social programs. Most people understand that poverty is a social ill and that governments have a role to play in providing benefits to at least some people. Instead, the main debate is about how many benefits the state should provide and who should be benefiting from them. Should social policy target the poor exclusively? Should resources be concentrated on a few people and a few programs to maximize the "bang for the buck"? Or are universal policies that provide generous benefits to everyone best to reduce inequality?

Based on the most successful experiences in both the developed and developing world, it is easy to answer these questions: providing generous benefits to everyone is best if the goal is to redistribute income and opportunities. Universal transfers and services usually have a larger impact on income distribution than targeted ones.[35] This may sound counterintuitive: surely providing money and services to the very poor is the most effective way to redistribute income? A now famous paper by Walter Korpi and Joaquim Palme shows why this is not the case.[36]

The two Swedish researchers identified "a paradox of redistribution": programs that benefit all social groups lead to more spending, thus leaving the poor better off as well. More recent studies have confirmed the initial findings, also demonstrating that the most equal countries in the world all have large welfare states that cover the poor, the middle class, and even the wealthy. Evidence on developing countries is scarcer, but some studies have also shown that countries with universal policies are also more redistributive.

The paradox of redistribution has its roots in politics. Programs that are exclusively for the poor tend to be poor programs because nobody else wants to support them. By contrast, both the poor and the middle class will be in favor of universal healthcare or education—leading to the creation of the kind of cross-class alliance that I discussed in Chapter 5. Also, the middle class has more resources—such as time, knowledge, and networks—to demand better hospitals, better teachers, or higher pensions.

The impact of universal policies on inequality goes beyond income. By treating every citizen equally, universal programs do not create stigma. Every individual has the right to health, pensions, and education, regardless of their race, gender, and class. By contrast, means-tested programs force the poor to demonstrate their lack of money and distinguish them from the rest of society. Peter Townsend, one of the giants of social policy studies, described the problem well: a program that targets the poor "fosters hierarchical relations of superiority and inferiority in society, diminishes rather than enhances the status of the poor, and has the effect of widening social inequalities ... it lumps the unemployed, sick, widowed, aged and others into one undifferentiated and inevitably stigmatized category."[37]

You may still be a little skeptical. Won't universal policies lead to bloated bureaucracies and less economic dynamism? And where will governments, particularly in developing countries, find the resources to fund universal healthcare and education and pensions and other transfers? Luckily there are answers for both of these questions.

Universal policies are likely to have a positive impact on sustainable economic growth and competitiveness. Generous social services and transfers can help countries confront external shocks, assisting people with becoming more entrepreneurial. It is easier to create your own company if you know that the state will support you when things do not go according to plan. Universal education will increase the amount of skilled workers—exactly what has been historically missing in Latin America. This kind of social policy can also help to expand aggregate demand, as more people have the resources to go to restaurants and buy computers, for example. These are not just theoretical arguments; in fact, some of the most competitive countries in the world—from Sweden to Finland—have large welfare states. In the developing world, countries like Mauritius have combined universal policies with high economic growth for decades.

Of course, universal policies are more expensive than targeted ones: guaranteeing healthcare or pensions to every citizen requires more resources than covering the poor alone. Yet many countries still have ample capacity to expand revenues to fund social programs, as demonstrated by a recent ILO study.[38] Some should focus on increasing taxes, others could expand their debt levels, and others could manage their foreign reserves more aggressively. In the specific case of Latin America, as we saw in Chapter 3, most countries raise fewer taxes than one would expect based on their income levels. My point is not that expanding revenues will be easy, but that the main obstacle is more political than economic.

Before I conclude this section, let me discuss a policy instrument that has become increasingly popular (even more in the age of COVID-19): the universal basic income (UBI).[39] The UBI is a cash transfer given to every citizen (or every resident) irrespective of their level of income or work status. Many consider it a necessary response to the rise of the robots and the lack of jobs in the future. "When you realize that we're in the midst of the greatest economic and technological transformation in the history of our country ... then you think okay, what can we do about that? What's a realistic countermeasure? And when I've dug into it, universal basic income was the most powerful response that we could adopt," explains the US millionaire, philanthropist, and presidential candidate Andrew Yang.[40] He promised that if he were elected president he would give every American a monthly transfer of US$1,000 until death. UBI proposals have been discussed in many other parts of the world, from Finland to Brazil.

UBI has plenty of both critics and defenders. Most critics focus on its high cost and negative work incentives. Why would people look for jobs if they have a guaranteed income? And why should the rich receive the same income as the poor? Proponents respond with many of the arguments I have already given in favor of universal policies: that UBI will have massive social support and that it is easier to implement than more targeted transfers. They also believe that it will give everyone the freedom to undertake their own projects, while not reducing people's willingness to work significantly.

In my view the UBI deserves serious attention. It constitutes an original response to a changing world. It can also contribute to simplifying the complex system of transfers many countries have, replacing minimum pensions, unemployment benefits, and accident insurance with a single payment. Yet some of the current proposals could end up doing more harm than good. In particular, if the UBI was to become the only social policy intervention and replace all social programs (including free health and education), gaps in income and opportunities would actually increase. While the wealthy could still attend the best schools and clinics, the poor would no longer have access to high-quality public services, relying on lower-quality private ones instead.

Where do we begin?

By now, you may be a little overwhelmed. I have provided a long list of potential policies that may have left you with more questions than answers. Why aren't countries implementing these policies already? Do they have the capacity to do it? Where should they begin? Let me briefly tackle a couple of these questions here, while leaving the discussion of politics for the next section.

Some progressive observers claim that we should focus on the labor market, while others believe that social policy is more important. Yet this is not a fruitful debate or one with a simple answer. Many of the recommendations I have made complement each other, creating virtuous circles. If we strengthen trade unions, we will have one more actor working toward universalism in social policy. If we improve healthcare and education, we may have a more competitive economy, capable of creating more jobs. Moreover, different countries will face different challenges: South Korea already has a robust industrial policy, so it should now focus on labor rights and universal social programs. By contrast, in, say, Uruguay, creating more good jobs is particularly urgent.

My proposals are not just a shopping list of disconnected policies. Instead, we should see them as components of a new model; together they constitute an alternative vision of what the good society is and what it requires. The conservative establishment believes that we need less regulation, more private initiative, and more individual rights. "The less the public sector interferes in the life of the citizens, the more freedom they have to promote their own initiatives, [and] the lower taxes they suffer, the higher the economy grows, the more society prospers and the higher the number of jobs created," proclaimed proudly a right-wing Spanish politician a few years ago.[41] We have heard similar statements from Margaret Thatcher, Ronald Reagan, Donald Trump, and Alberto Fujimori in recent decades, as well as many other politicians and business leaders.

Many of us believe that the economy is more inclusive, and also more dynamic, when states and markets work together. Society is more vibrant when socioeconomic rights are secured. Countries overcome dysfunctional inequality when financial markets are regulated and there are counterbalances to the economic elite. People can be happier when they are not treated as just individuals but as members of a broader community, one where everyone has access to well-paying jobs and high-quality health and education.

"Stop dreaming!," I can hear some of you shouting. "The policies you suggest may work in some wealthy economies. Yet many countries, particularly in the global South, lack the capacity to implement many of the suggestions," you may argue. Implementing active state policies is indeed challenging. Efficient bureaucracies and more effective checks and balances are vitally important.

Nevertheless, meeting this challenge is by no means impossible. We already have successful examples of state transformation in the South, from South Korea to Costa Rica and from Mauritius to Uruguay. More importantly, strengthening the state does not need to take place *before* countries begin implementing progressive policies. In most successful countries, the two processes have taken place simultaneously: policies and institutions have gradually improved and together resulted in higher economic growth and more equity.

Policies Without Politics Will Never Work

"Improving the distribution of income demands mobilization from below." This is what Ben Phillips, founder of the Fighting Inequality Campaign, kept telling me, every time we talked about inequality.[42] We were both spending some time at the Kellogg Institute of the University of Notre Dame writing books on inequality. I was writing this book based on my own research and understanding of Latin America, while his drew on his distinguished career as an activist and organizer in Europe and Africa.

He is right: designing good policies will be useless unless we also build the right politics. This book has shown as much: the power and influence of the elite explains why inequality has persisted in Latin

America. Why would the elite embrace the recommendations I have just made? Why would they have a change of heart and support higher taxes and more redistribution? Showing them that lower inequality could lead to higher growth and less violence will not be enough.

We must therefore think about the political conditions required to improve the distribution of income. How can we change the balance of power in already unequal regions like Latin America? How can we reverse the kind of politics that have led to the expansion of inequality in the US and parts of Europe? These are difficult questions with no easy answers. Pessimists like Walter Scheidel, author of *The Great Leveler*, argue that nothing is likely to change unless a major disruption such as a war takes place.[43] Others call for radical changes in our economic and political systems—changes that may be desirable but would take decades if not centuries to materialize.

As in the rest of the chapter, in this last section I do not offer radical new solutions. Instead I rely on some known but fundamental building blocks. I focus on three political conditions required to implement much-needed policies: deeper democracies, stronger progressive parties, and more active social movements. Past experiences also teach us that equitable outcomes are most likely when political parties and social movements work together—or at least their efforts do not go in opposite directions.

The importance of full democracies

Most philosophers and social scientists have traditionally assumed that there is a positive relationship between democracy and equality.[44] Democratic institutions have been linked to a more even distribution of social power and thus to a more inclusive economy. Electoral competition is believed to increase the influence of low-income voters— particularly in poor and unequal countries—and democratic institutions are thought to strengthen the power of workers in their struggle with the economic elites.

In recent decades, this positive influence of democracy has been questioned. Quantitative studies have found little reason to believe that income distribution is better in democracies than dictatorships. Democracies do not always contribute to a better distribution of wealth and assets either.[45] Citizens themselves have also become skeptical. A Pew Research Center survey across 27 developed and developing countries in 2018 found that more than half of respondents were dissatisfied with the working of democracy. Critics abounded in both developed countries such as Italy (where 70 percent were not happy with the way democracy worked), Spain (81 percent), and Greece (84 percent) as well as in developing countries such as South Africa (64 percent) and Tunisia (71 percent). Sixty percent of respondents across the whole sample also agreed that "no matter who wins an election, things do not change very much."[46]

How can we explain the contradiction between theoretical expectations and the reality on the ground? To answer this question, we just need to consider the experience of Latin America reviewed in Chapter 4. Latin American democracies have traditionally been limited and restrictive. Before the mid-twentieth century, many Latin Americans could not vote, freedom of the press was limited, and social mobilization was severely restricted. As a result, little redistribution took place. After the third wave of democratization in the 1980s, elections worked better and electoral participation was higher, but there were still many restrictions and problems.

Elections are thus no panacea. They can often be used by the elites to justify their power. "We chose leaders freely and the government is legitimate," they argue, without considering inequalities in access to political power, mass media ownership, and policy influence. Citizens across the world increasingly feel that their electoral choices are limited since the socioeconomic policies implemented by the right and the left look alike.

Yet a deeper and stronger democracy can make a significant contribution to a more equal distribution. Most cases of inequality reduction in peaceful environments—think about the Scandinavian countries in the first half of the twentieth century, Spain after 1978, or the US after the Great Depression—took place under democratic regimes.[47] Even in Latin America, despite institutional weakness, electoral competition in the 2000s intensified the pressures toward redistribution, and led to the reduction in Gini coefficients.

To be effective, democracy has to go beyond free, regular elections. Truly democratic institutions must provide political equality: every citizen must have access to high-quality information and to a say—at least potentially—in the political process. This means that mass media cannot be controlled by a few interest groups and that the right to mobilize, to protest, and to organize must be protected. Campaign financing has to be regulated so that powerful individuals cannot buy presidential candidates or congressional votes. Political parties must be both strong and diverse so that they can exert effective opposition when they are not in power and can also offer true policy alternatives to choose from.

Most countries are far from the ideal I have just described. Even well-established democracies show increasing strains: constraints on effective opposition, lack of real policy diversity, growing political influence of the wealthy, and weakened judiciaries are now common everywhere. Yet I am not sure these problems are unresolvable or incurable weaknesses of the system. Instead, I believe that we just need to continue fighting for effective institutions and stronger political parties. If democracy is still the best way to organize politics, then deepening democracy is more important and urgent than ever.

Progressive political parties: social democracy and beyond

Let me be a little controversial: it will be hard to improve the distribution of income significantly without strong progressive political parties. Let me be even more controversial: social democratic parties—those that try to effectively combine state and markets and defend liberal democracy as a potential instrument for change—still have a central role in the fight against inequality. This subsection justifies each of these two claims.

When you read the press these days, it would seem that everyone is concerned about inequality. The global elite in Davos, the *Financial Times* and other mainstream newspapers, conservative political parties—all agree on the need to reduce income concentration. Yet many of their recommendations lack credibility. It is hard to see how we are going to close the income gap with an expansion of markets and with lower taxes, precisely what many of these actors keep proposing.

By contrast, progressive/leftist parties have always placed equality at the heart of their political project. What truly distinguishes left and right, as famously argued the philosopher and political scientist Noberto Bobbio, "is the attitude . . . to the ideal of equality . . . The left is egalitarian and the right is inegalitarian."[48] These are not just theoretical beliefs: a large body of academic research demonstrates that progressive parties have been instrumental in the construction of redistributive social policies across the world.[49] Their presence in some countries and absence in others helps explain differences in the levels of inequality.

Progressive political parties contribute to the reduction of inequality in different ways. First, they have historically supported the kind of policies that improve the distribution of income, from higher minimum wages to more active labor market policies and universal welfare states. Second, by placing equality at the heart of political debates, they have forced all other parties to pay attention to it as well. Third, progressive political parties are more likely to work together with social movements and promote social mobilization—two important ingredients in reducing the power and influence of the wealthy.

Of course, there are progressive parties of many kinds: more or less populist, more or less market friendly. Why then do I highlight the role of social democratic parties in particular? There are several reasons.[50] Social democrats have traditionally accepted that markets have an important role to play, but only if they are properly managed and complemented by active state intervention. This perspective, I believe, makes sense: allowing people to follow their own personal projects and make their own decisions while simultaneously regulating markets has proven more effective than organizing the economy through central planning.

The most successful social democratic parties have been pragmatic in their means but radical in their aims. They have placed equality and social welfare at the heart of their agendas but have been willing to try different policies to achieve them. In many cases, they have also built close ties to trade unions and other social movements, thus successfully combining bottom-up and top-down approaches to politics. Empirically, it is also clear that social democrats have been behind most successful policies to reduce income distribution. Think about the Scandinavian countries during the second half of the twentieth century, the US Democratic Party in the 1940s and 1950s, Spain in the 1980s, or Costa Rica in the 1950s and 1960s.

If social democratic parties are so important, why have they failed so spectacularly in recent years? Why have they lost popular support and political influence in so many countries? Dealing with these questions in detail in a few pages is impossible; Spanish readers should take a look at the excellent book by the philosopher Borja Barragué, for a thorough discussion.[51] Richard Sandbrook's *Reinventing the Left in the Global South* provides a more global perspective in English on this question.[52] Here I offer only some clues, focusing on the changing social environment where parties operate as well as some mistakes they have made.

Social democratic parties face radically changed societies: in recent decades many countries, particularly in Europe, have become more culturally and ethnically diverse; their populations are now older and thus demand more from the welfare state; and the heterogeneity in labor markets has increased—with some professionals doing extremely well and many manual workers struggling to survive. In this new context, building the kind of cross-class coalitions that have historically supported social democrats has become harder and harder.

Unfortunately, parties and their leaders have also taken many wrong decisions. They have often embraced market liberalization, thinking that this would help to promote economic growth. They have weakened state bureaucracies instead of making them more effective and responsive. They have been timid with the wealthy, avoiding proposals to increase progressive taxation and regulate finance. They have also failed to protect trade unions and build strong links to new social movements. Too often, social democratic parties have become professional machines, whose only goal is to get as many votes as possible to remain in power. Their failure to renew their discourse has opened spaces for more radical parties—particularly from the far right—which are good at identifying clear enemies and proposing easy solutions.

In many parts of the developing world, social democratic parties—and the left more generally—have faced even more obstacles. At times they have been persecuted or faced significant financial constraints. In many countries they have failed to create strong party machineries, build stable political programs, or create links to social movements. When in government, they have often forgotten to implement measures to strengthen the state and fight corruption.

Given all these problems, it has become popular to argue that the division between left and right is no longer valid. Many observers have called for new parties that adopt more populist discourses and/or propose alternatives to capitalism. Both responses are, in my view, unsatisfactory. In the era of inequality, the distinction between left and right is more valid than ever. In the age of easy polarization, "utopian pragmatism"—that is, radical goals with credible means—can be particularly effective. Yet progressive parties must change. They need to recognize that income concentration at the top is one of the most significant challenges of our generation. Therefore, (re)distributing income and opportunities from the very rich to the rest should be a primary goal. Social democratic parties should not accept the still influential discourse that argues that redistribution and economic efficiency cannot be simultaneously achieved. They should offer solutions to those challenges shared by the poor and the middle class, including income volatility, low-quality social services, and high inequality. Both in government and in opposition, progressive leaders should also acknowledge the central role of the state, while simultaneously working to make it more efficient and more responsive. Finally, they need to build meaningful ties to society, creating more communication channels with social movements.

I realize that this is easier said than done. I also understand that advancing in this direction is more likely in some countries than others; it is still particularly hard in developing countries with weak political systems. Yet I believe that it is useful to have grand aspirations and clear roadmaps. Ambitious but pragmatic leftist parties should be at the center of any pro-equity strategy for the future.

The counterbalancing role of social mobilization from below

"What gives you hope that inequality can be beaten?" was a question we asked some of the social leaders and policymakers we invited to a conference on inequality at the Kellogg Institute.[53] They all offered similar responses:[54]

> People are organizing to challenge power (Winnie Byanyima, Oxfam International Executive Director).

> There are a lot of social movements and groups in civil society that are well organized to try to show the importance of inequality (Luis Felipe López-Calva, program director for Latin America and the Caribbean at UNDP).

> People in the street (Hector Castañón, Latin American coordinator of the Fighting Inequality Alliance).

> The possibility of finding common ground between [social] organizations (Thea Lee, president of the Economic Policy Institute).

> That there is a movement growing that is led by those who are most impacted (Liz Theoharis, Poor People's Campaign co-chair).

Their shared focus on social movements is not surprising. Every major success in the fight against socioeconomic inequalities from the US civil rights movement to the construction of the welfare state in Scandinavia has involved active mobilization. Neither the economic elites nor most governments ever moved from the status quo unless they felt the heat from below.

The leaders we interviewed, and many others, also shared a similar optimism about the future. They see growing social discontent against income concentration. Occupy Wall Street, the Spanish anti-austerity movement *Indignados*, Latin America's anti-mining movements: these are just some of the multiple examples of people clamoring for a more just world. Unfortunately, other trends are more negative. The weakness of trade unions, the disappointment with the political system, the heterogeneity of the middle class, and the power of the individualist culture all conspire against social activism.

It is imperative to strengthen social movements and to encourage more people to organize and protest across the world, while making sure that no state represses them. To achieve this goal, it is useful to remember some of the lessons from the previous chapter. There, we discussed how some social movements—from the Chilean students to the Brazilian landless movement—succeeded in shaping public opinion and influencing political debates. Their strategies provide at least five relevant lessons that are worth restating here.

Successful social movements focus on concrete needs, but successfully link them to broader social demands. They initially ask for lower bus fares, call for better social services, or occupy unused land—causes that mobilize a large number of people and result in quick improvements in their lives. Yet they also know how to place these demands within a broader agenda. In this way, little by little, they can encourage supporters to be more ambitious and mobilize for real structural change.

Success also requires linking the local and national spaces. Most protests start locally: they are organized in a large company or in a city or in a group of neighboring schools. These protests became most meaningful when they scale up and influence national debates. Moving from the local to the national can happen in a variety of ways: in Chile, students in most regions just followed the examples of those in the capital Santiago; in Brazil, the landless movement organized marches to the capital; in Mexico, the Zapatistas called for the solidarity of groups in other parts of the country.

Most meaningful mobilizations go beyond the spur of the moment. They lead to the creation of more or less stable organizations that can then develop a long-term strategy. If we move beyond Latin America for a second, we can use the civil rights movement in the US as an illustrative example. The movement planned its initial actions—including Rosa Parks's refusal to change seats in a Montgomery bus—for months and followed them up with subsequent protests. They were clear about their ultimate goal, but also knew they had to advance one step at a time.

Some of the most successful movements in Latin America—and beyond—were able to build a cross-class alliance. The Chilean students, who received support from both the poor and large segments of the middle class, constitute the most evident case. The *Indignados,* at least at the beginning, also secured support from broad segments of Spanish society. This kind of cross-class collaboration is particularly important in the fight against inequality.

The contribution of social movements goes beyond advancing political demands. At its best, indigenous groups, students, landless peasants, and trade unions create new narratives and new perspectives. This is particularly urgent at a time when too many people have adopted an individualist and meritocratic view of society. Social movements should help replace the idea that "my welfare depends on my individual hard work" and "I should just worry about me and by family" with "we are in this together" and "the good society is one with shared values where everyone wins." Moreover, successful mobilization can strengthen people's belief in their power to create a different world. "By ... recognising common grievances, puncturing neoliberal orthodoxy, celebrating hitherto marginalised identities and seeing widespread resistance to the status quo, many Latin Americans gained confidence in the possibility of social change," explained Alice Evans in her discussion of the region in the 2000s.[55]

The impact of social movements will be maximized when they are able to remain independent from political parties but also work with them. The example of Scandinavian countries is particularly illustrative in this regard. Social democratic parties and trade unions often collaborated to advance the equity agenda: for example, they negotiated moderate wage increases in exchange for the rapid expansion of the welfare state. They discussed alternatives together, but each knew their different role in society. Trade unions participated in many of the intra-party discussions but also opposed social democratic governments when needed. The Bolivian experience under Morales illustrates another way of linking a powerful party and social movements—and also highlights the dangers of becoming too close.

Conclusion

Inequality has become one of the challenges of our generation. If we do not tackle it soon, it could have significant, long-term economic, political, and social costs. The Latin American experience clearly shows that income concentration can reduce economic growth, contribute to financial crises, weaken the state's fiscal capacity, facilitate the emergence of populist leaders, and increase violence, among many other negative results. Moreover, when inequality is too high and too entrenched, it becomes harder to combat due to entrenched vicious circles.

Reducing inequality is increasingly difficult, but by no means impossible. If we combine the right policies with the right politics, we can gradually reverse course and create a more equal future. Under the right conditions, we could even break with centuries of inequality in Latin America and begin to improve the distribution of income in countries across the continent.

This chapter has made many proposals, from taxing wealth to strengthening social movements. For some, the discussion may sound utopian, almost naive. Each of the measures I have proposed will be difficult to implement in this era of globalization and income concentration. Together, they may constitute an almost unreachable dream.

However, the usefulness of the chapter goes beyond each of the proposals I have discussed. Several underlying messages are more important than any specific policy proposal. First, fighting inequality is not about finding a magic solution. It is not enough to implement a universal basic income or to define new sustainable development goals. Improving income distribution is a long-term struggle that will demand efforts from many people in many different areas—from policy to politics.

Second, improving the distribution of income is primarily a political challenge. Of course, we need to implement the type of policies discussed here. These policies, however, will only be adopted if we gradually change the distribution of social power. This is why strengthening our unions, mobilizing in the streets, and participating in formal and informal politics is so important. This is also why we cannot get discouraged and must understand that this will be a long and at times painful battle.

Finally, and most importantly, I hope the chapter provides suggestions of how to think about the good society and the right policy mix. The still dominant narrative tells us that markets should be as free as possible, that states should not overreach, that people want to accumulate as much wealth as possible, and that inequality is the product of a meritocratic race. Instead, I hope we use the COVID-19 pandemic and our response to it to recognize that unregulated markets only create inequality and instability, that successful societies always have strong states, that shared prosperity is particularly rewarding, and that meritocracy is a myth. Recognizing that a better distribution of income, wealth, and opportunities can benefit everyone may be the first and most important step to build a more humane society in Latin America and beyond.

NOTES

Chapter 1

1   Wolf, M. (2019), "Why Rentier Capitalism is Damaging Liberal Democracy," *Financial Times*, September 18.

2   There is an intense debate in academia and policy circles about the labels we should use for different countries (developed and developing, global South and North, center and periphery). Despite their problems, in this book I often use the terms "developed" and "developing" simply because they are still the most common terms in the popular press.

3   Fabrikant, G. (2005), "Old Nantucket Warily Meets the New," *New York Times,* June 5, https://www.nytimes.com/2005/06/05/us/class/old-nantucket-warily-meets-the-new.html.

4   Obama, B. (2013), "Speech on Inequality," *Politico*, December 4, https://www.politico.com/story/2013/12/obama-income-inequality-100662.

5   Freeland, C. (2012), *Plutocrats: The Rise of the New Global Super-Rich and the Fall of Everyone Else*, London: Penguin Press.

6   Nolan, B., E. Rahbari, M. Richiardi, L. Rivera, and B. Nabarro (2017), "Inequality and Prosperity in the Industrialized World: Addressing a Growing Challenge," *Citi GPS: Global Perspectives & Solutions*, https://www.oxfordmartin.ox.ac.uk/downloads/Citi_GPS_Inequality.pdf.

7   Vogel, C. (2010), "Warhol and Rothko Lead a Big Night at Sotheby's," *New York Times*, May 12, https://www.nytimes.com/2010/05/13/arts/design/13auction.html.

8   Zeveloff, J. (2013), "Andy Warhol Painting Sets a New Record with $105 Million Sale," *Business Insider,* November 13, https://www.businessinsider.com/andy-warhol-painting-sets-a-new-record-with-105-million-sale-2013-11.

9   Wilkinson, R., and K. Pickett (2011), *The Spirit Level: Why Greater Equality Makes Societies Stronger*, London: Bloomsbury, p. 11.

10 Hacker, J., and P. Pierson (2010), *Winner-Take-All Politics: How Washington Made the Rich Richer—And Turned Its Back on the Middle Class*, New York: Simon & Schuster.

11 Hopkin, J., and J. Lynch (2016), "Winner-Take-All Politics in Europe? European Inequality in Comparative Perspective," *Politics & Society* 44(3): 335–43.

12 Cuadros, A. (2016), *Brazillionares: Wealth, Power, Decadence, and Hope in an American Country*, New York: Spiegel & Grau.

13 Bárcena Ibarra, A., and W. Byanyima (2016), "América Latina es la región más desigual del mundo. ¿Cómo solucionarlo?," *World Economic Forum*,

January 17, https://es.weforum.org/agenda/2016/01/america-latina-es-la-region-mas-desigual-del-mundo-asi-es-como-lo-solucionamos/.

14 World Bank (2003), *Inequality in Latin America: Breaking with History?*, Washington, DC: World Bank Group.

15 Eduardo, D. (2017), "10 of the Richest People in Latin America," *Latin American Post*, https://latinamericanpost.com/index.php/letters/16518-10-of-the-richest-people-in-latin-america. The Brazilian Eduardo Severin, Facebook's co-founder, would seem to be the exception. Yet he comes from a wealthy family with interests in clothing, shipping, and real estate—hardly the most innovative economic activities—lives in Singapore and has limited economic links to Latin America.

16 Sánchez-Ancochea, D., and I. Morgan (eds) (2009), *The Political Economy of the Public Budget in the Americas,* London: Institute for the Study of the Americas.

17 OECD (2018), *Revenue Statistics in Latin America and the Caribbean 2018*, Paris: OECD.

18 Martínez Franzoni, J., and D. Sánchez-Ancochea (2016), *The Quest for Universal Social Policy in the South: Actors, Ideas and Architectures*, Cambridge: Cambridge University Press.

19 Martínez Franzoni, J., and D. Sánchez-Ancochea (2018), "Overcoming Segmentation in Social Policy? Comparing New Early Education and Childcare Efforts in Costa Rica and Uruguay," *Bulletin of Latin American Research* 38(4): 423–37.

20 Berg, J. (2011), "Laws or Luck? Understanding Rising Formality in Brazil in the 2000s," in S. Lee and D. McCann (eds), *Regulating for Decent Work: Advances in Labour Studies*, London: Palgrave Macmillan, pp. 123–50.

21 Engbom, N., and C. Moser (2018), "Earning Inequality and the Minimum Wage: Evidence from Brazil," *Opportunity & Inclusive Growth Institute Working Paper 7 2018-3*, Federal Reserve Bank of Minneapolis.

Chapter 2

1 Meinhardt, M. (2015), "The Romantic Scientist: Alexander von Humboldt Under the Palm Trees," *Guernica*, https://www.guernicamag.com/maren-meinhardt-the-romantic-scientist-alexander-von-humboldt/.

2 Von Humboldt, A. (1811), *Political Essay on the Kingdom of New Spain*, vol. 1, New York, p. 138.

3 Esquivel Hernández, G. (2015), "Desigualdad extrema en México: Concentración del poder económico y político," Oxfam México, http://trazandoelrumbo.ibero.mx/wp-content/uploads/2015/08/desigualdadextrema_informe.pdf.

4 Capgemini (2018), *World Wealth Report, 2018*, https://www.worldwealthreport.com/.

5 Oxfam International, "Brazil: Extreme Inequality in Numbers," https:// www.oxfam.org/en/even-it-brazil/brazil-extreme-inequality-numbers.

6 Cobham, A., and A. Sumner (2013), "Putting the Gini back in the Bottle? 'The Palma' as a Policy-Relevant Measure of Inequality," unpublished manuscript, King's College, London.

7 CEPAL (2017), "La elevada desigualdad en América Latina constituye un obstáculo para el desarrollo sostenible," press release, https://www.cepal. org/es/comunicados/cepal-la-elevada-desigualdad-america-latina-constituye-un-obstaculo-desarrollo.

8 Torche, F. (2005), "Unequal but Fluid: Social Mobility in Chile in Comparative Perspective," *American Sociological Review* 70(3): 422–50. See also López, R., E. Figueroa, and P. Gutiérrez (2013), "La Parte del León: Nuevas estimaciones de la participación de los súper ricos en el ingreso de Chile," Working Paper 379, Facultad Economía y Negocios, Universidad de Chile, Departamento de Economía; and Solimano, A. (2012), *Chile and the Neoliberal Trap: The Post-Pinochet Era*, Cambridge: Cambridge University Press.

9 Fairfield, T., and M. Jorratt (2014), "Top Income Shares, Business Profits, and Effective Tax Rates in Contemporary Chile," *Review of Income and Wealth* 62(51): S120–S144.

10 World Bank, *Inequality in Latin America*.

11 Cañete Alonso, R. (2015), "Privilegios que niegan derechos: Desigualdad extrema y secuestro de la democracia en América Latina y El Caribe," https://www.oxfam.org/sites/www.oxfam.org/files/file_attachments/ reporte_iguales-oxfambr.pdf.

12 Alexander, H. (2011), "Carlos Slim: At Home with the World's Richest Man," *Daily Telegraph*, February 19, https://www.telegraph.co.uk/ finance/8335604/Carlos-Slim-At-home-with-the-worlds-richest-man.html.

13 Esquivel Hernández, "Desigualdad extrema en México."

14 See Sotheby's International Realty's website at https://www.sothebysrealty. com/eng/sales/detail/180-l-4339-hgds6t/duplex-garden-vila-nova-conceicao-sao-paulo-sp-04513100, and BBC Mundo (2018), "¿Cuáles son los barrios más caros de América Latina?," http://www.t13.cl/noticia/ negocios/mundo/bbc/cuales-son-los-barrios-mas-caros-de-america-latina.

15 Novais, A. (2012), "Most Expensive Neighbourhoods in São Paulo City," *Brazil Business*, http://thebrazilbusiness.com/article/most-expensive-neighborhoods-in-sao-paulo-city.

16 The Borgen Project (2018), "Revamping Favelas: Top 10 Facts about Poverty in São Paulo," https://borgenproject.org/revamping-favelas-top-10-facts-about-poverty-in-sao-paulo/.

17 The following discussion is based on Jefferson, A., and P. Lokken (2011), *Daily Life in Colonial Latin America*, Santa Barbara, CA: Greenwood. See also Cardoso, E., and A. Hewlege (1995), *Latin America's Economy: Diversity, Trends and Conflicts*, Cambridge, MA: MIT Press.

18 Jefferson and Lokken, *Daily Life in Colonial Latin America*, p. 179.

19 Engergman, S., and K. Sokoloff (1994), "Factor Endowments, Institutions, and Differential Paths of Growth Among New World Economies: A View from Economic Historians of the United States," NBER Historical Working Paper 66.

20 Acemoglu, D., and J. Robinson (2012), *Why Nations Fail: The Origins of Power, Prosperity and Poverty*, New York: Profile.

21 Williamson, J. (2009), "Five Centuries of Latin American Inequality," NBER Working Paper 15305.

22 Bértola, L., and J. Williamson (2006), "Globalization in Latin America before 1940," in V. Bulmer-Thomas, J. Coatsworth, and R. Cortés Conde (eds), *The Cambridge Economic History of Latin America*, vol. 2, Cambridge: Cambridge University Press, pp. 11–57.

23 Bértola, L., C. Castelnovo, J. Rodríguez Weber, and H. Willebald (2010), "Between the Colonial Heritage and the First Globalization Boom: On Income Inequality in the Southern Cone," *Revista de Historia Económica – Journal of Iberian and Latin American Economic History* 28(2): 307–41.

24 Coatsworth, J. (2005), "Structures, Endowments, and Institutions in the Economic History of Latin America," *Latin American Research Review* 40(3): 126–44.

25 Rodríguez Weber, J. (2018), "High Inequality in Latin America: Since When and Why?," MPRA Paper 87619; and Bulmer-Thomas, V. (1987), *The Political Economy of Central America since 1920*, Cambridge: Cambridge University Press.

26 OECD (2011), "An Overview of Growing Income Inequalities in OECD Countries: Main Findings," in *Divided We Stand: Why Inequality Keeps Rising*, Paris: OECD.

27 UNDP (2015), *Humanity Divided: Confronting Inequality in Developing Countries*, New York: UNDP. The increase in inequality is calculated based on a population-weighted average of all developing countries for which data is available.

28 Hsu, S. (2016), "High Inequality Still Festering in China," *Forbes*, November 18, https://www.forbes.com/sites/sarahsu/2016/11/18/high-income-inequality-still-festering-in-china/#28a8ae251e50

29 Chancel, L., and T. Piketty (2017), "Indian Income Inequality, 1922–2015: From British Raj to Billionaire Raj?," WID Working Paper 2017/11.

30 For China, see Ambler, P. (2017), "Where Young Chinese Billionaires are Making Their Wealth and Spending It," *Forbes*, October 30, https://www.forbes.com/sites/pamelaambler/2017/10/30/where-young-chinese-billionaires-are-making-their-wealth-and-spending-it/#16417fcd7fb6. For India, Crabtree, J. (2018), *The Billionaire Raj: A Journey Through India's New Gilded Age*, London: Tim Duggan; and Patnaik, P. (2018), "Why is India's Wealth Inequality Growing So Rapidly?," *Aljazeera*, January 28, https://www.aljazeera.com/indepth/opinion/india-wealth-inequality-growing-rapidly-180125084201143.html.

31 Quoted in Roden, L. (2017), "Sweden's Wealth Inequality Exposed by New Research," *The Local*, February 16, https://www.thelocal.se/20170216/ swedens-wealth-inequality-exposed-by-new-research.

32 Turula, T. (2017), "The Number of Millionaires in Sweden and Norway is Growing Fast," *Business Insider*, October 3, https://www.businessinsider. com/the-number-of-millionaires-in-sweden-and-norway-is-growing-fast-2017-10?r=US&IR=T.

Chapter 3

1 Mankiw, N.G. (2013), "Defending the One Percent," *Journal of Economic Perspectives* 27: 21–34.

2 Bértola and Williamson, "Globalization in Latin America before 1940".

3 Ossenbach Sauter, G. (1993), "Estado y educación en América Latina a partir de su independencia (siglos XIX y XX)," *Revista Iberoamericana de Educación*, https://rieoei.org/historico/oeivirt/rie01a04.htm.

4 Bulmer-Thomas, V. (2014), *The Economic History of Latin America Since Independence*, Cambridge: Cambridge University Press, 3rd edition, chapter 5.

5 Ibid., p. 140.

6 Ibid.

7 World Bank, *Inequality in Latin America*, p. 117.

8 Gvirtz, S., and J. Beech (2008), *Going to School in Latin America*, Westport, CT: Greenwood.

9 Ibid., p. 186.

10 Frankema, E. (2009), *Has Latin America Always Been Unequal?* Leiden: Brill, p. 104.

11 Ibid.

12 Gómez, K. (2016), "Las universidades que producen más millonarios, una es mexicana," *Dinero en Imagen*, August 30, https://www.dineroenimagen. com/2016-08-30/77316.

13 Tecnológico de Monterrey, "Our History," https://tec.mx/en/about-us/ our-history, and ITAM, "Historia del ITAM," https://www.itam.mx/es/ historia-del-itam.

14 McGuire, J. (2014), "The Politics of Development in Latin America and East Asia," in C. Lancaster and N. Van Der Walle (eds), *Oxford Handbook of the Politics of Development*, Oxford: Oxford University Press, pp. 567–95.

15 Jones, H. (2017), *Breaking the Intergenerational Cycle of Poverty? Young People's Long-Term Trajectories in Brazil's Bolsa Família Programme*, DPhil thesis, Oxford Department of International Development, University of Oxford, quotes from pp. 107, 115.

16 Ibid., p. 126.

17 Rivas, A. (2015), *América Latina después de PISA: Lecciones aprendidas de la educación en siete países (2000–2015)*, Buenos Aires: CIPPEC Instituto Natura.

18 UNESCO (2014), *Regional Report about Education for All in Latin America and the Caribbean*, Santiago: UNESCO, http://www.unesco.org/new/fileadmin/MULTIMEDIA/HQ/ED/ED_new/pdf/LAC-GEM-2014-ENG.pdf.

19 Sehnbruch, K. (2006), *The Chilean Labor Market: A Key to Understanding Latin American Labor Markets*, London: Palgrave Macmillan.

20 Schneider, B. (2013), *Hierarchical Capitalism in Latin America: Business, Labor, and the Challenges of Equitable Development*, New York: Cambridge University Press.

21 See, for example, a discussion of the network of Argentinian secondary schools at Infobae (2013), "Colegios secundarios de excelencia: dónde se forma la elite," February 16, https://www.infobae.com/2013/02/16/696783-colegios-secundarios-excelencia-donde-se-forma-la-elite/.

22 Economía Hoy (2014), "Tres colegios latinoamericanos entre los mejores del mundo," November 22, https://www.economiahoy.mx/rankings-eAm-mexico/noticias/6254276/11/14/Tres-colegios-latinoamericanos-entre-los-mejores-del-mundo.html.

23 https://checkinprice.com/average-minimum-salary-in-sao-paulo-brazil/ and http://www.stpauls.br/about-us.

24 https://www.newton.edu.pe/index.html.

25 Wolff, L., and C. de Moura Castro (2003), "Education and Training: The Task Ahead," in J. Williamson and C. Moura Castro (eds), *After the Washington Consensus*, Washington, DC: IIE, pp. 181–210. At the university level, many leave their own countries and go to the United States. The list of the richest men in Latin America reads like a who's who of the best universities, particularly in the United States. In Central America alone, the Nicaraguan Carlos Pellas and the Salvadorean Ricardo Poma—both worth more than US$1 billion—studied in Stanford and Princeton, while others went to Texas, New York, and Europe. See Pantaleón, I. (2017), "¿Dónde estudiaron los millonarios de Centroamérica?," *Forbes México*, https://www.forbes.com.mx/donde-estudiaron-los-millonarios-de-centroamerica/.

26 For Chile, see Sánchez-Ancochea, D. (2017), "The Political Economy of Inequality at the Top in Contemporary Chile," in L. Bértola and J. Williamson (eds), *Has Latin American Inequality Changed Direction?*, New York: Springer, pp. 339–63, and the bibliography included there.

27 Rebossio, A. (2013), "La concentración económica en Latinoamérica," *El País*, March 2, http://blogs.elpais.com/eco-americano/2013/03/la-concentración-económica-en-latinoamérica.html.

28 Schneider, *Hierarchical Capitalism in Latin America*, p. 45.

29 Alarco, G., and P. del Hierro (2010), "Crecimiento y concentración de los principales grupos empresariales en México," *Revista de la Cepal* 101: 179–97.

30 Rebossio, "La concentración económica en Latinoamérica."
31 Fazio, H. (1999), *La transnacionalización de la economía chilena: Mapa de la extrema riqueza al año 2000*, Santiago: LOM; and Ruiz, C., and G. Boccardo (2010), "Problemas sociales de la concentración económica (vistos desde la crisis)," *Análisis del año* 12: 31–53.
32 We should remember that Slim's wealth is primarily a result of the privatization of TELMEX, which left the Mexican government without a major asset and gave Slim a "gold mine." Other Mexican billionaires also owe their wealth to close links to the state: Ricardo Salinas Pliego is the owner of several TV channels and Germán Larrea and Alberto Baillères received several mining concessions. See "Las clases de la clase alta," *Chilango*, October 24, 2018, https://www.chilango.com/noticias/reportajes/las-clases-de-la-clase-alta/.
33 Carmona, E. (2002), *Los dueños de Chile*, Santiago: La Huella.
34 Family business groups in Latin America still specialize in traditional sectors. According to a recent study of eight Latin American countries (and Spain), their sales come primarily from trade (31 percent), food and beverage processing (24 percent), mining (11 percent), and financial services (9 percent). See Fernández Pérez, P., and A. Lluch (2015), *Familias empresarias y grandes empresas familiares en América Latina y España: Una visión de largo plazo*, Bilbao: Fundación BBVA.
35 Meller, P., and J. Gana (2016), "Perspectives on Latin American Technological Innovation," in A. Foxley and B. Stallings (eds), *Innovation and Inclusion in Latin America: Strategies to Avoid the Middle-Income Trap*, London: Palgrave Macmillan, pp. 91–117.
36 World Bank (2014), *El emprendimiento en América Latina: Muchas empresas y poca innovación*, Washington, DC: World Bank.
37 World Bank (2013), "Latin America: Entrepreneurs' Lack of Innovation Curbs Creation of Quality Job," *World Bank News*, http://www.worldbank.org/en/news/feature/2013/12/05/latin-america-many-entrepreneurs-little-innovation-growth.
38 Fernández Pérez and Lluch, *Familias empresarias y grandes empresas familiares*, p. 96. All quotations from Spanish sources in the book have been translated by the author.
39 Infante, R., and O. Sunkel (2009), "Chile: Towards Inclusive Growth," *ECLAC Review* 97: 133–52.
40 Islam, A. (2014), "Do Latin American Firms Invest in R&D?," http://blogs.worldbank.org/developmenttalk/do-latin-american-firms-invest-rd.
41 Meller and Gana, "Perspectives on Latin American Technological Innovation."
42 The discussion on Chile comes from Fairfield, T. (2010), "Business Power and Tax Reform: Taxing Income and Profits in Chile and Argentina," *Latin American Politics and Society* 52(2): 37–71.
43 Fairfield, T. (2015), *Private Wealth and Public Revenue in Latin America: Business Power and Tax Politics*, Cambridge: Cambridge University Press.

44 López, R. (2011), "Fiscal Policy in Chile: Promoting Faustian Growth?," Working Paper 11-01, University of Maryland.
45 López, R., and S. Miller (2008), "Chile: The Unbearable Burden of Inequality," *World Development* 36(12): 2679–95.
46 Fairfield and Jorratt, "Top Income Shares, Business Profits and Effective Tax Rates."
47 Sánchez-Ancochea and Morgan, *The Political Economy of the Public Budget in the Americas.*
48 Gómez, J. (2006), "Evolución y situación tributaria actual en América Latina: una serie de temas para la discusión," in CEPAL (2006), *Tributación en América Latina: En busca de una nueva agenda de reformas,* Santiago: CEPAL.
49 Cornia, G.A. (2014), *Falling Inequality in Latin America: Policy Changes and Lessons,* Oxford: Oxford University Press for UN-WIDER.
50 According to a 2016 UN report, taxes contributed to a 17 percent reduction of inequality in OECD countries, but a negligible 3 percent reduction in Latin America. See Bárcena, A., and A. Prado (2016), *El imperativo de la igualdad: Por un desarrollo sostenible en América Latina y el Caribe,* Buenos Aires: Siglo Veintiuno.
51 CEPAL and Oxfam (2016), "Tributación para un crecimiento inclusivo," https://repositorio.cepal.org/bitstream/handle/11362/39949/S1600238_es.pdf, p. 11.
52 Oxfam (2014), "Justicia fiscal para reducir la desigualdad en Latinoamérica y el Caribe," https://cdn2.hubspot.net/hubfs/426027/Oxfam-Website/oi-informes/bp-LAC-fiscal-justice-100914-es.pdf.
53 CEPAL and Oxfam (2016), "Tributación para un crecimiento inclusivo."
54 Ibid.
55 Ibid.
56 Oxfam, "Justicia fiscal para reducir la desigualdad en Latinoamérica y el Caribe."
57 Oxfam Intermón (2018), "El fenómeno de la captura: Desenmascarando el poder," https://www.oxfamintermon.org/sites/default/files/documentos/files/OXFAM_Intermon_Metodolog%C3%ADa_captura_2018.pdf; and Cañete, R. (2018), "Democracias capturadas: El gobierno de unos pocos," https://oxfamilibrary.openrepository.com/bitstream/handle/10546/620600/rr-captured-democracies-16118-summ-es.pdf?sequence=2&isAllowed=y.
58 "Odebrecht pagó irregularmente $3 mil millones para campañas políticas en Latinoamérica," *Aristegui Noticias,* March 7, 2017, https://aristeguinoticias.com/0703/mundo/odebrecht-pago-irregularmente-3-mil-millones-para-campanas-politicas-en-latinoamerica/.
59 Cañete, "Democracias capturadas."
60 ILO (2018), *Women and Men in the Informal Economy: A Statistical Picture,* 3rd edition, Geneva: ILO.
61 Martínez Franzoni, J., and D. Sanchez-Ancochea (2013), *Good Jobs and Social Services: How Costa Rica Achieved the Elusive Double Incorporation,*

New York: Palgrave Macmillan; Sandbrook, R., M. Edelman, P. Heller, and J. Teichman (2007), *Social Democracy in the Global Periphery: Origins, Challenges, Prospects*, Cambridge: Cambridge University Press; and Mkandawire, T. (ed.) (2004), *Social Policy in a Development Context*, London: Palgrave Macmillan.

62 Bulmer-Thomas, V. (2014), *The Economic History of Latin America Since Independence*, Cambridge: Cambridge University Press, 3rd edition, chapter 11.

63 Simons, M. (1982), "Mexican Peso Devalued for 2nd Time in 6 Months," *New York Times*, August 7, https://www.nytimes.com/1982/08/07/business/mexican-peso-devalued-for-2d-time-in-6-months.html.

64 Bulmer-Thomas, *The Economic History of Latin America Since Independence*, chapter 11.

65 Kaminsky, G., and C. Reinhart (1998), "Financial Crises in Asia and Latin America: Then and Now," *American Economic Review* 88(2): 444–48.

66 Rodrik, D. (2004), "Development Strategies for the 21st Century", in A. Kohsaka (ed.), *New Development Strategies: Beyond the Washington Consensus*, London: Palgrave Macmillan, pp. 13–39, quote from p. 17.

67 Rodrik, D. (1999), "Where Did All the Growth Go? External Shocks, Social Conflict, and Growth Collapses," *Journal of Economic Growth* 4(4): 385–412.

68 Martínez Franzoni and Sánchez-Ancochea, *Good Jobs and Social Services*, p. 11.

69 Ocampo, J.A. (2004), "Latin America's Growth and Equity Frustrations During Structural Reforms," *Journal of Latin American Perspectives* 18(2): 67–88.

70 Psacharopoulos, G., S. Morley, A. Fiszbein, H. Lee, and W.C. Wood (1995), "Poverty and Income Inequality in Latin America During the 1980s," *Review of Income and Wealth* 41(3): 245–64.

71 Psacharopoulos, G., S. Morley, A. Fiszbein, H. Lee, and W.C. Wood (1997), "Poverty and Income Distribution in Latin America: The Story of the 1980s," World Bank Working Paper, Washington, DC: World Bank.

72 Huber, E., and F. Solt (2004), "Successes and Failures of Neoliberalism," *Latin American Research Review* 39(3): 150–64, quote from p. 156.

73 Third World Network, "The Financial Crisis of Latin America and the New International Financial Architecture," https://www.twn.my/title/twr122f.htm.

74 Stiglitz, J. (2012), *The Price of Inequality: How Today's Divided Society Endangers Our Future*, New York: W.W. Norton, p. 3.

75 Hacker and Pierson, *Winner-Take-All Politics*.

76 Scocco, S. (2018), "Why Did the Populist Far Right In Sweden Make Gains?," *Social Europe*, https://www.socialeurope.eu/why-did-the-populist-far-right-in-sweden-make-gains.

77 Kuntz, V. (2016), "Germany's Two-Tier Labor Market," *Handelsblatt Today*, December 9, https://www.handelsblatt.com/today/politics/temporary-workers-germanys-two-tier-labor-market/23540762.html?ticket=ST-1143617-49LVTSkWQr7aG6cjgakd-ap2.

78 OECD (2017), "The Great Divergence(s): The Link between Growing Productivity Dispersion and Wage Inequality," Directorate for Science, Technology and Innovation Policy Note.

79 McCue, T.J. (2018), "57 Million US Workers Are Part Of The Gig Economy," *Forbes*, August 31; and Wilson, B. (2017), "What is the Gig Economy?," BBC News, February 10, https://www.bbc.co.uk/news/business-38930048.

80 Mian, E. (2016), "In Praise of the Gig Economy," *Daily Telegraph*, January 21, https://www.telegraph.co.uk/technology/uber/12086500/In-praise-of-the-gig-economy.html.

81 Landy, B. (2012), "Graph: Did Income Inequality Cause the Financial Crisis?," Century Foundation, https://tcf.org/content/commentary/graph-did-income-inequality-cause-the-financial-crisis/?agreed=1&session=1; Rajan, R. (2010), *Fault Lines: How Hidden Fractures Still Threaten the World Economy*, Princeton, NJ: Princeton University Press; and Van Treeck, T. (2013), "Did Inequality Cause the US Financial Crises?," *Journal of Economic Surveys* 28(3): 421–48.

Chapter 4

1 This description of the 1945 protests is based on James, D. (1988), "October 17th and 18th, 1945: Mass Protest, Peronism, and the Argentine Working Class," *Journal of Social History* 21(3): 421–61.

2 Ibid., p. 449.

3 Inequality has been connected to other negative features of Latin American institutions, including clientelism (through which political parties secure electoral support through individual favors instead of institutionalized policies) and the use of the state as an instrument for wealth accumulation. I thank Salvador Martí for reminding me of both factors. I do not discuss them here because they are less relevant for current political debates, particularly in developed countries, but promise to consider them in future books.

4 See Palma, G. (2011), "Homogeneous Middles vs. Heterogeneous Tails, and the End of the 'Inverted-U': It's All About the Share of the Rich," *Development and Change* 42(1): 87–153.

5 Drake, P. (2009), *Between Tyranny and Anarchy: A History of Democracy in Latin America, 1800–2006*, Stanford, CA: Stanford University Press, chapter 5.

6 Posada-Carbo, E. (1997), "Limits of Power: Elections Under the Conservative Hegemony in Colombia, 1886–1930," *The Hispanic American Historical Review* 77(2): 245–79.

7 Ibid., p.277.

8 Skidmore, T. (2010), *Brazil: Five Centuries of Change*, Oxford: Oxford University Press, p. 140.

9 Drake, *Between Tyranny and Anarchy*, p. 99.

10 Deas, M. (1996), "The Role of the Church, the Army and the Policy in Colombian Elections, c.1850–1930," and Valenzuela, S. (1996), "Building Aspects of Democracy before Democracy: Electoral Practices in Nineteenth Century Chile," both in E. Posada-Carbó (ed.), *Elections before Democracy: The History of Elections in Europe and Latin America*, London: Institute of Latin American Studies.

11 Drake, *Between Tyranny and Anarchy*, table 2.3.

12 Engerman, S., and K. Sokoloff (2002), "Factor Endowments, Inequality, and Paths of Development among New World Economies," *Economía* 3(1): 41–109.

13 Examples from Collier, R., and D. Collier (1991), *Shaping the Political Arena*, Princeton, NJ: Princeton University Press.

14 Arroyo, L., and P. Lindert (2017), "Fiscal Redistribution in Latin America since the Nineteenth Century," in Bértola and Williamson (eds), *Has Latin American Inequality Changed Direction?*, pp. 265–66.

15 Mesa-Lago, C. (1978), *Social Security in Latin America: Pressure Groups, Stratification and Inequality*, Pittsburgh, PA: University of Pittsburgh Press; and Filgueira, F. (2007), "The Latin American Social States: Critical Juncture and Critical Choices," in Y. Bangura (ed.), *Democracy and Social Policy*, New York: Palgrave/UNRISD, pp. 136–63.

16 The account about Quadros comes from Skidmore, *Brazil*, and Barron, J. (1992), "Janio Quadros, 75, Dies; Leader of Brazil Yielded Office in 60's," *New York Times*, February 18.

17 Cited in Dulles, J. (1967), *Vargas of Brazil: A Political Biography*, Austin, TX: University of Texas Press, p. 9.

18 See Skidmore, *Brazil*, and Alexander, R. (1962), *Prophets of the Revolution: Profiles of Latin American Leaders*, New York: Macmillan.

19 Dulles, *Vargas of Brazil*, pp. 334–35.

20 Jorrín, M., and J. Martz (1970), *Latin-American Political Thought and Ideology*, Chapel Hill, NC: University of North Carolina Press, chapter 8.

21 Alexander, *Prophets of the Revolution*.

22 Navarro, M. (1982), "Evita's Charismatic Leadership," in M. Conniff (ed.), *Latin American Populism in Comparative Perspective*, Alburquerque, NM: New Mexico University Press, pp. 47–67.

23 Tamarin, D. (1982), "Yrigoyen and Perón: The Limits of Argentine Populism," in Conniff (ed.), *Latin American Populism in Comparative Perspective*, p. 41.

24 Mainwaring, S., and A. Pérez-Liñán (2013), *Democracies and Dictatorships in Latin America: Emergence, Survival and Fall*, Cambridge: Cambridge University Press.

25 Levitsky, S., and D. Ziblatt (2018), *How Democracies Die: What History Reveals About Our Future*, New York: Penguin.

26 Mainwaring and Pérez-Liñán, *Democracies and Dictatorships in Latin America*, p. 136.

27 The term "populism" has been used to characterize two different features of politics during this period. The first refers to a political movement led by a charismatic leader who developed a nationalist discourse and benefited from support from urban workers (at times in alliance with industrialists). The second refers to a specific kind of political discourse which emphasizes the direct appeal to the "people" without any intermediation. See Cammack, P. (2000), "The Resurgence of Populism in Latin America," *Bulletin of Latin American Research* 19(2): 149–61. Note that both of these features resulted from Latin America's inequality and the previous lack of political representation of the working majority.

28 Knight, A. (1994), "Cardenismo: Juggernaut or Jalopy?," *Journal of Latin American Studies* 26(1): 73–107; see especially pp. 80, 84.

29 "The Return of Populism," *Economist*, April 16, 2006, https://www. economist.com/the-americas/2006/04/12/the-return-of-populism.

30 De la Torre, C. (1994), "Velasco Ibarra and 'La Revolución Gloriosa': The Social Production of a Populist Leader in Ecuador in the 1940s," *Journal of Latin American Studies* 26(3): 683–711.

31 De la Torre, C. (1997), "Populism and Democracy: Political Discourses and Cultures in Contemporary Ecuador," *Latin American Perspectives* 24(3): 12–24.

32 Stein, S. (1982), "Populism in Peru: APRA, The Formative Years," in Conniff (ed.), *Latin American Populism in Comparative Perspective*, pp. 113–34.

33 Haya de la Torre, V. (1945), "El gran desafío de la democracia," lecture in the Municipal Theater of Lima, October 6, text at https://www.scribd.com/ doc/59039390/1945-Haya-de-la-Torre-El-gran-desafio-de-la-democracia, translation by the author.

34 Tamarin, "Yrigoyen and Perón," p. 42.

35 Drake, *Between Tyranny and Anarchy*, p. 192.

36 Allende, S. (1973), "The Last Speech in Radio Magallanes," text at https:// en.wikisource.org/wiki/Salvador_Allende%27s_Last_Speech.

37 O'Brien, P., and J. Roddick (1983), *Chile: The Pinochet Decade: The Rise and Fall of the Chicago Boys*, London: Latin American Bureau.

38 Drake, *Between Tyranny and Anarchy*, p. 164.

39 This discussion relies primarily on Grieb, K. (1976), "The Guatemalan Military and the Revolution of 1944," *The Americas* 32(4): 524–43.

40 Handy, J. (1994), *Revolution in the Countryside: Rural Conflict and Agrarian Reform in Guatemala, 1944–1954*, Chapel Hill, NC: University of North Carolina Press.

41 Ibid. p. 38.

42 Ibid., p. 33.

43 Drake, *Between Tyranny and Anarchy*, p. 166.

44 Most international institutions and 61 percent of Hondurans agreed that Zelaya's removal from office constituted a coup. See: Pérez, O., J. Booth, and M. Seligson (2010), "The Honduran 'Catharsis,'" *Americas Barometer Insights* 45.

45 Ruhl, J. (2010), "Trouble in Central America: Honduras Unravels," *Journal of Democracy* 21(2): 93–107.

46 Hetherington, K. (2012), "Paraguay's Ongoing Struggle Over Land and Democracy," *NACLA Report on the Americas* 45(3): 8–10.

47 Ezquerro-Cañete, A., and R. Fogel (2017), "A Coup Foretold: Fernando Lugo and the Lost Promise of Agrarian Reform in Paraguay," *Journal of Agrarian Change* 17(2): 279–95.

48 Szucs, R. (2014), "A Democracy's Poor Performance: The Impeachment of Paraguayan President Fernando Lugo," *George Washington International Law Review* 46: 409–36.

49 Drake, *Between Tyranny and Anarchy*, p. 199.

50 Smith, P. (2005), *Democracy in Latin America: Political Change in Comparative Perspective*, Oxford: Oxford University Press.

51 Collier, R. (1999), *Paths Toward Democracy: The Working Class and Elites in Western Europe and Latin America*, Cambridge: Cambridge University Press.

52 Examples from Bartell, E., and L. Payne (1995), *Business and Democracy in Latin America*, Pittsburgh, PA: Pittsburgh University Press.

53 Paige, J. (1998), *Coffee and Power: Revolution and the Rise of Democracy in Central America*, Cambridge, MA: Harvard University Press.

54 Weyland, K. (2004), "Neoliberalism and Democracy in Latin America: A Mixed Record," *Latin American Politics and Society* 46(1): 135–57.

55 Drake, *Between Tyranny and Anarchy*, p. 205.

56 Examples from Grugel, J., and P. Riggirozzi (2012), "Post-neoliberalism in Latin America: Rebuilding and Reclaiming the State after Crisis," *Development and Change* 43(1): 1–21.

57 Encarnación, O. (2018), "The Rise and Fall of the Latin American Left," *Nation*, May 9, https://www.thenation.com/article/the-ebb-and-flow-of-latin-americas-pink-tide/.

58 Data from Roberts, K. (2003), "Social Correlates of Party System Demise and Populist Resurgence in Venezuela," *Latin American Politics and Society* 45(3): 35–57.

59 Comás, J. (2002), "Hugo Chávez: 'El neoliberalismo es el camino que conduce al infierno,'" *El País*, May 17, https://elpais.com/diario/2002/05/17/internacional/1021586404_850215.html; and Fair, H. (2013), "La revolución democrática en el discurso de Hugo Chávez (1999–2002)," *Textos e Debates Boa Vista* 23: 53–67.

60 Steve Ellner offered an informative evaluation of the contradictory record of Chávez's social programs in his 2017 article "Social Programs in Venezuela Under the Chavista Governments." See https://thenextsystem.org/learn/stories/social-programs-venezuela-under-chavista-governments#footnoteref3_ageiws1.

61 The MAS and its global relevance as a party-movement are discussed in more detail in Chapter 6.

62 Rico, M. (2005), "Victoria arrolladora de Evo Morales," *El País*, December 20, https://elpais.com/diario/2005/12/20/internacional/1135033202_850215.html.

63 Farthing, L. (2017), "Evo's Bolivia: The Limits of Change," https://
thenextsystem.org/learn/stories/evos-bolivia-limits-
change#footnote6_13taebf.

64 IMF (2016), "IMF Executive Board Concludes 2016 Article IV
Consultation with Bolivia," https://www.imf.org/en/News/
Articles/2016/12/22/PR16577-Bolivia-IMF-Executive-Board-Concludes-
2016-Article-IV-Consultation.

65 Reuters (2016), "Bolivia's Morales Says He May Run for Fourth Term
despite Referendum Loss," December 18, https://www.reuters.com/article/
us-bolivia-politics-morales/bolivias-morales-says-he-may-run-for-fourth-
term-despite-referendum-loss-idUSKBN14802G.

66 Encarnación, "The Rise and Fall of the Latin American Left."

67 In Argentina, the conservative Mauricio Macri only lasted four years in
power, in which he failed to promote economic growth and secure
macroeconomic stability. In the 2019 elections, Macri was replaced by the
Peronist Alberto Fernández, with the former president Cristina Kirschner
as his vice-president.

68 Gethin, A., and M. Morgan (2017), "Brazil Divided: Hindsights on the
Growing Politicisation of Inequality," *World Inequality Lab Policy Brief*
2018/3.

69 BBC Mundo (2010), "El legado de los ocho años de Lula en el poder,"
December 27, https://www.bbc.com/mundo/noticias/2010/12/101214_
lula_fin_periodo_presidencial.

70 Encarnación, O. (2017), "The Patriarchy's Revenge: How Retro-Macho
Politics Doomed Dilma Rousseff," *World Policy Journal* 34(1): 82–91.

71 Sanchez-Ancochea, D. (2018), "Bolsonaro, nuevo traspié para la democracia
en América," *Agenda Pública*, http://agendapublica.elpais.com/bolsonaro-
nuevo-traspie-para-la-democracia-en-america/.

72 Llaneras, K. (2018), "Bolsonaro arrasa en ciudades blancas y ricas: un mapa
del voto en 5.500 municipios," *El País*, October 25, https://elpais.com/
internacional/2018/10/23/actualidad/1540291997_116759.html.

73 Zovatto, D. (2017), "El financiamiento político en América Latina," *Studia
Politicae* 40: 7–52.

74 Boas, T. (2013), "Mass Media and Politics in Latin America," in J.
Domínguez and M. Shifter (eds), *Constructing Democratic Governance in
Latin America*, 4th edition, Baltimore, MD: Johns Hopkins University
Press, pp. 48–78.

75 González, P. (2013), "Guatemala," in D. Sánchez-Ancochea and S. Martí (eds),
Handbook of Central American Governance, London: Routledge, p. 405.

76 Eliana Cardoso, E., and A. Helwege (1992), "Populism, Profligacy and
Redistribution," in R. Dornbusch and S. Edwards (eds), *The
Macroeconomics of Populism in Latin America*, Chicago: University of
Chicago Press, pp. 45–70.

77 Bresser Pereira, L.C. (1991), "Populism and Economic Policy in Brazil,"
Journal of Interamerican Studies and World Affairs 33(2): 1–21, p. 7.

78 This point has been consistently advanced by Ben Phillips, co-founder of the Fighting Inequality Alliance, https://www.fightinequality.org/. For Ben Phillips's presentation on the role of social movements in the reduction of inequality, see https://www.youtube.com/watch?v=RrtmziaJBIc&t=176.

79 De la Torre, C. (2014), "La promesa y los riesgos del populismo," *El País*, August 13, https://elpais.com/internacional/2014/08/14/ actualidad/1407971608_590649.html.

80 Benites, A. (2014), "Report Says Brazil's Dictatorship Was Responsible for 421 Deaths," *El País*, November 14, https://elpais.com/elpais/2014/11/14/ inenglish/1415985145_550698.html.

81 See Palma, "Homogeneous Middles vs. Heterogeneous Tails".

82 Gaulard, M. (2011), "Balance sobre la cuestión de la desigualdad en Brasil," *Problemas del Desarrollo* 166(42): 111–34.

83 Human Rights Watch (2010), *Después del Golpe de Estado: Continúan la violencia, la intimidación y la impunidad en Honduras*, https://www.hrw. org/sites/default/files/reports/honduras1210spWebVersion_1.pdf.

84 Johnson, J., and S. Lefebvre (2013), *Honduras Since the Coup: Economic and Social Outcomes*, Washington, DC: Center for Economic and Policy Research, http://cepr.net/documents/publications/Honduras-2013-11-final.pdf.

85 Piketty, T. (2018), "Brahmin Left vs Merchant Right: Rising Inequality and the Changing Structure of Political Conflict (Evidence from France, Britain and the US, 1948–2017)," WID.world Working Paper Series, 2018/7.

86 "Transcript: Donald Trump Victory Speech," *New York Times*, November 9, 2016, https://www.nytimes.com/2016/11/10/us/politics/trump-speech-transcript.html.

87 "France's Le Pen Says the People Revolting against the Elite," *Dayton Daily News*, April 25, 2017, https://www.daytondailynews.com/news/france-pen-says-the-people-revolting-against-the-elite/PnNOnT28n0CDlRJZiX62pN/.

88 Levitsky and Ziblatt, *How Democracies Die*.

89 Bershidsky, L. (2018), "Orban's Economic Model Is Trump's Dream," *Bloomberg*, April 13, https://www.bloomberg.com/opinion/articles/ 2018-04-13/orban-s-economic-model-in-hungary-is-trump-s-dream.

90 Velasco, A. (2018), "Populism Is Rooted in Politics, not Economics," *Project Syndicate*, https://www.project-syndicate.org/commentary/political-not-economic-roots-of-populism-by-andres-velasco-2018-11.

91 Kulwin, N. (2018), "Steve Bannon on How 2008 Planted the Seed for the Trump Presidency," *New York Magazine*, August 10.

Chapter 5

1 "Inequality . . . in a Photograph," *Guardian*, November 29, 2017, https:// www.theguardian.com/cities/2017/nov/29/sao-paulo-injustice-tuca-vieira-inequality-photograph-paraisopolis.

2 World Bank (2014), "Está demostrado: con menos desigualdad se tiene menos crimen," http://www.bancomundial.org/es/news/feature/2014/09/03/latinoamerica-menos-desigualdad-se-reduce-el-crimen.

3 Muggah, R., and K. Aguirre (2018), *Citizen Security in Latin America: Facts and Figures*, Rio de Janeiro: Igarapé Institute, p. 10.

4 Szalavitz, M. (2017), "The Surprising Factors Driving Murder Rates: Income Inequality and Respect," *Guardian*, December 8, https://www.theguardian.com/us-news/2017/dec/08/income-inequality-murder-homicide-rates.

5 Sánchez Inzunza, A., and J.L. Pardo Veiras (2017), "¿Por qué en América Latina se mata más?," *New York Times*, June 4, https://www.nytimes.com/es/2017/06/04/por-que-en-america-latina-se-mata-mas/?rref=collection%2Fsectioncollection%2Fnyt-es.

6 Muggah and Aguirre, *Citizen Security in Latin America*, p. 9.

7 Chioada, L. (2017), *Stop the Violence in Latin America: A Look at Prevention from Cradle to Adulthood*, Washington, DC: World Bank.

8 Perlman, J. (2006), "The Metamorphosis of Marginality: Four Generations in the Favelas of Rio de Janeiro," *Annals of the American Academy of Political and Social Science* 606: 154–77. See also Perlman (2010), *Favelas: Four Decades of Living on the Edge of Rio de Janeiro*, Oxford: Oxford University Press.

9 Levenson, D. (2013), *Adios Niño*, Ithaca, NY: Cornell University Press, p. 67.

10 Ibid., p. 78.

11 "El Salvador: Homicidios intencionados," https://datosmacro.expansion.com/demografia/homicidios/el-salvador; and Caldentey, D. (2016), "El Salvador ya iguala en cifras de muertes violentas a las víctimas de la guerra siria," *La Información*, March 9.

12 Rodgers, D., and R. Muggah (2009), "Gangs as Non-state Armed Groups: the Central American Case," *Contemporary Security Policy* 30(2): 301–17.

13 Segovia, A. (2018), *Economía y poder: Recomposición de las élites económicas salvadoreñas*, San Salvador: F&E, p. 8.

14 Moodie, E. (2012), *El Salvador in the Aftermath of Peace*, Philadelphia, PA: University of Pennsylvania Press, p. 40.

15 Levenson, *Adios Niño*, p. 95.

16 Denyer Willis, G. (2015), *The Killing Consensus: Police, Organized Crime, and the Regulation of Life and Death in Urban Brazil*, Berkeley, CA, and London: University of California Press, p. 9.

17 Levenson, *Adios Niño*, p. 105.

18 Caldeira, T. (2000), *City of Walls: Crime, Segregation and Citizenship in São Paulo*, Berkeley, CA, and London: University of California Press, p. 137.

19 Desmond Arias, E., and D. Goldstein (eds) (2010), *Violent Democracies in Latin America*, Durham, NC: Duke University Press, pp. 201–26.

20 Pardo Veiras, J.L., and A. Sánchez Inzunza (2017), "Los policías de Rio de Janeiro: Servir, proteger, matar y morir," *New York Times*, July 19, https://www.nytimes.com/es/2017/07/10/los-policias-de-rio-de-janeiro-servir-proteger-matar-y-morir/?rref=collection%2Fsectioncollection%2Fnyt-es.

21 Rodgers and Muggah, "Gangs as Non-state Armed Groups."

22 Muggah and Aguirre, *Citizen Security in Latin America.*

23 Gender Observatory for Latin America and the Caribbean, "Femicide or Feminicide," https://oig.cepal.org/en/indicators/femicide-or-feminicide.

24 Christian Aid (2017), *El escándalo de la desigualdad 2: Las múltiples caras de la desigualdad en América Latina y el Caribe,* London: Christian Aid.

25 Gender Observatory for Latin America and the Caribbean, "Femicide or Feminicide."

26 "En 25 años van 1,779 feminicidios en Ciudad Juárez," *Heraldo de México,* February 15, 2018.

27 CEPAL (2019), "In 2018, At Least 3,529 Women Were Victims of Femicide in 25 Latin American and Caribbean Countries," press release, https://www.cepal.org/en/pressreleases/2018-least-3529-women-were-victims-femicide-25-latin-american-and-caribbean-countries.

28 Christian Aid, *El escándalo de la desigualdad 2.*

29 Boamo, C., and B. Desmaison (2016), "A Wall in Lima Explains Latin America's Gated-community Problem," *The Conversation,* February 11, https://theconversation.com/limas-wall-of-shame-and-the-gated-communities-that-build-poverty-into-peru-53356; and see https://www.youtube.com/watch?v=mfFoYq5p0co.

30 Caldeira, T. (1996), "Building Up Walls: The New Pattern of Spatial Segregation in São Paulo," *International Social Science Journal* 48(1): 55–66.

31 Caldeira, "Building Up Walls."

32 All quotes from Bayón, M.C., G. Saraví, and M. Ortega Breña (2013), "The Cultural Dimensions of Urban Fragmentation: Segregation, Sociability, and Inequality in Mexico City," *Latin American Perspectives* 40(2): 35–52. The names they use are not the real ones.

33 Bayón, Saraví, and Ortega Breña, "The Cultural Dimensions of Urban Fragmentation," p. 43.

34 Ibid., p. 47.

35 Ibid., p. 45.

36 Ibid., p. 48.

37 Perlman, "The Metamorphosis of Marginality."

38 Lépore, E., and S. Simpson Lapp (2018), "Concentrated Poverty and Neighbourhood Effects: Youth Marginalisation in Buenos Aires' Informal Settlements," *Oxford Development Studies* 46(1): 28–44.

39 Caldeira, "Building Up Walls," p. 64.

40 The following discussion relies on my previous work on the subject together with Juliana Martínez Franzoni from the University of Costa Rica. See, in particular, "The Relationship between Universal Social Policy and Inequality: A Comparative Political Economy Approach," UNDP Working Paper, 2019; "Achieving Universalism in Developing Countries," 2016 UNDP Human Development Report Background Paper, 2016; and "Undoing Segmentation? Latin American Health Care Policy During the Economic Boom," *Social Policy and Administration* 52(6): 1181–1200, 2018.

41 "Salud: tendencias e innovación, un debate que reunió a los protagonistas del sector," *Infobae*, December 6, 2018, https://www.infobae.com/salud/2018/12/06/salud-tendencias-e-innovacion-un-debate-que-reunio-a-los-protagonistas-del-sector.

42 Larrañaga, O., and M.E. Rodríguez (2014), "Clases medias y educación en América Latina," PNUD-Chile Working Paper, July.

43 Arcidiácono, M., G. Cruces, L. Gasparini, D. Jaume, M. Serio, and E. Vázquez (2014), "La segregación escolar público-privado en América Latina," CEDLAS Working Paper 167, p. 21.

44 Nogueira, K. (2018), "VÍDEO: na Câmara, Bolsonaro defendeu esterilização dos pobres," *DCM*, June 11, https://www.diariodocentrodomundo.com.br/video-na-camara-bolsonaro-defendeu-esterilizacao-dos-pobres/.

45 Queirolo, R., M.F. Boidi, and M. Seligson (2013), *Cultura política de la democracia en Uruguay y en las Américas, 2012: Hacia la igualdad de oportunidades*, USAID funded report, Vanderbilt University.

46 See her TED talk in Bahía Blanca (Argentina) on August 22, 2018, at https://www.youtube.com/watch?v=4JDu69Jy41Y.

47 Inter-American Development Bank (2019), "How Trust Impacts your Quality of Life," https://www.iadb.org/en/improvinglives/how-does-trust-impact-your-quality-life.

48 Perlman, "The Metamorphosis of Marginality," p. 174. See also Perlman, *Favelas*.

49 Latinobarómetro (2018), *Informe 2018*, Santiago of Chile.

50 Mafalda is probably the most popular Latin American cartoon character. Created by Joaquín Salvador Lavado Tejón "Quino," she comes from a progressive middle-class family in Buenos Aires, hates soup, and is concerned with the future of humanity and world peace. The cartoon described in the text is available at http://www.unitedexplanations. org/2013/06/18/las-35-mejores-vinetas-de-mafalda-de-satira-politica/.

51 Latinobarómetro (2018), *Informe 2018*, Santiago. The situation is particularly worrying in the two largest Latin American countries, Brazil and Mexico, where only one in ten people believe that the government rules for the benefit of everyone.

52 Hilbink, L., J. Gallagher, J. Restrepo Sanin, and V. Salas (2019). "Engaging Justice amidst Inequality in Latin America," https://www.openglobalrights. org/engaging-justice-amidst-inequality-in-latin-america/.

53 Viga Gaier, R. (2019), "Brazil's Bolsonaro Says Democracy, Liberty Depend on Military," Reuters, March 7, https://www.reuters.com/article/us-brazil-politics/brazils-bolsonaro-says-democracy-liberty-depend-on-military-idUSKCN1QO2AT.

54 Spinetto, J.P., and B. Douglas (2019), "Military Revival in Latin America Stirs Unease over Past Abuses," *Bloomberg*, January 30, https://www. bloomberg.com/news/articles/2019-01-30/military-revival-in-latin-america-stirs-unease-over-past-abuses.

55 "Ejército, decisivo para pacificar al país: AMLO," *La Razón*, February 19, 2019, https://www.razon.com.mx/mexico/amlo-ejercito-fuerzas-armadas-guardia-nacional-celebracion-dia-coahuila-inseguridad-violencia; and Pérez, A.L. (2018), "Guardia Nacional militarizada: un 'error colosal' de AMLO, dicen expertos," *Newsweek en español*, November 25, https://newsweekespanol.com/2018/11/guardia-nacional-militarizada-amlo/.

56 Spinetto and Douglas, "Military Revival in Latin America Stirs Unease."

57 Muggah and Aguirre, *Citizen Security in Latin America*.

58 World Bank (2018), *Afro-descendants in Latin America: Toward a Framework of Inclusion*, Washington, DC: World Bank.

59 Hasenbalg, C. (1996), "Racial Inequalities in Brazil and throughout Latin America: Timid Responses to Disguised Racism," in E. Jelin and E. Hershberg (eds), *Constructing Democracy: Human Rights, Citizenship and Society in Latin America*, Oxford: Westview Press, chapter 9; and Telles, E. (2014), *Pigmentocracies: Ethnicity, Race and Color in Latin America*, Chapel Hill, NC: University of North Carolina Press.

60 Levenson, *Adios Niño*, p. 13.

61 Vasconcelos, J. (1948 [1925]), *La Raza Cósmica*, Mexico City: Espasa Calpe Mexicana, p. 30.

62 Telles, *Pigmentocracies*.

63 Morrison, J. (2015), "Behind the Numbers: Race and Ethnicity in Latin America," *Americas Quarterly*, Summer, https://www.americasquarterly. org/fulltextarticle/behind-the-numbers-race-and-ethnicity-in-latin-america/#:~:text=Indigenous%20and%20Afro%2Ddescendant%20 peoples,the%20poorest%20of%20the%20poor.

64 In 2009, the poverty rate for Afro-descendants was 45 percent compared to 20 percent for whites. Data from Queirolo, Boidi, and Seligson, *Cultura política de la democracia en Uruguay y en las Américas, 2012*.

65 Richmond, S., and G. Drinkwater (2018), "Race Matters: The Reality of Inequality in Latin America and the Caribbean," World Economic Forum Blog Series Christian Aid, January 23, https://news.christianaid.org.uk/ race-matters-the-reality-of-inequality-in-latin-america-and-the-caribbean-baabb9a231ee.

66 Zizumbo-Colunga, D., and I. Flores Martínez (2017), "Study Reveals Racial Inequality in Mexico, Disproving its 'Race-blind' Rhetoric," *The Conversation*, December 13. See also Zizumbo-Colunga, D., and I. Flores Martínez (2017), "Is Mexico a Post-Racial Country? Inequality and Skin Tone across the Americas," USAID and Vanderbilt University.

67 Fowks, J. (2018), "El racismo y el clasismo en Perú, ante el espejo," *El País*, September 28; and "¿Qué dijo Saga Falabella por esta publicidad considerada racista?," *Capital*, December 4, 2014.

68 Jones, C. (2019), "La publicidad en México perpetúa el racismo y el clasismo," *Nuevatribuna*, May 5.

69 "Los insultos racistas a Yalitza Aparicio, la actriz indígena nominada a los Oscars por *Roma*," *La Voz de Galicia*, February 21, 2019. *Roma*'s success was celebrated by most in Mexico and the rest of Latin America, partly because of its intelligent treatment of discrimination and ethnic relations in Mexico.

70 Wilkinson and Pickett, *The Spirit Level*, p. 168.

71 This paragraph relies on a discussion in Caumartin, C., and D. Sánchez-Ancochea (2011), "Explaining a Contradictory Record: The Case of Guatemala," in A. Lange, F. Stewart, and R. Venegupal (eds), *Horizontal Inequalities and Post-Conflict Development*, Basingstoke: Palgrave Macmillan, pp. 158–86.

72 Jonas, S. (2000), *Of Centaurs and Doves: Guatemala's Peace Process*, Oxford: Westview Press, chapter 8.

73 "Gobierno interino de Bolivia anunció ruptura de relaciones con Venezuela," *El País de Uruguay*, November 16, 2019, https://www.elpais.com.uy/mundo/gobierno-interino-bolivia-anuncio-ruptura-relaciones-venezuela.html.

74 Alesina, A., and E. Glaeser (2004), *Fighting Poverty in the US and Europe: A World of Difference*, New York: Oxford University Press, p. 134.

75 Sánchez-Ancochea, D. (2020), "Beyond a Single Model: Explaining Differences in Inequality within Latin America," Kellogg Institute Working Paper no. 434.

76 Tuchin, F. (2018), "Las grandes desigualdades del sistema sanitario en Argentina," *El País*, June 13.

77 Izquierdo, A., C. Pessino, and G. Vulletin (2018), *Better Spending for Better Lives: How Latin America and the Caribbean Can Do More with Less*, Washington, DC: Inter-American Development Bank.

78 Watts, J. (2015), "Latin America Leads World on Murder Map, but Key Cities Buck Deadly Trend," *Guardian*, May 6, https://www.theguardian.com/world/2015/may/06/murder-map-latin-america-leads-world-key-cities-buck-deadly-trend.

79 Sánchez Inzunza and Pardo Veiras, "¿Por qué en América Latina se mata más?"

80 Kinosian, S., and J. Bosworth (2018), "Security for Sale: Challenges and Good Practices in Regulating Private Military and Security Companies in Latin America," American Dialogue Rule of Law Program Report, https://www.thedialogue.org/wp-content/uploads/2018/03/Security-for-Sale-FINAL-ENGLISH.pdf.

81 The growth of private security is a particularly worrisome phenomenon. Instead of strengthening the state—and funding proper police investigations—through taxation, the wealthy prefer to spend on individual protection. The state security forces are thus forced to compete for trained staff with private companies, which often pay better. In several countries, the police are also moonlighting in the private sector, further eroding public institutions (and trust).

82 Data from OECD Better Life Index at http://www.oecdbetterlifeindex.org/topics/safety/.

83 Ingraham, C. (2018), "How Rising Inequality Hurts Everyone, even the Rich," *Washington Post*, February 6.

84 Wilkinson and Pickett, *The Spirit Level*; and Metz, N., and M. Burdina (2018), "Neighbourhood Income Inequality and Property Crime," *Urban Studies* 55(1): 133–50.

85 Putman, R. (2001), *Bowling Alone: The Collapse and Revival of the American Community*, New York: Simon & Schuster.

86 See Uslaner, E. (2002), *The Moral Foundations of Trust*, New York: Cambridge University Press; and Rothstein, B. (2018), "How the Trust Trap Perpetuates Inequality," *Scientific American*, November 1, https://www. scientificamerican.com/article/how-the-trust-trap-perpetuates-inequality/.

87 Riley, T. (2012), "The Social Consequences of Inequality," May 13, https:// billmoyers.com/2012/05/13/the-social-consequences-of-inequality/.

88 Alfageme, A (2019), "El negocio de la sanidad privada se dispara tras los recortes en el sistema público," *El País*, January 29.

Chapter 6

1 "Pope Francis Canonises Óscar Romero and Pope Paul VI," *Guardian*, October 14, 2018.

2 The following paragraphs rely in part in Moodie, *El Salvador in the Aftermath of Peace*, pp. 32–33.

3 Maier, M. (2016), "Monseñor Romero y la teología de la liberación," *Revista Latinoamericana de Teología* 99: 201–14.

4 Moodie, *El Salvador in the Aftermath of Peace*, p. 33.

5 The document was first published in Spanish in 1949 with the title "El desarrollo económico de la América Latina y algunos de sus principales problemas." It can be found at https://repositorio.cepal.org/bitstream/ handle/11362/40010/4/prebisch_desarrollo_problemas.pdf. It was published in English by the United Nations one year later with the same title, "Economic Development in Latin America and Some of its Main Problems," https://repositorio.cepal.org/bitstream/handle/11362/ 29973/002_en.pdf?sequence=1&isAllowed=y.

6 Prebisch, R. (2008), "Más allá de la transformación," *Revista de la CEPAL* 96: 27–71, p. 32.

7 "Documento final de Medellín," published in 1968 and available at http:// www.diocese-braga.pt/catequese/sim/biblioteca/publicacoes_online/91/ medellin.pdf.

8 This list only includes men because liberation theology was initially male dominated. It was not until the 1980s that progressive theologians began paying more attention to gender issues and opening more spaces for women thinkers.

9 Vigil, J.M., "La opción por los pobres: Evaluación crítica," http:// servicioskoinonia.org/relat/112.htm.

10 Gutiérrez, G. (1994) [1972], *Teología de la Liberación: Perspectivas*, Salamana: Sígueme, p. 325.
11 Congregation for the Doctrine of the Faith (1984), *Instruction on Certain Aspects of "Theology of Liberation,"* Vatican City.
12 It took the Vatican more than three decades to reverse course. While not formally embracing liberation theology, the Argentinian Pope Francis celebrated mass jointly with Gustavo Gutiérrez, made Óscar Romero a saint, lifted Cardenal's suspension as a priest, and adopted much of its radical pro-poor discourse. See Kirchgaessner, S., and J. Watts (2015), "Catholic Church Warms to Liberation Theology as Founder Heads to Vatican," *Guardian*, May 11. See also the reflections of the Spanish theologian Juan Tamayo on Pope Francis and liberation theology in Tamayo, J.J. (2013), "La teología de la liberación, hoy," *Diario de Córdoba*, September 8.
13 Bentley, L. (1999), "A Brief Biography of Paulo Freire," https://ptoweb.org/aboutpto/a-brief-biography-of-paulo-freire/.
14 Freire, P. (1970) [2000], *The Pedagogy of the Oppressed*, New York: Continuum, p. 72.
15 Freire, P. (1996), *Letters to Cristina: Reflections on my Life and Work*, New York: Routledge, p. 16.
16 Ibid., p. 29.
17 Ibid., p. 118.
18 Schulson, M. (2017), "Fifty Years Later, Religious Progressives Launch a New Poor People's Campaign," *Religion & Politics*, https://religionandpolitics.org/2017/11/27/fifty-years-later-religious-progressives-launch-a-new-poor-peoples-campaign/.
19 Blakeley, G. (2019), "How Millennial Socialism Went Global," *New Statesman*, April 17.
20 https://twitter.com/alfgunvald/status/1119864577120985089?s=11.
21 Of course, periodic opposition to the ruling elite started during colonial times and continued after independence in many countries. The beginning of the twentieth century witnessed the Mexican Revolution and later revolutionary protests across the region. Mythical progressive leaders such as Nicaragua's Augusto Sandino and El Salvador's Farabundo Martí rebelled—and were killed—in the 1930s. Unfortunately, discussing the regional history of social protests and uprisings would require a whole book. Instead, this section focuses on the anti-neoliberal movements, contrasting them with the violent guerrilla response of the previous generation.
22 Crowley-Wickham, T. (2014), "Two 'Waves' of Guerrilla-Movement Organizing in Latin America, 1956–1990," *Comparative Studies in Society and History* 56(1): 215–42.
23 Ruíz Fernández, T. (1977), "El fracaso de la guerrilla en Latinoamérica," *Tiempos de Historia* 30: 84–91.
24 During the 1970s, there were also large guerrilla movements in Colombia and Peru. In Colombia, a conflict that had begun more than a decade

before was intensified, resulting in a long low-intensity civil war. A peace accord between the main guerrilla organization and the government was not signed until 2016 and its ultimate success is still in question. In Peru, *Sendero Luminoso* (Shining Path), a leftist revolutionary movement inspired by Maoist ideas, initially succeeded in weakening the state in the context of an economic crisis. The army's virulent response led to thousands of deaths of innocent peasants, also triggering *Sendero's* further radicalization. The late 1980s and early 1990s were a dark period in Peruvian history, with thousands of people—including social activists and progressive politicians—dying in the crossfire between two extremely violent forces. *Sendero* gradually lost popular support and collapsed after its main leader, Abimael Guzmán, was captured in 1992. Given the weakening of Peruvian democratic institutions, social movements, and progressive political parties, *Sendero's* long-term impact on the fight against inequality was particularly negative. See Burt, J-M. (2007), *Political Violence and the Authoritarian State in Peru: Silencing Civil Society*, London: Palgrave, for a fascinating account of the human rights catastrophe during this period of Peruvian history.

25 Martí, S., and D. Sánchez-Ancochea (2013), "Central America's Triple Transition and the Persistent Power of the Elite," in Sánchez-Ancochea and Martí (eds), *Handbook of Central American Governance*, pp. 4–23.

26 Stronzake, J., and W. Wolford (2016), "Brazil's Landless Workers Rise Up," *Dissent*, 63(2): 48–55.

27 Ondetti, G. (2006), "Repression, Opportunity, and Protest: Explaining the Takeoff of Brazil's Landless Movement," *Latin American Politics and Society* 48(2): 61–94.

28 Reader, S. (2014), "The Landless Workers Movement Report back from VI Congress," World Development Movement Solidarity Briefing, May, p. 2.

29 Hammond, J. (1999), "Law and Disorder: The Brazilian Landless Farmeworkers' Movement," *Bulletin of Latin American Research* 18(4): 469–89.

30 Carter, M. (2010), "The Landless Rural Workers Movement and Democracy in Brazil," *Latin American Research Review* 45: 186–217; and Watts, J. (2014), "Brazil's Landless Workers Movement Renews Protest on 30th Anniversary," *Guardian*, February 13.

31 Brazil is responsible for a fifth of all pesticide consumption in the world—more than any other country. Additionally, Brazil is second (after the United States) in the amount of land cultivated with genetically modified crops. See Mano, A. (2018), "Brazil Boasts World's Second Largest Genetically Modified Crop Area," Reuters, June 27.

32 Stronzake and Wolford, "Brazil's Landless Workers Rise Up."

33 Gonçalves, J. (2017), "Cooperativa cumple 20 años; la celebración, en Rio Grande do Sul, será marcada por diversos eventos y talleres," *Resumen Latinoamericano*, November 30.

34 Carter, "The Landless Rural Workers Movement and Democracy in Brazil."

35 Ibid.; and Reader, "The Landless Workers Movement Report back from VI Congress."

36 Carballo López, M. (2011), "Vem, Teçamo a Nossa Liberdade: Mujeres líderes en el Movimiento sin Tierra (Ceará-Brasil)," unpublished PhD thesis, Universitat Autónoma de Barcelona.

37 Watts, "Brazil's Landless Workers Movement Renews Protest on 30th Anniversary."

38 Betim, F. (2019), "Los 'sin tierra' de Brasil afrontan la embestida de Bolsonaro," *El País*, January 9; and "Bolsonaro atribuye caída de invasiones de tierra en Brasil al porte de armas," *El Diario*, April 16.

39 General Command of the EZLN (1993), "First Declaration of the Lacandon Jungle," December 31. Available at https://en.wikisource.org/wiki/First_ Declaration_of_the_Lacandon_Jungle.

40 Rovira, G. (2005), "El Zapatismo y la red transnacional," *Razón y Palabra* 10: 47.

41 Salazar Rodríguez, P. (2014), "20 frases del subcomandante Marcos," *Chilango*, January 1, https://www.chilango.com/cultura/20-frases-del- subcomandante-marcos.

42 Inclán, M. (2018), *The Zapatista Movement and Mexico's Democratic Transition: Mobilization, Success, and Survival*, Oxford: Oxford University Press.

43 Stahler-Sholk, R. (2019), "Zapatistas and New Ways of Doing Politics," *Oxford Research Encyclopedias*, available online at oxfordre.com/politics.

44 The account of the student movement relies in part on two papers published in the *Journal of Latin American Studies*, which I co-edited between 2015 and 2019. See Donoso, S. (2013), "Dynamics of Change in Chile: Explaining the Emergence of the 2006 Pingüino Movement," *Journal of Latin American Studies* 45(1): 1–29; and Palacios-Valladares, I. (2017), "Internal Movement Transformation and the Diffusion of Student Protest in Chile," *Journal of Latin American Studies* 49(3): 579–607.

45 BBC Mundo (2011), "En fotos: las protestas de Chile en carteles," https:// www.bbc.com/mundo/noticias/2011/08/110822_fotos_carteles_chile_ estudiantes_nc.

46 "Crisis de la educación en Chile," Argentinian public TV, June 25, 2011, at https://www.youtube.com/watch?v=TCzrwMKMAi0.

47 Bellei, C., C. Cabalin, and V. Orellana (2014), "The 2011 Chilean Student Movement against Neoliberal Educational Policies," *Studies in Higher Education* 39(3): 426–40.

48 Proponents and critics are divided on the significance of Bachelet's reforms. They were "an adjustment to the market-based education model . . . but not deep changes," argues the President of the Association of Teachers. The reforms "were able to modify the field in the education game and opened the door for newer and better reforms," responds the Chilean political scientist Kenneth Bunker. Overall, they were probably a pragmatic but incomplete modification of one of the most neoliberal and unequal

education systems in Latin America. For newspaper analysis and expert comments, see Almazabar, D. (2018), "Expertos analizan: ¿Qué dejó pendiente la reforma educacional del Gobierno de Bachelet?," *Emol.com*, February 7; and Pardo, D. (2018), "Por qué el segundo gobierno de Michelle Bachelet es considerado por muchos el más importante en décadas en Chile," BBC Mundo, March 11. For a more detailed evaluation of the efforts to secure free higher education, see Delisle, J., and A. Bernasconi (2018), "Lessons from Chile's Transition to Free College," *Evidence Speaks Reports*, 2(43), Economic Studies at Brookings.

49 "Crisis de la educación en Chile," https://www.youtube.com/watch?v=TCzrwMKMAi0.

50 IRS (2007), "El movimiento estudiantil en Chile, o la marcha de 'los pingüinos,'" http://www.institut-gouvernance.org/fr/analyse/fiche-analyse-348.html.

51 Silva, E. (2012), "The Winter Chilean Students Said, Enough," https://mobilizingideas.wordpress.com/2012/05/02/the-winter-chilean-students-said-enough/.

52 The video is worth watching: https://www.youtube.com/watch?v=iJAmHgUvd_c&list=RDiJAmHgUvd_c&start_radio=1&t=27.

53 Bellei, Cabalin, and Orellana, "The 2011 Chilean Student Movement against Neoliberal Educational Policies."

54 Harten, S. (2010), *The Rise of Evo Morales and the MAS*, London: Zed, chapter 3.

55 Do Alto, H. (2008), "El MAS-IPSP boliviano, entre movimiento social y partido politico," *Análisis Político* 21(62): 25–43.

56 Chaplin, A., and J. Crabtree (2013), *Bolivia: Processes of Change*, London: Zed, p. 97.

57 Do Alto, H. (2011), "Un partido campesino en el poder: Una mirada sociológica del MAS boliviano," *Nueva Sociedad* 234: 95–111.

58 Harten, *The Rise of Evo Morales and the MAS*, pp. 86–87.

59 Anria, S. (2013), "Social Movements, Party Organization, and Populism: Insights from the Bolivian MAS," *Latin American Politics and Society* 55(3): 19–46.

60 Zuazo, M. (2010), "¿Los movimientos sociales en el poder? El gobierno del MAS en Bolivia," *Nueva Sociedad* 227: 120–35.

61 "Historias de vida y testimonios reflejan el origen ideológico y político del MAS," *Periódico Digital de Investigación sobre Bolivia*, November 9, 2015, http://www.pieb.com.bo/nota.php?idn=9974.

62 Anria, S. (2018), *When Movements Become Parties: The Bolivian MAS in Comparative Perspective*, New York: Cambridge University Press, p. 4.

63 Anria, "Social Movements, Party Organization, and Populism," p. 38.

64 This section is partly informed by a recent paper I wrote on the subject: Sánchez-Ancochea (2019), "The Surprising Reduction of Inequality during a Commodity Boom: What do we Learn from Latin America?," *Journal of Economic Policy Reform*.

65 "The Party is Ending in Latin America," *Financial Times*, October 30, 2014, https://www.ft.com/content/e9d02da2-5e9f-11e4-b81d-00144feabdc0.
66 Two books sponsored by UN institutions were particularly influential: López Calva, L., and N. Lustig (eds) (2010), *Declining Inequality in Latin America: A Decade of Progress?*, Washington, DC: Brookings Institution; and Cornia, *Falling Inequality in Latin America*. The IMF position is summarized here: https://blogs.imf.org/2018/06/21/how-the-commodity-boom-helped-tackle-poverty-and-inequality-in-latin-america/.
67 López Calva and Lustig (eds), *Declining Inequality in Latin America*.
68 Messina, J. (2017), "Latin America: The Story Behind Falling Inequality," *IADB Ideas Matter*, https://blogs.iadb.org/ideas-matter/en/why-inequality-declined-in-latin-america/.
69 For a discussion of efforts to expand formal jobs, see, for example, Berg, "Laws or Luck? Understanding Rising Formality in Brazil in the 2000s," in Lee and McCann (eds), *Regulating for Decent Work: Advances in Labour Studies*; and Maurizio, R. (2014), "Labour Formalization and Declining Inequality in Argentina and Brazil in the 2000s: A Dynamic Approach," ILO Research Paper no. 9; and Weller, J., and C. Roethlisberger (2011), "La calidad del empleo en América Latina," *Macroeconomía del Desarrollo* 110, Santiago: CEPAL.
70 Cornia, *Falling Inequality in Latin America*, p. 35.
71 For a critical perspective on the role of minimum wages in Latin America, see the work of the Inter-American Development Bank, some of which is reviewed at https://blogs.iadb.org/ideas-matter/en/why-inequality-declined-in-latin-america/. For the opposite view, see Maurizio, R., and G. Vázquez (2016), "Distribution Effects of the Minimum Wage in Four Latin American Countries: Argentina, Brazil, Chile and Uruguay," *International Labour Review* 155(1): 97–131, as well as Cornia, *Falling Inequality in Latin America*. The Argentinian economist Nora Lustig is carefully supportive of this latter position, arguing that "in some countries, increases in the minimum wage and union-friendly governments have contributed as well." See Lustig, N. (2011), "The Decline in Inequality in Latin America: Policies, Politics or Luck?," *Americas Quarterly* 5(4): 43–46.
72 World Bank (2013), "One in Every Four Latin Americans is Covered by Programs Such as the Bolsa Família and Oportunidades," http://www.worldbank.org/en/news/feature/2013/07/15/Brazil-Latin-America-covered-social-safety-nets.
73 The academic literature evaluating Bolsa Família and other CCTs is very large. Two useful references are: IPEA (2009), "Desigualdade e pobreza no Brasil metropolitano durante a crise internacional," Comunicado da Presidência, August 25; and Soares S. (2006), "Distribuição da renda no Brasil de 1976 a 2004 com ênfase no período entre 2001 e 2004," IPEA Texto para Discussão, 1.166.
74 On the politics of inequality reduction, see Evans, A. (2017), "How Latin America Bucked the Trend of Rising Inequality," *The Conversation*,

December 17. One of the best academic accounts of the links between democratization and social policy is Garay, C. (2016), *Social Policy Expansion in Latin America*, New York: Cambridge University Press.

75 Lewis, P., S. Clarke, and C. Barr (2019), "Revealed: Populist Leaders Linked to Reduced Inequality," *Guardian*, March 7; Lustig, N., and D. McLeod (2009), "Are Latin America's New Left Regimes Reducing Inequality Faster? Addendum to Poverty, Inequality and the New Left in Latin America," Woodrow Wilson International Center for Scholars Working Paper; and Milanović, B. (2019), "Market Income Inequality, Left-Wing Political Parties, and Redistribution in Latin America," AFD Research Paper Series, no. 2019–106.
76 Evans, "How Latin America Bucked the Trend of Rising Inequality."
77 Morgan, M. (2017), "Extreme and Persistent Inequality: New Evidence for Brazil Combining National Accounts, Surveys and Fiscal Data, 2001–2015," WID Working Paper Series, no. 2017/12.

Chapter 7

1 Casillas Bermúdez, K. (2018), "Desigualdad: la eterna tragedia de América Latina," *Vice.com*, February 8.
2 Hacker, J. (2011), "The Institutional Foundations of a Middle-Class Society," *Policy Network*, May 6.
3 See Kay, C. (2001), "Asia's and Latin America's Development in Comparative Perspective: Landlords, Peasants and Industrialization," Institute of Social Studies Working Paper no. 336; and "For Asia, the Path to Prosperity Starts with Land Reform," *Economist*, October 12, 2014.
4 "For Asia, the Path to Prosperity Starts with Land Reform," *Economist*.
5 Cañete Alonso, "Privilegios que niegan derechos."
6 Deininger, K. (2014), "Cultivating Equality: Land Reform's Potential and Challenges," *World Politics Review*, April 8.
7 Roberts, C., G. Blakeley, and L. Murphy (2018), "A Wealth of Difference: Reforming the Taxation of Wealth," IPPR Discussion Paper.
8 "Wealth Inequality in the United States" at https://inequality.org/facts/wealth-inequality/; and Huddleston, C. (2019), "58% of Americans Have Less Than $1,000 in Savings, Survey Finds," *Yahoo! Finance*.
9 "A Hated Tax, but a Fair One: The Case for Taxing Inherited Assets is Strong," *Economist*, November 23, 2017; "Taxing Inheritances is Falling out of Favour But the Benefits of Cutting these Levies are Overstated," *Economist*, November 23, 2017; and Sánchez-Ancochea and Morgan (eds), *The Political Economy of the Public Budget in the Americas*.
10 IPPR Commission on Economic Justice (2018), *Prosperity and Justice: A Plan for the New Economy*, London: Polity; Wilson, S. (2018), "Land Value Tax: The Least-Bad Tax," *MoneyWeek*, November 3; and Wolf, M. (2006), "A Strong Case for a Tax on Land Values," *Financial Times*, January 5.

11 Piketty, T. (2019), "Wealth Tax in America," https://www.lemonde.fr/blog/
    piketty/2019/02/12/wealth-tax-in-america/; Saez, E., and G. Zucman
    (2019), "How Would a Progressive Wealth Tax Work? Evidence from the
    Economics Literature," http://gabriel-zucman.eu/files/saez-zucman-
    wealthtaxobjections.pdf; and Yglesias, M. (2019), "Elizabeth Warren's
    Proposed Tax on Enormous Fortunes, Explained," *Vox*, January 24.

12 Piketty, T. (2014), *Capital in the 21st Century*, Cambridge, MA: Harvard
    University Press, p. 515 (Kindle edition).

13 Barragué, B. (2019), *Larga vida a la Social Democracia: Cómo evitar que el
    crecimiento de la desigualdad acabe con la democracia*, Madrid: Ariel; and
    IPPR Commission on Economic Justice, *Prosperity and Justice*.

14 Milberg, W., and D. Winkler (2013), *Outsourcing Economics: Global Value
    Chains in Capitalist Development*, New York: Cambridge University Press,
    p. 115.

15 Baker, J., and S. Salop (2015), "Antitrust, Competition Policy, and
    Inequality," *Georgetown Law Journal Online* 104(1): 1–28.

16 IPPR Commission on Economic Justice, *Prosperity and Justice*, p. 150.

17 The literature both in the popular press and academia on this topic is large.
    See, for example, Berg, J., and D. Kuzera (2008), *In Defence of Labour
    Market Institutions: Cultivating Justice in the Developing World*, New York:
    Palgrave Macmillan; Helm, T. (2018), "Rising Inequality Linked to Drop in
    Union Membership," *Guardian*, June 10; Standing, G. (2011), *The Precariat:
    The New Dangerous Class*, London: Bloomsbury; Van der Hoeven, R.
    (2000), "Labor Markets and Income Inequality: What Are the New Insights
    after the Washington Consensus?," UNU-Wider Working Paper no. 209;
    and Western, B., and J. Rosenfeld (2011), "Unions, Norms and the Rise in
    US Wage Inequality," *American Sociological Review* 76(4): 513–37.

18 Krugman, P. (2015), "Liberals and Wages," *New York Times*, July 17. For a
    review of the literature on minimum wages in developing countries, see
    Eyraud, F., and C. Saget (2008), "The Revival of Minimum Wage Setting
    Institutions," in Berg and Kuzera (eds), *In Defence of Labour Market
    Institutions: Cultivating Justice in the Developing World*, pp. 100–118.

19 High Pay Centre (2014), *Reform Agenda: How to Make Top Pay Fairer*,
    London: High Pay Centre; Martínez Franzoni, J., and D. Sánchez-Ancochea
    (2013), "Falling Inequality in Latin America: How Much? How
    Sustainable?," *Global Dialogue Newsletter* 3(5): 27–29; and Pizzigati, S.
    (2018), "For Minimum Decency, a Maximum Wage," https://inequality.org/
    great-divide/minimum-decency-need-maximum-wage/.

20 Linker, D. (2014), "Why We Need a Maximum Wage?," *The Week*, April 22;
    Shotter, J. (2013), "Swiss Poll Stirs Debate on Executive Pay," *Financial
    Times*, November 12; and Wren-Lewis, S. (2014), "If Minimum Wages, Why
    Not Maximum Wages?," https://mainlymacro.blogspot.com/2014/07/
    if-minimum-wages-why-not-maximum-wages.html.

21 Ford, M. (2015), *The Rise of the Robots: Technology and the Threat of a
    Jobless Future*, New York: Basic Books, pp. xii, xvi.

22 Paus, E. (2018), "The Future Isn't What it Used to Be," in E. Paus (ed.), *Confronting Dystopia: The New Technological Revolution and the Future of Work*, Ithaca, NY: Cornell University Press, p. 7.

23 OECD (2019), "The Future of Work in Figures," https://www.oecd.org/els/emp/future-of-work/data/.

24 Ford, *The Rise of the Robots*, p. xvi.

25 See, among many others, Amsden, A. (2001), *The Rise of "The Rest": Challenges to the West from Late-Industrializing Economies*, Oxford: Oxford University Press; Chang, H-J. (2002), *Kicking Away the Ladder: Development Strategy in Historical Perspective*, London: Anthem Press; and Rodrik, D. (2004), "Industrial Policy for the 21st Century," https://drodrik.scholar.harvard.edu/files/dani-rodrik/files/industrial-policy-twenty-first-century.pdf.

26 Mazzucato, M. (2015), *The Entrepreneurial State: Debunking Public vs. Private Sector Myths*, London: Public Affairs.

27 Economists Howard Pack and Kamal Saggi provide a more rigorous definition which has become rather popular among academics. Industrial policy is "any type of selective government intervention or policy that attempts to alter the structure of production in favour of sectors that are expected to offer better prospects for economic growth (and good jobs we would add) in a way that would not occur in the absence of such intervention in the market equilibrium." See Pack, H., and K. Saggi (2006), "Is There a Case for Industrial Policy? A Critical Survey," *World Bank Research Observer* 21(2): 267–97.

28 For a summary of the problem, particularly in Latin America, see Sánchez-Ancochea, D., and K. Shadlen (2008), *The Political Economy of Hemispheric Integration: Responding to Globalization in the Americas*, London: Palgrave Macmillan.

29 Martínez Franzoni and Sánchez-Ancochea, *Good Jobs and Social Services*; and Sánchez-Ancochea, D. (2006), "Development Trajectories and New Comparative Advantages: Costa Rica and the Dominican Republic under Globalization," *World Development* 34(6): 996–1015.

30 Perez, C. (2010), "Technological Dynamism and Social Inclusion in Latin America: A Resource-based Production Development Strategy," *CEPAL Review* 100: 121–42; and Martínez Franzoni, J., and D. Sánchez-Ancochea (2013), "The Double Challenge of Market and Social Incorporation: Progress and Bottlenecks in Latin America," *Development Policy Review* 32(3): 275–98.

31 Eatwell, J., and L. Taylor (2000), *Global Finance at Risk: The Case for International Regulation*, New York: New Press.

32 Collins, M. (2015), "Wall Street and the Financialization of the Economy," *Forbes*, February 4.

33 Tannal, J., and D. Waldenström (2016), "Does Financial Deregulation Boost Top Incomes? Evidence from the Big Bang," IZA Discussion Paper Series no. 9684.

34 The following discussion relies heavily on some of my joint academic and policy-oriented work with Juliana Martínez Franzoni. See, in particular, the following papers: Martínez Franzoni, J., and D. Sánchez-Ancochea (2014), "Should Policy Aim at Having All People on the Same Boat? The Definition, Relevance and Challenges of Universalism in Latin America," Desigualdades.net Working Paper no. 70; Martínez Franzoni, J., and D. Sánchez-Ancochea (2016), "Achieving Universalism in Developing Countries," http://hdr.undp.org/sites/default/files/franzoni_sanchez_layout. pdf; and Sánchez-Ancochea, D., and J. Martínez Franzoni (2019), "The Relationship between Universal Social Policy and Inequality: A Comparative Political Economy Approach," background paper for the UNDP Human Development Report 2019. These three papers include some of the most significant literature on universalism and income distribution from a political economy perspective.

35 Programs relying on means testing require beneficiaries to demonstrate that their income is below a certain level. The government can use individual surveys or target regions with a high share of low-income households.

36 Korpi, W., and J. Palme (1998), "The Paradox of Redistribution and Strategies of Equality: Welfare State Institutions, Inequality, and Poverty in the Western Countries," *American Sociological Review* 63(5): 661–87.

37 As quoted in Walker, C. (2011), "For Universalism and Against the Mean Test," in A. Walker, A. Sinfield, and C. Walker (eds), *Fighting Poverty, Inequality and Injustice: A Manifesto Inspired by Peter Townsend*, Bristol: Policy Press, p. 142.

38 Ortiz, I., M. Cummins, and K. Karunanethy (2017), "Fiscal Space for Social Protection and the SDGs: Options to Expand Social Investments in 187 Countries," ESS Working Paper no. 48, ILO, UNICEF, and UN-Women.

39 For one of the most recent and comprehensive academic defenses of the UBI, see Van Parijs, P., and Y. Vanderborght (2017), *Basic Income: A Radical Proposal for a Free Society and a Sane Economy*, Cambridge, MA: Harvard University Press. For an academic review of this book and other literature, see Calsamiglia, C., and S. Flamand (2019), "A Review on *Basic Income: A Radical Proposal for a Free Society and a Sane Economy* by Philippe Van Parijs and Yannick Vanderborght," *Journal of Economic Literature* 57(3): 644–58.

40 Vietor, T. (2019), "2020: Andrew Yang on the Universal Basic Income and Why He Hates the Penny," https://crooked.com/podcast/andrew-yang-on-the-universal-basic-income-and-why-he-hates-the-penny/.

41 Aguirrre, E. (2017), "Los impuestos bajos como pilar de la prosperidad," *Expansión*, April 24.

42 See Phillips, B. (2018), "How to Move Mountains on Inequality," https://www.gpidnetwork.org/2018/02/12/how-to-move-mountains-on-inequality/?fbclid=IwAR1ftulD3rPkV_hX00uysJDNT43tXDlnPW0W29UnzjsjzBixvEyehfscwFo.

43 Scheidel, W. (2017), *The Great Leveler: Violence and the History of Inequality from the Stone Age to the Twenty-First Century*, Princeton, NJ: Princeton University Press.

44 The academic literature on the positive role of democracy is large. For one of the most influential and powerful discussions, see Boix, C. (2003), *Democracy and Redistribution*, Cambridge: Cambridge University Press. Gradstein, M., and B. Milanović (2004), "Does Liberté = Egalité? A Survey of the Empirical Links between Democracy and Inequality with Some Evidence on the Transition Economies," *Journal of Economic Surveys* 18: 515–37, offer a good review of the literature.

45 See, for example, Acemoglu, D., S. Naidu, P. Restrepo, and J. Robinson (2015), "Democracy, Redistribution, and Inequality," in A. Atkinson and F. Bourguignon (eds), *Handbook of Income Distribution*, vol. 2, London: Elsevier, pp. 1885–966; and Albertus, M. (2015), *Autocracy and Redistribution: The Politics of Land Reform*, New York: Cambridge University Press.

46 Wike, R., L. Silver, and A. Castillo (2019), "Many Across the Globe Are Dissatisfied with How Democracy Is Working," https://www.pewresearch.org/global/2019/04/29/many-across-the-globe-are-dissatisfied-with-how-democracy-is-working/.

47 East Asian countries such as South Korea and Taiwan were exceptions. Yet some of the preconditions for redistribution (such as the land reforms I discussed above) took place under occupation. Moreover, both countries were at the frontier of the Cold War and faced dangerous neighbors for decades.

48 Bobbio, N. (1996), *Left and Right: The Significance of a Political Distinction*, London: Polity, pp. 62–63.

49 See, for example, Bradley, D., E. Huber, S. Moller, F. Nielsen, and J. Stephens (2003), "Distribution and Redistribution in Post-industrial Democracies," *World Politics* 55: 193–228; Hicks, A. (1999), *Social Democracy and Welfare Capitalism: A Century of Income Security Policies*, Ithaca, NY: Cornell University Press; Huber, E., and J. Stephens (2001), *Development and Crisis of the Welfare State: Parties and Policies in Global Markets*, Chicago: University of Chicago Press; Pribble, J. (2013), *Welfare and Party Politics in Latin America*, Cambridge: Cambridge University Press; and Sandbrook et al., *Social Democracy in the Global Periphery*.

50 I am not just talking about labels here. What we need are parties that follow the social democratic ideas. In practice, many parties using the name have actually become conservative parties in disguise. Other parties that present themselves as radical are really advancing a social democratic agenda.

51 Barragué, *Larga vida a la Social Democracia*.

52 Sandbrook, R. (2014), *Reinventing the Left in the Global South: The Politics of the Possible*, Cambridge: Cambridge University Press.

53 The conference was jointly organized by Raymond Offenheiser, Victoria Paniagua, Ben Phillips, and me, with funding from the Kellogg Institute

and the Notre Dame Initiative for Global Development. It aimed to encourage more active debate between academics, activists, and policymakers—three groups that speak with each other less often than they should. You can find more information at https://kellogg.nd.edu/democracy-and-inequality-americas.

54 See their short videos at https://twitter.com/i/moments/1163046913513537536.

55 Evans, "How Latin America Bucked the Trend of Rising Inequality."

INDEX

Page numbers: Figures are given in *italics* and notes as [page number] n. [note number].